TEACHING, LEARNING AND STUDY SKILLS

TEACHING, LEARNING AND STUDY SKILLS

A GUIDE FOR TUTORS

Tom Burns and Sandra Sinfield

$ SAGE Publications

London • Thousand Oaks • New Delhi

A SAGE Publications Company
1 Oliver's Yard
55 City Road
London EC1Y 1SP

SAGE Publications Inc
2455 Teller Road
Thousand Oaks, California 91320

SAGE Publications India Pvt Ltd
B-42, Panchsheel Enclave
Post Box 4109
New Delhi 110 017

Library of Congress Control Number: available

A catalogue record for this book is available from the
British Library

ISBN 1 4129 0068 9
ISBN 1 4129 0069 7 (pbk)

Production by Deer Park Productions, Tavistock, Devon
Typeset by TW Typesetting, Plymouth, Devon
Printed in Great Britain by TJ International Ltd,
Trecerus Industrial Estate, Padstow, Cornwall

Contents

List of resources

Biographical details

Tom Burns has been a Visiting Lecturer at the University of North London, now London Metropolitan University, since 1994. He has taught Media, Sociology and Literature but now focuses mainly on developing study and academic skills support, programmes and resources for students from foundation to postgraduate level.

Sandra Sinfield has been a Visiting Lecturer at London Metropolitan University since 1990. In November 2000 she was appointed Senior Lecturer and Co-ordinator for Learning Development (North). She has taught Literature and Media but now focuses on supporting the access, retention, progression and achievement of university students.

With thanks to our families
for their encouragement and support.

Introduction and how to use this book

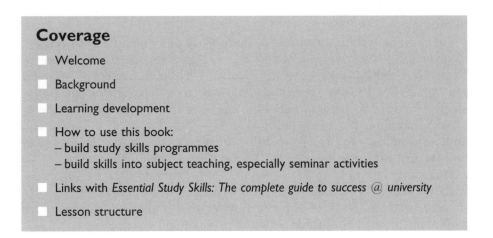

Coverage

- Welcome
- Background
- Learning development
- How to use this book:
  – build study skills programmes
  – build skills into subject teaching, especially seminar activities
- Links with *Essential Study Skills: The complete guide to success @ university*
- Lesson structure

Welcome

Welcome to *Teaching, Learning and Study Skills: A guide for tutors*. This is our second book for Sage and while it operates as a completely autonomous text, it can also function as a companion text to our student handbook *Essential Study Skills: The complete guide to success @ university*.

Background

For over thirty years (combined) our practice has revolved around facilitating the academic success of those that were typically not expected to succeed: older students and those from working-class and minority ethnic communities. We have undertaken this work on GNVQ, AS, A level and access programmes and across the whole continuum of university programmes – from foundation to postgraduate. There is no one stereotypical non-traditional student to whom we can point and say, there, if you can understand him or her you will have the key to teaching in this climate of widening participation. As with traditional students, our students come in all shapes and sizes, with various degrees of motivation, commitment and study 'readiness'. However, if forced to generalise, we would say that, yes, we have found that typically the more mature of our students do tend to be more highly motivated and committed towards their studies. At the same time, while mature students bring strengths and experiences with them from the worlds of work and home where they may have already proven themselves powerful or successful, they tend to experience often crippling self-doubt in the academic context. This latter is the rationale for Chapter 6 on how to promote self-confidence.

For non- or traditional students there is no one quick fix with respect to promoting study success just as there is no one correct way to teach. Typically teaching and learning involve a complex interplay between aspects of the learner (personal, political, social, psychological, philosophical) with the various academic contexts in which they find themselves, including personal, political, social, psychological, philosophical and pedagogical aspects of the tutor. However, the activities, exercises and lecture contents detailed in this text have proven themselves to be useful starting points in dialogues and engagements that we have had with our students over the years, and we intend this handbook to operate in very practical ways to support further and higher education tutors with their practice and their personal professional development.

Resources

We have designed photocopiable resources to support the activities and exercises detailed throughout this guide. For ease of photocopying these are all gathered together in the Resources section at the end of the book.

Study skills, teaching and learning development

The authors of this text have both worked in further and higher education with a special focus on working with non-traditional students. Both now work in learning development in London Metropolitan University. The university itself has some 30,000 students and has a commitment to following a widening participation brief.

Learning development, as with teaching or professional development and alongside psychological and pedagogical research, is perhaps gaining a greater 'voice' as universities embrace widening participation in the move towards a mass higher education system.

In our university learning development itself operates:

▓ practically with students – running drop-in workshops, teaching accredited and unaccredited study and academic skills programmes and developing learning resources including on-line resources;

▓ practically with staff – contributing to staff induction and staff development activities, producing staff newsletters, generating and disseminating teaching and learning resources and working with staff to design and deliver integrated skills and HE orientation programmes;

▓ strategically with respect to groups across the university that contribute to the development of teaching, learning, retention and diversity strategies and practice, and that operate on a continuum of levels from practitioner discussion groups to academic committees;

▓ nationally with respect to learning development practitioners across the country – in the South East England Network and the Learning Development in Higher Education Network (*http://www.jiscmail.ac. uk/lists/LDHEN.html*).

And while this text is the practical manual that we suggest above, we do reference out to wider educational debates especially where these transect with issues relating to widening participation and the experiences of the non-traditional student.

How to use this book

This handbook has a special focus on HE orientation, that is it is designed to make transparent the forms and processes of academic discourse and to introduce a variety of strategies that enable students to become successfully inducted into academic practice, especially within higher education. The majority of the chapters contain suggestions for teaching practice and particular activities that, with the photocopiable resources, can be delivered straight from the page to supplement your subject teaching at any level. This is designed to be a very practical handbook and it is intended that tutors could teach a particular topic using the lesson plans, resources and lecture notes that are given here either as complete source material or as a detailed guide or introduction to a specific topic.

Further, the materials in the book can be drawn together to compose an accredited study and academic skills programme – and we offer a model of one such programme in Chapter 15. While our study and academic skills programme is accredited at preliminary or first-year level, it is a programme that we have delivered to access and foundation students to prepare them for university, and that is also undertaken by postgraduate students in a bid to either refresh or develop their personal skills and practice; we take this as an indication that the practices described in this text have been proven to work with (university) students of all levels.

Tutor tips: Lesson structure

When we teach the various activities laid out in this text we tend to adopt the following strategies:

- **Agenda:** Write the lesson agenda on the board before students arrive. Eventually students utilise the agenda as a way of focusing on and tuning into the session.

- **Brainstorm:** Prior to commencing a session, we require that students brainstorm either individually or collectively on the session topic such that they become focused upon and tuned into the topic. Occasionally we vary this by getting students to write one or two things that they expect to take away from a session or utilise in their assignment.

- **Delivery +/− activities:** Typically we teach a session via a mixture of lecture, discussion and some form of student interaction or activity.

- **Check learning:** where possible we circulate to check that activity – and hopefully learning – is taking place during the session.

- **Student – reflect on learning:** We utilise learning logs (see Chapter 14) to structure student reflection upon the session.

- **Tutor – reflect on session:** We reflect on the session ourselves along the lines of what went well and why, and what went badly and why, in a bid to continually develop our own practice.

Essential Study Skills

With all the sections in this text, we will make reference to the relevant sections in our companion student handbook *Essential Study Skills: The complete guide to success @ university* (published by Sage, 2003). For example, Chapter 10 on how to promote effective presentations contains references to ESS 9: How to prepare better assignments and ESS 7: How to build your confidence, indicating that Chapters 9 and 7 of *Essential Study Skills* (ESS) will offer supporting material. This is for your convenience; it is simply a means to quickly indicate which sections of that handbook relate to this one. At the same time, while students can use that text to facilitate their development and support any study and academic skills work that you undertake, you can teach from this text separately from that one.

Finally

We do hope that you enjoy using the activities in this handbook with your students – and we would be interested in gathering feedback on your experiences of doing so. You can contact us, Tom Burns and Sandra Sinfield, via the Learning Development in Higher Education Network, e-mail: *LDHEN@jiscmail.ac.uk*.

2 University teaching, widening participation and study skills

Introduction – but is it 'education'?

While traditionally higher education may pivot around pure research or be linked to social prosperity and social justice, many of our fellow practitioners argue that, government policy notwithstanding, universities are concerned with 'Education'. Here tutors speak of the something 'other', the something indefinable, un-pin-downable and almost unknowable that happens for students in the best of circumstances (Noble, 2002; Satterthwaite, 2004). This is a something that perhaps cannot be captured and measured in our current audit culture nor in government white papers, teaching and learning strategy documents or the sorts of aims and learning outcomes that we are expected to generate to define our teaching and learning goals (Clegg and Ashworth, 2004; Noble, 2002). Whatever your own thoughts about the role that higher education could and should play in society today, in this section of the text we explore some of the key issues affecting higher education (HE) at this moment, paying particular attention to the government White Paper, *The future of higher education* (2003). In the process we consider the relationship between government policy and university practices and how this may impact on tutor – and eventually on student – experiences.

What is happening to university education?

For many lecturers these are challenging times. Traditionally, university lecturers have enjoyed considerable autonomy in their research with their pedagogical practice part of their personal remit as domain experts and recruitment strategy a matter of departmental policy. However, ongoing governmental intervention has worked to change the HE environment. The White Paper (2003) urges universities in effect to focus either on research, associations with business or their approaches to teaching and learning. At the same time that all universities are supposed to generate an access policy and play their part in the move to a mass HE system, there is a drive to concentrate research into the Russell Group of universities with a focus in the newer universities on the implicitly lower-status relationships with business or on a preoccupation with teaching and learning. These drives not only involve a paradoxical separation of roles that many lecturers see as intricately connected, they are arguably creating a two-tier higher education system while simultaneously moving university management towards a much more hands-on approach to the evolution of strategies concerned with teaching, learning and recruitment.

Management generation of strategy

In many universities teaching and learning strategy is becoming generated from the centre in terms of overall broad targets and smaller, staged goals. Such strategies may determine the curricular and co-curricular activities with which students have to engage – and thus the pedagogical strategies that lecturers have to adopt. Coupled with an insistence that new university lecturers have to undertake teaching qualifications, many professionals may feel that the sorts of pedagogical practices with which they wish to engage are being determined centrally by government policy and management intervention.

While many domain and teaching and learning experts within universities have long sought the elevation of the status of university teaching and learning, that good teaching practice be as valued as a strong research portfolio, earlier developments in pedagogical innovation were driven by educational and psychological research, while changes determined by management, instigated through government policy, move pedagogy out of the domain of professionalism and into the realm of institutional and even party politics. The reality is that while many lecturers are happy to develop their pedagogical practices, there may be resistance to the ways in which they are now compelled to do so.[1]

Widening participation

A significant factor in HE at the moment is the move towards a mass higher education system. Unfortunately, the very fact that this is a centralist thrust rather than an institution's own mission can have negative implications for the widening participation (WP) student who is caught in the government/academic cross fire. Here we discuss WP and its implications for staff and, more significantly, for students.

The move to mass HE has been offered as a major initiative in the government's 'education, education, education' agenda, with the goal of achieving the participation of 50% of 18–30 year olds in higher education by 2010. Margaret Hodge, when Labour Minister for Lifelong Learning (2002–3), placed widening participation in the context of resolving the conflict between the previous left-wing agenda out of office that focused on education for equality and social justice, and the far more centre-right policy once elected that emphasised instead the role of education in fostering economic prosperity. Hodge acknowledged the tension between these two competing objectives in education policy and offered New Labour's third way: that prosperity is predicated upon social inclusion – hence mass higher education.

While some doubt the notion of a mass higher education programme as an obvious social good, Hodge's critics note the 'assurance' that not all of these new graduates would be able to take up 'graduate jobs' (Hodge, 2002). For them the 'massification' of HE is seen as a move towards a bipartite HE system with an elite higher education for some – and an inferior, vocational HE for the mass. This negative perception is exacerbated if one considers the diminishing unit of resource that has been directed at HE in recent years, for at the same time as arguing for widening participation, successive British governments have systematically reduced the unit of resource available: between 1976 and 1986 funding was reduced by 29%, with a further reduction of 38% by 1999 (Leathwood and O'Connell, 2003). Thus class sizes rose and staff/student ratios worsened as increasing numbers of perhaps less academically inducted[2] students began to enter universities and mixed-ability teaching became increasingly common (Bennett, 2002).

Widening participation – it's a struggle

While WP students, as with successive governments, typically do support the notion of education for personal and social prosperity, often citing HE as a way of increasing control over their lives, their economic prosperity and their career advancement (Sinfield et al., 2004; Leathwood and O'Connell, 2003), many have negative experiences when entering HE for the first time. Non-traditional students often experience HE as a series of interlocking and cumulative struggles (Anie, 2001; Leathwood and O'Connell, 2003). The new WP student, perched so precariously on the cusp between known and unknown worlds, struggles to raise a family, perhaps, and to work and study full time. These students are very aware that such work damages their grades and limits their opportunities for postgraduate study and for well-paid employment; the non-traditional student understands that they are the least likely to actually get the graduate job that will free them of debt:

> Working-class students recognise that cheaper degrees from new
> universities are worth less in the job market, but they are restricted to
> studying there because they are unwilling to take on large debts.
> (Archer, 2002)

Typically such students struggle to adjust to the occult demands of academic discourse, a struggle worsened by the negative stereotypes that the university, perhaps, and the wider society have of them. For the Widening Participation debate as conducted in the press reveals a fear of the non-traditional student and its pollutant qualities. Lillis (2001) specifically links ongoing debates about the 'crisis' in education and the preoccupation with 'skills' and 'standards' to the reaction to the widening participation student (see also Chapter 4 on understanding our students). She critiques HE for not adopting a broader frame of reference to the contexts of its participants and to its own practices. Moreover there is a formidable body of research (Anie, 2001; Bourdieu and Passeron, 1979; Burn and Finnigan, 2003; hooks, 1994; Leathwood and O'Connell, 2003; Lillis, 2001; Luttrell, 1997; Medhurst, 2000; Munt, 2000; Reay, 1998; Sinfield et al., 2004; Tett, 2000) that records responses towards the non-traditional student that are classed, raced, aged and gendered – responses that pathologise and denigrate these students. Taken together with the unequal power relations of educational discourse itself, it is at this time of widening participation that the academic environment has arguably never been more hostile for the non-traditional student.

Our experience with non-traditional students in further and higher education tells us that while education does constitute a struggle, it is a struggle in which students can be helped to succeed. And that while some do fail needlessly (Cottrell, 2001; Leathwood and O'Connell, 2003) there are positive changes that we in higher education can make that will facilitate student success. Ironically, such changes, often because they introduce a more transparent and varied teaching and learning environment, also serve to promote the success of what we often term the traditional student (Warren, 2002). Typically the locus for much of this change has been the introduction of study and academic skills or learning development initiatives and we move on to consider that debate.

Changing HE – the discourses of learning development

Study and academic skills, key skills, capabilities and now graduate attributes are all terms that have been coined over recent years to describe variously the practices, techniques, qualities or attributes that, typically non-traditional, students will need to succeed first in HE itself and then in the graduate job market. As indicated above, this is heavily contested ground (see Holmes, 2001, 2002; Lea and Street, 1998; Lillis, 2001). Lillis (2001) argues that this very debate is a negative response to WP per se and suggests that rather than problematising the student, HE should problematise its own practices. Further, the argument is that when 'skills' are sought in graduates they are really used as a code for the cultural capital associated with being white, male and middle class: non-traditional students will never gain that particular aspect of cultural capital and if we engage in the skills debate at all then we are engaged in a deception that itself plays a part in conferring an inferior position on our non-traditional students.

At the same time there are practitioners, often in learning development (LD), that have harnessed these debates in their attempts to get academic staff to recognise that just being in an academic environment is typically not sufficient to confer either success or a 'graduate identity' (Holmes, 2001, 2002) on their students. Here the argument is that if we allow our own 'ideological purity' (LDHEN ongoing debate, 2003) to prevent us from engaging in the same debate that employers and influential others are having, it will be our very own non-traditional students who suffer the greatest disadvantage. Here it is argued that it is only the 'skills debate', flawed as it is, that has opened up study, academic and learning development initiatives within universities – and that these spaces do offer students the opportunity to discover the tricks of the trade, the practices and attributes that successful graduates employ. Here, it is argued that, just as academics – and especially 'once working-class academics' – have made 'their own accommodation with discourses of belonging, identity and power' (Medhurst, in Munt, 2000:

31), it is for our students to decide whether or not to adopt such strategies, whether or not to make the changes in their own behaviours – and whether or not they are prepared to pay the price attached to making those changes.

Learning development and 'skills'

In drawing up our own study and academic skills programmes we called first on our experience of 'study skills' on access programmes. As discussed above, 'study skills' is a term that is now heavily contested, but within the Open College Network (OCN) study skills were and are seen quite differently. OCN access programmes linked 'study skills' with equal opportunities and acknowledged that while it is also necessary to make transparent the forms and processes of academic discourse – to adopt an emancipatory pedagogy (Thompson, 2000) – the non-traditional student can benefit from a targeted and safe introduction to that discourse – one that introduces them to and rehearses them in successful (constituent) academic, study, learning and communication practices. This introduction was termed 'study skills', it was universally delivered and it was central to the notion of access. In this context study skills was not framed as remedial nor were the students seen as deficit (Sinfield, 2003).

HE and the skills agenda

Given the contested nature of the 'skills' debate per se, the learning development debate in HE tends to revolve around whether there should be study skills, academic socialisation or academic literacies programmes (Lea and Street, 1998) – and whether or not such programmes should be sessional or pre-sessional, semi- or fully integrated, universal, bolt-on or remedial (Warren, 2002). Those concerned with LD and teaching and learning in higher education argue for a resolution that acknowledges that, for everyone, entering HE means embarking on a journey that is emotionally charged and academically challenging – and that learning development is the responsibility of all professional staff. At its best 'learning development' is expressed through creative and academically rigorous programmes, through teaching and learning expertise, through HE orientation courses or parts of courses, especially if universally delivered; and LD can take place through study and academic skills programmes, workshops and the generation and use of teaching and learning resources. Warren (2002) argues that such programmes will necessitate staff development if the emphasis is indeed to fall on the facilitation of significant learning (Rogers, 1994) for all students.

Further, it could arguably also require a paradigm shift in all universities, not just those committed to 'teaching and learning', such that lecturers on all programmes are valued for their prowess as educators, as well being judged as academics.

Resolution

If education is more than formulaic policy, strategy or learning outcomes, if it can constitute some sort of transcendent experience (Satterthwaite, 2004), we have found that it is often the reviled non-traditional student, dismembered and dislocated by the discourses of derision, who is the most moved and the most changed by their educational experience. In fact, despite the falling unit and poor targeting of resource, despite Hodge relegating the majority of students to educational backwaters and (implicitly less respected) vocational degrees, it is the widening participation student who is embracing risk, engaging in the modernisation project and rewriting their life narratives through educational struggle (Giddens, 1996).

And while the government might seek a separation between research, teaching and learning and relations with business, it is perhaps only a continuation of these relationships for all universities that will militate against the development of a bipartite higher education system with its consequent negative ramifications, especially for the non-traditional student. For, while research does remain the key to the identity and practice of many universities, the majority also acknowledge the role that pedagogical practice plays in a university's success. Further, all research, even if applied, perhaps to pedagogic practice, say, rather than pure, can be fed into course delivery such that students feel the exhilaration of being on the cutting edge of discovery.

What can the HE practitioner do?

Whatever your attitude towards HE and government intervention in HE per se – and the ramifications of that for your institution and your own practice – there are some practical steps that you can take to help your own personal professional development – and the development of your students.

Show you know

You are advised to discover your institution's research, access/recruitment and teaching and learning strategy documents. Discover who in your department, and your institution as a whole, is responsible for the delivery of such strategies – and from where you can expect support, including teaching and learning development support. When generating your own performance review targets and indicators, use the language of the relevant institutional documentation and detail how far you have played a role in helping your institution meet its research, recruitment and teaching and learning targets.

Teaching and learning practice

In order to improve the learning development and academic success of your students, we would also recommend that you utilise the practices, strategies and techniques detailed in this tutor's handbook. The information, activities and exercises in this text have been developed over more than thirty years of practical work – typically with non-traditional students. While there cannot be one quick-fix solution to the various study issues with which *any* of your students may present, the ones here, if introduced and then rehearsed in a variety of contexts, have been proven to facilitate student understanding of the forms and processes of academic discourse – and to encourage students to master them for themselves.

Notes

1 For a more detailed discussion of the changing management practices in HE see also Sinfield et al. (2004).
2 We use the term 'less academically inducted' throughout to indicate not that these students are academically deficient but that they have not been inducted into successful academic practice.

Bibliography and further reading

Anie, A. (2001) *Widening Participation – Graduate Employability Project.* University of North London (now London Metropolitan University).

Archer, L. (2002) '*Access elite*', *Times Higher Education Supplement*, 18 January.

Archer, L., Hutchings, M. and Ross, A. (2003) *Higher Education and Social Class: Issues of Exclusion and Inclusion.* London and New York: Routledge Falmer.

Bennett, R. (2002) 'Lecturers' attitudes to new teaching methods', *International Journal of Management Education*, 2 (1): 42–57.

Bourdieu, P. and Passeron, J.-C. (1979) *Reproduction in Education, Society and Culture.* London: Sage.

Burn, E. and Finnigan, T. (2003) 'I've made it more academic by adding some snob words from the thesaurus', in Satterthwaite, J., Atkinson, E. and Gale,

K. (eds), *Discourse, Power, Resistance: Challenging the Rhetoric of Contemporary Education*. Stoke-on-Trent: Trentham Books.

Burns, T. and Sinfield, S. (2003) *Essential Study Skills: The complete guide to success @ university*. London: Sage.

Clegg, S. and Ashworth, P. (2004) 'Contested practices: learning outcomes and disciplinary understandings', in Satterthwaite et al. (eds), *The Disciplining of Education: New Languages of Power and Resistance*. Stoke-on-Trent: Trentham Books.

Cottrell, S. (2001) *Teaching Study Skills and Supporting Learning*. Basingstoke: Palgrave.

Giddens, A. (1996) *Consequences of Modernity*. Cambridge: Polity Press.

Hodge, Margaret, Secretary of State for Education (2002) Keynote speech: *What Is College and University Education for?* Church House, Westminster, Education Conference, 24 January.

Hodge, Margaret (2003) quoted in Claire Saunders, 'Fact: term jobs damage grades', *Times Higher Education Supplement*, 7 February.

Holmes, L. (2001) 'Reconsidering graduate employability: the "graduate identity" approach', *Quality in Higher Education*, 7 (2): 111–19.

Holmes, L. (2002) Available from: *www.re-skill.org.uk/thesis/*, accessed February 2002. (See also: *www.re-skill.org.uk*; *www.graduate-employability.org.uk*; *www.odysseygroup.org.uk*.)

hooks, b. (1994) *Teaching to Transgress*. London: Routledge.

LDHEN (2003) Learning Development in Higher Education Network discussion at: *http://www.jiscmail.ac.uk/lists/LDHEN.html*.

Lea, M.R. and Street, B. (1998) 'Student writing in Higher Education: an academic literacies approach', *Studies in Higher Education*, 23 (2): 157–72.

Leathwood, C. and O'Connell, P. (2003) ' "It's a struggle": the construction of the "new student" in higher education', in *Journal of Educational Policy*, 18 (6).

Lillis, T. (2001) *Student Writing, Access, Regulation, Desire*. London: Routledge.

Luttrell, W. (1997) *Schoolsmart and Motherwise*. London: Routledge.

Medhurst, A. (2000) 'If anywhere: class identifications and cultural studies academics', in Munt, S. (ed.), *Cultural Studies and the Working Class*. London: Cassell.

Munt, S. (ed.) (2000) *Cultural Studies and the Working Class*. London: Cassell.

Noble, D. (2002) *Digital Diploma Mills: The Automation of Higher Education*. New York: Education Monthly Review Press.

Reay, D. (1998) *Class Work*. London: UCL Press.

Rogers, C. (1994) *Freedom to Learn*. Upper Saddle River, NJ: Merrill.

Satterthwaite, J. (2004) 'Learning in the clouds: learning beyond knowledge', in Satterthwaite, J. et al. (eds), *Educational Counter-Cultures: Confrontations, Images, Vision*. Stoke-on-Trent: Trentham Books (due 2004).

Satterthwaite, J., Atkinson, E. and Gale, K. (eds) (2003) *Discourse, Power, Resistance: Challenging the Rhetoric of Contemporary Education*. Stoke-on-Trent: Trentham Books.

Sinfield, S. (2003) 'Teaching older learners: an opportunity not a problem', *Investigations in Teaching and Learning in Higher Education*, 1 (1): 35–40.

Sinfield, S., Burns, T. and Holley, D. (2004) 'Outsiders looking in or insiders looking out?', in Satterthwaite, J. et al. (eds), *The Disciplining of Education: New Languages of Power and Resistance*. Stoke-on-Trent: Trentham Books (due 2004).

Tett, L. (2000) 'I'm working class and proud of it – gendered experiences of non-traditional participants in higher education', *Gender and Education*, 1 (2): 183–94.

Thompson, J. (ed.) (2000) *Stretching the Academy: The Politics and Practice of Widening Participation in Higher Education*. Leicester: NIACE.

Warren, D. (2002) 'Curriculum design in a context of widening participation in higher education', *Arts and Humanities in Higher Education*, 1 (1): 85–99.

White Paper (2003) *The future of higher education*. Available from *http://www.dfes.gov.uk/highereducation/hestrategy/pdfs/DfES-HigherEducation.pdf* (accessed 16 March 2004).

3 How to assess – a short preface on assessment

Coverage

- Assessment today:
  - Formative/summative
  - Active learning, HE induction and orientation, managing students
  - The changing HE environment – modularisation of work

- *ESS 9*: How to prepare better assignments

- *ESS 7*: How to build your confidence

- Bibliography and further reading

Introduction

This chapter discusses assessment in a time of widening participation and, alongside the further reading indicated below, is offered as a preface to all the chapters exploring student potential and actual assessment practices, such as effective research, reading and note-making practices, group work, presentations, seminars, essays, reports and exams, that are covered elsewhere in this handbook.

Assessment per se

Arguably, for the majority of lecturers assessment is not a problem in itself; if we have an education system that awards qualifications then there must be assessment devices that can determine what the student has learned and at what level. In this way certificates, diplomas and degrees can be awarded appropriately and fairly.

Typically, for many of us the natural impulse in the past may have been to opt for written assessments – in the form of essays, reports, papers and/or exams – that we as tutors would evaluate. Increasingly, however, the situation is becoming more complex with an emphasis on formative and summative assessments – and on opening up the range of assessment devices offered to students: to stimulate active learning, to stimulate the forms of critical and analytical thinking that we wish students to develop, to provide variety and, sometimes, even to 'police' the new students.

Some assessment devices

A quick survey of some of the modules with which we interact at the university reveal, alongside the essay, report and paper, the following assessment strategies in use:

- Learning log

- Critical reflection upon an organisation and time management exercise

- Annotated bibliography

- Critical 'reading record'

- Abstract writing

- Exams with time constraints of varying length from one hour upwards, seen or unseen, open or closed book

- Exams with word constraints from three, 400-word answers to two 750-word answers

- Presentations and seminars, individual or group, the latter awarding either an individual or a group mark.

Model it: Arguably each assessment device requires the student to adopt different practices and adapt to different academic forms or genres. If you intend students to learn through a struggle with content rather than form, offer models or case study exemplars, of good practice.

How will I assess that?

When considering which mode of assessment to choose we might reflect upon the nature of our subject or discipline – does it inherently merit one form of assessment over another, a presentation rather than an essay, say? And perhaps also consider the level of the unit, module or course that we are running – maybe being happier with self- or peer-assessment at the lower levels of a programme of study rather than at the higher. Perhaps more importantly we will consider our particular aims, objectives and teaching and learning goals – specifically, we might consider the benefit we would like our students to derive from the assessment process itself, rather than focusing on the end product of assessment alone.

As well as developments in assessment per se, in many institutions assessment is being revisited in the context of widening participation and the move to mass higher education. In these instances tutors may be building in staged assessment activities designed to promote learning or understanding, rather than relying on one definitive assessment at the end of a unit, module or programme of study. Typically the tutor will use these activities to help the student develop understanding of a particular concept and/or to practice an academic or study skill, such as goal setting, reference finding, note-making, paragraph or summary writing. Here lecturers are using these interventions to promote active learning and understanding, as well as to rehearse students in good academic practice, including the development of critical and analytical thinking skills.

Still other lecturers may be using these interventions as policing devices. With the latter, particular assignments may be set during a specific lecture or seminar session and while the activity may be used to gradually acclimatise the less academically inducted student to good study and academic practice, the emphasis on these mini-assessments is to ensure the student's attendance at that lecture or seminar. Of course this is a complex area in terms of good practice and of ethics or ideology.

Some issues with respect to assessment

Lecturers in the Learning Development in Higher Education Network revealed the following concerns with respect to assessment:

- Formative activities are an essential part of the teaching/learning process – but many of my classes are too big to allow for this.

- I believe that we over-assess our students – we are only giving them more opportunities to fail.

- Students are becoming very assessment-focused – if it isn't assessed, they won't do it.

- I'm not comfortable with assessment as policing – this is not a secondary school, it's a university.

- Many of our students are working over twenty hours a week – just how are they supposed to do all the work that we set?

Interactionist, cognitive and social theories of teaching and learning stress that it is essential that all students, not only those that are non-traditional, have the space to engage with the ideas, concepts and practices of their subject and thus there is a need for formative activities, whether or not they are actually assessed. Perhaps it is where **all** the formative activities are graded and count toward the student's grade for a particular module or course that de facto leads us to over-assess our students and, worse, to increase opportunities for failure rather than opportunities for learning. Further, there is the argument that using such formative assessment practices to regulate student behaviour moves us towards a policing of the **implicitly transgressive student** (Sinfield et al., 2004), which fundamentally changes the university ethos and damages the trust relationship that ought to exist between tutor and student.

The changing HE environment

Further, assessment processes exist within the dynamic environment that is HE. Not only have the introduction of fees and the replacement of student grants with loans pushed students into paid employment so that they have less time for independent study, the move to modularisation – the Americanisation of the British HE system – has also had an impact. That is, the drive to make education a global commodity has caused many universities – especially the new universities that attract the widening participation student – to move to 15-week modular programmes instead of the one-year course. Typically, while the latter has an assessment load that is spread over an academic year, the 15-week module offers 12 teaching weeks wherein assessed coursework is typically generated, followed by three weeks for revision and examinations. Hence you have a system where the typically less academically inducted student engages with a new topic, at a new level, for just 12 weeks before engaging in assessments that will eventually (after the preliminary year) lead to their degree classification.

Often these students are encountering a multiplicity of assessment devices in their various modules: individual or group presentations or seminars, essays, reports, reading records, summary or abstract writing, annotated bibliographies, seen or unseen exams and so forth. Thus the student has to grapple with new material and a diversity of potentially new and frequently changing assessment devices in very short spaces of time. Further, given that this student has to take four modules per semester, they may be engaging with a bewildering diversity of assessment devices at one and the same time. Typically, the student – and we are arguing that this affects mainly the non-traditional, less academically inducted widening participation student – has little time to engage with course content – and no time to become familiar with the multiplicity of assessment devices with which they are faced. Hence it is precisely the new widening participation student that is increasingly handicapped in this system.

Conclusion

Assessment per se is not simple. The increasing participation of perhaps less academically inducted students in higher education has also seen the evolution of pedagogic practice with a concurrent shift towards a greater use of formative assessment mechanisms. Apart from the traditional essay, report or paper, currently there are a multiplicity of coursework assessment devices proliferating: as part of the HE induction/orientation process, as part of good teaching and learning practice, to police the student or as a consequence of modularisation. On some courses the examination – the assessment device with which the older tutor is typically the most familiar – is being omitted altogether. Typically, when deciding on assessment devices tutors consider the value of the processes in which they wish students to engage, as well as the end product that they will adjudge. In all instances those of us in learning development also argue for the evolution of an emancipatory pedagogy that reveals the forms and processes of academic discourse. Here, the use of models or case study exemplars will facilitate student understanding of and performance in the requisite assessment mechanism, and that thus it will be possible to use assessment proactively to promote student learning and student success.

Bibliography and further reading

Beckwith, J. (1991) 'Approaches to learning, their context and relationship to assessment performance', *Higher Education*, 22: 17–40.

Bennett, R. (2002) 'Lecturers' attitudes to new teaching methods', *International Journal of Management Education*, 2 (1): 42–57.

Biggs, J. (1999) *Teaching for Quality at University*. Buckingham: Open University Press.

Bourdieu, P. and Passeron, J.-C. (1979) *Reproduction in Education, Society and Culture*. London: Sage.

Burns, T. and Sinfield, S. (2003) *Essential Study Skills: The complete guide to success @ university*. London: Sage.

Cottrell, S. (2001) *Teaching Study Skills and Supporting Learning*. Basingstoke: Palgrave.

Gibbs, G. (1992) 'Improving the quality of student learning through course design', in Barnett, R. (ed.), *Learning to Effect*. Buckingham: SRHE and OUP.

Holmes, L. (2002) Available from: *www.re-skill.org.uk/thesis/*, accessed February 2002. (See also: *www.re-skill.org.uk*; *www.graduate-employability.org.uk*; *www.odysseygroup.org.uk*.)

Jenkins, A., Breen, R., Lindsay, R. and Brew, A. (2003) *Reshaping Teaching in Higher Education: Linking Teaching with Research*. London: Kogan Page.

Kahn, P. and Baume, D. (eds) *A Guide to Staff and Educational Development*. London: Kogan Page.

Lave, J. and Wenger, E. (1991) *Situated Learning: Legitimate Peripheral Participation*. Cambridge: CUP.

LDHEN (2003) Learning Development in Higher Education Network discussion at : *http://www.jiscmail.ac.uk/lists/LDHEN.html*.

Lea, M. and Stierer, B. (2002) *Student Writing in Higher Education*. Buckingham: SRHE and OUP.

Lea, M.R. and Street, B. (1998) 'Student writing in Higher Education: an academic literacies approach', *Studies in Higher Education*, 23 (2): 157–72.

Leathwood, C. and O'Connell, P. (2003) ' "It's a struggle": the construction of the "new student" in higher education', in *Journal of Educational Policy*, 18 (6).

Lillis, T. (2001) *Student Writing, Access, Regulation, Desire*. London: Routledge.

Martinez, P. (2001) *Improving Student Retention and Achievement*. London: Learning and Skills Development Agency.

Noble, D. (2002) *Digital Diploma Mills: The Automation of Higher Education*. New York: Education Monthly Review Press.

Prosser, M. and Trigwell, K. (1999) *Understanding Learning and Teaching*. Buckingham: SRHE and OUP.

Race, P. (2002) *The Lecturer's Toolkit*, 2nd edn. London: Kogan Page.

Ramsden, P. (1992) *Learning to Teach in Higher Education*. London: Routledge.

Rogers, C. (1994) *Freedom to Learn*. Upper Saddle River, NJ: Merrill.

Satterthwaite, J., Atkinson, E. and Gale, K. (eds) (2003) *Discourse, Power, Resistance: Challenging the Rhetoric of Contemporary Education*. Stoke-on-Trent: Trentham Books.

Satterthwaite, J. et al. (eds) (2004) *The Disciplining of Education: New Languages of Power and Resistance*. Stoke-on-Trent: Trentham Books.

Sinfield, S., Burns, T. and Holley, D. (2004) 'Outsiders looking in or insiders looking out?', in Satterthwaite, J. et al. (eds), *The Disciplining of Education: New Languages of Power and Resistance*. Stoke-on-Trent: Trentham Books.

Squires, G. (2203) *Trouble-shooting Your Teaching: A Step-by-Step Guide to Analysing and Improving Your Practice*. London: Kogan Page.

Thompson, J. (ed.) (2000) *Stretching the Academy: The Politics and Practice of Widening Participation in Higher Education*. Leicester: NIACE.

Warren, D. (2002) 'Curriculum design in a context of widening participation in higher education', *Arts and Humanities in Higher Education*, 1 (1): 85–99.

Wisker, G. and Brown, S. (2001) *Enabling Student Learning: Systems and Strategies*. London: Kogan Page.

4 How to understand our students

Our students

Our university has a widening participation brief and actively recruits those that are deemed 'non-traditional' students. This is not an homogenous group but consists of:

- Mature students
- International students
- English speakers of other languages
- Those typically excluded from or not encouraged into higher education
- Those where HE is not an 'embedded' way of life
- Those from the local working-class and ethnic minority communities
- Those who have suffered previous education rebuff
- Those lacking in self-confidence and self-esteem, especially with respect to higher education

▩ Those that are often highly motivated

▩ And those that just want to survive: 'I'll be happy with a C,' 'I just want to pass.'

The QAA *Subject Review for Business* (2002) noted that of our students just 12% entered at 18 with the typical A level profile; the rest – that is 88% – were classified as mature. Seventy-four per cent of our students had no previous family member through HE, 60% did not pay fees. Further, many of our students speak of painful educational experiences at school – and the majority suffer low self-esteem and self-confidence. Leathwood and O'Connell (2003) note that this continual feeling of not being 'good enough' relates to 'systems of oppression' within society rather individual traits or personality failings and constitutes further evidence of the struggle faced by non-traditional students.

In this chapter we draw on informal interviews that we have had with our students over several years as we attempt to explain the non-traditional student in their own words. We draw particularly on the experiences of students accessing learning development support either in HE orientation modules or drop-in workshops as we consider student aims, the attitudes of others towards our students, student self-perception, various modes of learning development (LD) and support, and whether or not LD makes a difference to student success.

WP students' expressed aims

Self-development and improvement ... and financial reward have all been offered as reasons for entering HE, both in the wider research literature and from our internal research:

▩ I wanted to follow up [my subject], I wanted more.

▩ I needed to bring myself up to speed and see if I had a brain.

▩ I'm at the top of my [pay] scale] ... and I can't go any further.

These goals did seem to alter as students moved through their programmes of study; further, many students reported that they felt changed by their educational experiences:

▩ I feel it's part of my life now.

▩ You feel so special. You really feel marvellous. You think, gosh, I can be clever again. It's a good, a good feeling.

▩ No, no. My reason is now for myself and to try and change things.

▩ I want to do more. I want to have my ideas ... I want to be on top.

■ It was very good for my confidence as well and also, to tell you the truth, anything I learn on the modules actually complements my work. So I take it back into the workplace.
(Sinfield, 2003; Sinfield et al., 2004)

Attitudes to our students

See also Chapter 1.

■ Research here and beyond (Bourdieu and Passeron, 1979; Burn and Finnegan, 2003; hooks, 1994; Leathwood and O'Connell, 2003; Lillis, 2001; Luttrell, 1997; Medhurst, 2000; Munt, 2000; Reay, 1998; Sinfield, 2003; Skeggs, 1997; Tett, 2000) record responses that are classed, aged, raced and gendered – pathologising and denigrating non-traditional (staff and) students. This has been captured by Starkey: 'There are Mickey Mouse students for whom Mickey Mouse degrees are quite appropriate.'

■ Lillis (2001) specifically links debates about the 'crisis' in education and the preoccupation with 'skills' and 'standards' to the reaction to widening participation.

■ On the one hand, some warn that we are actually harsher towards our students: 'I think we give them opportunities to fail …' 'I'm an external examiner for other institutions and I know that we are harsher here' (Sinfield et al., 2004).

■ At the same time, many tutors here report their enthusiasm for our students.

Self-perception

Becoming a student was a very emotionally charged activity for all the students interviewed. While there was a sense of anticipation and excitement, the overriding emotional experience was of fear and anxiety. Common words to describe initial experiences are: apprehensive, het-up, nervous, nerve racking, inadequate, frightened, terrified:

■ I thought they were all looking at me and thinking what is that old woman doing here?

■ I was glad but scared. I thought you stupid idiot, why didn't you leave things as they were?

■ Why, why, why couldn't you be happy just going to work?
(Sinfield et al., 2004).

Fear and a lack of self-confidence have a real impact on the quality of the student learning experience and affect that learning:

▥ But that week when you did that ... I hated that and I was really uncomfortable the whole lesson ... I was so unsure and not confident ... I thought, I don't know what the hell she wants me to do. And you know, as soon as you're in that position, you can't learn anything, you can't take anything in ... and it was awful. It was horrible. I didn't like that at all. I found that really hard.

(Sinfield et al., 2004).

But these feelings can change:

▥ I don't feel that way about myself anymore. I feel quite confident now. I can go for most things, you know?

▥ It's my university now!

(Sinfield et al., 2004).

As argued throughout this text, there is no one quick-fix way of helping students change from their initial feelings of fear – even despair – to those of self-confidence. It will not be one perfect learning development experience or one exquisitely designed HE orientation module that will 'do the trick' but rather a multiplicity of responses and practices are required in order to reach out to our multiple and diverse student body. Below we have detailed some of the techniques that can be put into place to facilitate the student transition into – and success with – the HE environment (see also Chapter 15 on how to promote overall success).

Embedding learning development – helping our students succeed in HE

1 **Interesting and creative programmes:** Arguably the best way of enabling all students to succeed in HE is the design and delivery of interesting, creative and academically rigorous programmes that stimulate students to learn and, where necessary, to reach out for the study and academic skills and practices that will enable them to do so. Nothing will more harm the HE experiences of the non-traditional student than the wholesale development of homogenised, remediating curricula.

2 **Teaching and learning expertise:** Teaching and learning practice that facilitates students' active engagement with ideas is another key facet of an embedded approach to learning development. We argue that staff have to reveal and discuss the epistemological practices and

ontological roots of their disciplines and that this, coupled with making transparent the forms and processes of academic discourse itself, is a prime mechanism for facilitating the entry into HE discourse of all students, including the less academically inducted student.

3 **HE orientation** (see also Chapter 15): Teaching and learning development practitioners have long discussed the benefits of making transparent the forms and processes of academic discourse (Lillis, 2001) and of devising and delivering intensive, well-designed academic programmes that reveal epistemological practices coupled with an emphasis on study, communication and academic 'skills'. Warren (2002) indicates that rather than constituting a 'dumbing down' of university education, all students benefit from such HE orientation initiatives.

4 **Learning development:** Many universities now have Learning Development, Teaching and Learning Development or Study and Academic Skills units[1] with advisers that can work directly with students and/or staff. Typically such units will offer some form of study and academic skills provision for students and may run training or development activities for staff. As well as raising awareness of the strengths and needs of non-traditional students, resource generation may form one of the functions of units such as these.

5 **Learning resources:** As mentioned above, many universities do have learning development provision of some form or another. Typically such provision will include the production of teaching and learning resources – either for direct dissemination to students – or for dissemination through subject staff and subject tuition. Typically LD resources will not serve to replace sensitive one-to-one or small-group engagement between students and experienced staff – but they can definitely supplement good teaching. Both this text and our companion text *Essential Study Skills* have produced supplementary learning resources for use with students.

6 **Integrated skills:** As well as LD being a locus for the development of study and academic skills, some institutions build student awareness of study and academic skills and strategies within specific modules – this is sometimes known as an integrated skills approach. Whether designed and delivered by subject staff alone, or by subject and LD staff in collaboration, the purpose of such tuition is to self-consciously and overtly develop and rehearse an awareness of study and academic skills in the participating students.

7 **Academic consistency:** Not only do students often find the terms essay, report, paper, presentation, seminar, etc. confusing in the first

instance, they tend to become further confused when every member of staff uses these terms in idiosyncratic ways. It can help students if we demystify these terms in our practice, and if there is some uniformity to the way that we use the terms across an institution. However, the latter is not as necessary as the tutor at least making overt what they expect when they ask for an essay, paper, literature review, etc.

8 **Pedagogical innovation:** Many non-traditional students have not benefited from successful early educational experiences. It may be that innovative pedagogical practice may be needed to harness these students' potential. Some institutions are experimenting with e-learning (electronic or virtual learning environments) or blended learning (an appropriate mixture of direct tuition and e-learning) in order to harness the potential and meet the needs of the non-traditional student. One caveat here would be that just as students can need help with the transition into HE discourse per se, they will benefit from help with the transition to e- or blended learning approaches.

Does HE orientation and learning development make a difference?

Both in longitudinal studies and in smaller qualitative studies, students have been asked what has made a difference to them in their success at university. Particular mention has been made of the benefits of the opportunity to learn and rehearse specific academic skills and practices, for example:

- organisation and time management
- targeted research and reading
- pattern notes (mind maps)
- decoding assessments – and explaining the importance of learning outcomes and assessment criteria
- building presentation skills
- developing essay and report writing skills, including paragraph construction
- positive thinking.

Caveat – be a SWOT

In our own experiences we have noted that many of the practices that we wish to teach students in the first instance actually appear threatening to those students and increase their stress. For example, our ten-step approach to assignment success (see Chapter 10) appears to be a very time-consuming approach that students will feel they simply cannot afford to adopt, even if it does appear to embody good practice. It may be that tutors will need to employ seminar time in order to facilitate student adoption of successful strategies.

● **Tutor tips:**
● Use seminar time to rehearse successful strategies.
● Help students adopt a successful strategy by having a SWOT session with students on the strategy. That is, make the time to discuss the **S**trengths, **W**eaknesses, **O**pportunities and **T**hreats of the new system. Get students themselves to suggest ways of tackling the weakness/threat elements of the strategy.

What made a difference – in their own words

- I was thinking about all those books on the booklist. I was thinking I had to read every single one of those books and I didn't know how I was going to manage it ... When you did that bit about the books [work on successful research and active reading strategies – see Chapter 8] ... I found that very valuable.

- I use mind maps all the time on all modules and throughout my work [see Chapter 9].

- I felt that I needed that space just to build the confidence up and to know that I was doing things right [see Chapter 15].

- I think I have gained the confidence to speak in public ... So I feel that confidence is the main thing.

- [Study skills] gave me the structure to go back to, to hold on to and work from there. Particularly useful when I feel I don't know anything!

- And it opened up learning strategies, different strategies [see Chapter 12 on revision and exam techniques] ... And now I don't feel inferior ... when I came out of school ... I just viewed myself as a not very intelligent person really.

- I pay much more attention to the assessment criteria now [Chapter 5].

- (On grades:) I'm really lucky; mostly it's made me feel up there. And it, and it – and you go, **yes**, and it really spurs you on.

Grade note: While grades per se do – and arguably must – matter to our students, it is necessary to explain to new students the difference between university grades and previous grades that they have achieved. For example, while a strong tutor-directed essay might receive a high B or even an A grade in pre-degree programmes or at AS, A2 or GNVQ, such a piece might receive a mid-range C grade (or lower) in HE. For B and A grades students will have to undertake significant research, going beyond the recommended reading and typically accessing upwards of ten sources of information for a B and 15 plus for an A – even in first year programmes.

Typically, once students enter HE they will be expected to undertake independent thought and independent study – but we must make this clear to students.

Student recommendations

■ 'Tell us what you mean by a "child study" or a report or whatever!'

● **Tutor tip:** Use models or case study exemplars of good practice. Tell students precisely what **form** an essay, presentation or paper should take. Reveal your requirements – this is not cheating!

■ 'Give us small pieces of work to do so that we know we are "on the right track." '

● **Tutor tip:** Give small assignments with formative feedback – this alleviates anxiety and allows students to take control of their work. Many students do realise that high student numbers made this problematic on some courses/ modules.

■ 'I didn't know this support was available – you should advertise it more!'

● **Tutor tip:** Work to raise awareness of learning development and support.

Final comments

■ Higher education presents (non-traditional) students with what appear to be insurmountable obstacles (Anie, 2001; Archer, 2002; Leathwood and O'Connell, 2003)

■ Many tutors feel that our (non-traditional) students have been failed by the education system. Whilst pathologised by policy-makers, the keepers of the academy and influential others, they are neither failures nor 'remedial' – but they are engaged in 'struggle' (Anie, 2001; Leathwood and O'Connell, 2003; Lillis, 2001).

▪ The widening participation student, rather than being part of diluting or weakening HE, is often over-assessed – and more harshly assessed than students in the old universities (Sinfield et al., 2004).

▪ The success of much of our teaching is due to the diversity of our student body and the high levels of motivation, commitment and enthusiasm that the students themselves bring to the university. Working with our students can be joyful and inspiring.

▪ We do need to raise awareness of the value and needs of the non-traditional student; and the potential of the **right sort** of support to improve the quality of the student learning experience and to help students negotiate a potentially hostile academic environment. Such support can include:
  – Working directly to build self-confidence.
  – Opportunities to practise writing – with models of good practice.
  – Formative assessments and feedback (formative feedback also underpins 'write to learn' as opposed to 'learn to write' approaches).
  – Decoding learning outcomes and clarifying assessment criteria.
  – Consistency: **either** we all mean the same thing by essay, report, paper, learning log, reading record, bibliography, references, the Harvard system, a presentation, a seminar, **or**, where we diverge, we know that we have and we explain the divergence to the student.

Conclusion

For (non-traditional) students, entering HE can be an almost disabling experience fraught with 'struggle' (Leathwood and O'Connell, 2003). While Lillis (2001) warns that the skills agenda itself is partly responsible for disabling the non-traditional student, learning development in practice can and does support students in their transition into academic discourse and can work to promote their success in the HE environment. Students with whom we have worked recommend direct tuition in research, reading, note-making and assignment preparation (including the use of formative feedback). Further, non-traditional students report their appreciation of direct attempts to build their self-confidence.

Learning development, we argue, is not just the responsibility of a university's LD unit (by whatever name) but is the responsibility of all professional staff, and this is manifest in the design and delivery of exciting courses, in teaching and learning expertise and in the appropriate direct addressing of learning development – which can take place via integrated skills work, in HE orientation modules, in study and academic skills programmes and workshops and with the support of well-designed teaching and learning resources.

We argue that non-traditional students enrich the academic environment with our teaching and learning processes facilitated by the interest and motivation of a diverse student body. Typically the (adult) student wants to understand their subject – de facto, to engage with its epistemology – and to become a successful graduate. This interest and engagement is fostered when we in HE make transparent and problematic the forms and processes of education itself – and yet learn to trust the student, allowing them to 'reach their own accommodation with discourses of belonging, identity and power' (Medhurst, in Munt, 2000: 31).

Note

1 The year 2003 saw the evolution of the Learning Development in Higher Education Network. This is a group of practitioners interested in sharing approaches to learning development work. If you are interested in joining the LDHEN contact *LDHEN@jiscmail.ac.uk* web address.

Bibliography and further reading

Anie, A. (2001) *Widening Participation – Graduate Employability Project*. University of North London (now London Metropolitan University).

Bourdieu, P. and Passeron, J.-C. (1979) *Reproduction in Education, Society and Culture*. London: Sage.

Burn, E. and Finnigan, T. (2003) 'I've made it more academic by adding some snob words from the thesaurus', in Satterthwaite, J., Atkinson, E. and Gale, K. (eds), *Discourse, Power, Resistance: Challenging the Rhetoric of Contemporary Education*. Stoke-on-Trent: Trentham Books.

Burns, T. and Sinfield, S. (2003) *Essential Study Skills: The complete guide to success @ university*. London: Sage.

Holmes, L. (2001) 'Reconsidering graduate employability: the "graduate identity" approach', *Quality in Higher Education*, 7 (2): 111–19.

Holmes, L. (2002) Available from: *www.re-skill.org.uk/thesis/*, acessed February 2002. (See also: *www.re-skill.org.uk*; *www.graduate-employability.org.uk*; *www.odysseygroup.org.uk*.)

hooks, b. (1994) *Teaching to Transgress*. London: Routledge.

Leathwood, C. and O'Connell, P. (2003) ' "It's a struggle": the construction of the "new student" in higher education', *Journal of Educational Policy*, 18 (6).

Lillis, T. (2001) *Student Writing, Access, Regulation, Desire*. London: Routledge.

Luttrell, W. (1997) *Schoolsmart and Motherwise*. London: Routledge.

Medhurst, A. (2000) 'If anywhere: class identifications and cultural studies academics', in Munt, S. (ed.), *Cultural Studies and the Working Class*. London: Cassell.

Munt, S. (ed.) (2000) *Cultural Studies and the Working Class*. London: Cassell.

QAA (2002) *Subject Review for Business*. London Metropolitan University.

Reay, D. (1998) *Class Work*. London: UCL Press.

Sinfield, S. (2003) 'Teaching older learners: an opportunity not a problem', *Investigations in Teaching and Learning in Higher Education*, 1 (1): 35–40.

Sinfield, S., Burns, T. and Holley, D. (2004) 'Outsiders looking in or insiders looking out?', in Satterthwaite, J. et al. (eds), *The Disciplining of Education: New Languages of Power and Resistance*. Stoke-on-Trent: Trentham Books.

Skeggs, B. (1997) *Formations of Class and Gender*. London: Sage.

Tett, L. (2000) *'I'm working class and proud of it – gendered experiences of non-traditional participants in higher education'*, *Gender and Education*, 1 (2): 183–94.

Warren, D. (2002) 'Curriculum design in a context of widening participation in higher education', *Arts and Humanities in Higher Education*, 1 (1): 85–99.

5 How to promote an effective transition to HE

Introduction

The experience of going to university is a profound one for all students, wrought with more fears and stresses than we can imagine. Cast your mind back to your own thoughts, fears and misconceptions about university . . . remember for a moment how powerful they were and what effect they had on you. It is useful for us as tutors to understand the emotional and practical implications of the move to university for the student. This chapter explores how potential and actual university students can be helped in their transition to university, with a special focus on raising their awareness of what is expected of them not by problematising the student, but by making explicit the forms and practices of HE itself – and of our own particular subject or discipline.

Problematising HE not the student

Going to university – and arguably who goes to university – has ramifications for both students and staff. For students, their lives will change dramatically – such changes will be felt particularly by those who are the first in the family to undertake this venture. For staff, changes in pre-degree syllabi and ever increasing moves to widening participation, may lead us to feel that we no longer know how academically inducted our students are, nor what subject knowledge we can expect of them when they arrive at university. For the student, the new university environment of fees, student loans and part-time employment is a much more hostile one than most of us who are (older) lecturers at the moment have had to endure. For staff there may be a tendency to focus on the lowering of academic standards – with GCSEs and A levels 'not what they used to be' – rather than recognising the often heroic nature of student struggle (see also Chapter 1). We may be tempted to view our students only in terms of the problems with which they present us in that they are under-prepared for university per se and for our course in particular, and we may resent having to undertake what we consider to be remedial teaching just to bring students 'up to speed'. However, whether or not an institution has a commitment to widening participation, we argue that efforts on our behalf to help students make an effective transition to HE are emblematic of ethical good practice and benefit all our students (Warren, 2002). This book as a whole explores ways of facilitating student success in HE – and this chapter explores how we can better prepare students for university by making more explicit aspects of HE that we perhaps take for granted.

Choosing a university

Perhaps one of the most basic questions that we would expect students to ask is this – which university should I choose? If you are a sixth-form teacher or a tutor in further education, whether or not your students do ask this crucial question, you may need to discuss with them the nature of university per se – and the different types of university that exist. Students do need this information in order to make informed choices – even if in the end financial constraints will force them to attend the university nearest to home. If you are a university lecturer welcoming students into your institution, it may help to lay out this information for your students such that they better understand the institution of which they will be a member for a significant length of time.

Information that you might like to give to students on this topic could include some of the following:

- Higher education in England typically takes place in what are termed the 'old' and the 'new' universities – although some does take place in higher education institutions – perhaps attached to FE colleges.

- The old universities range from the Russell Group to the modern campus of East Anglia. These universities are primarily research-based institutions – sometimes with strong links to local or other industries, the industries that draw on the research base of the university. Think of Microsoft and the reasons that it chose to locate in Cambridge. Tutors at the old universities are expected to have a strong research focus such that they become the 'leaders in the field' of their chosen subject. That means that they will be the ones taking the knowledge (or knowledge-claims) of their subject forward. While the old universities may be criticised for being rather monocultural (Leathwood, 2004), if students choose to study at such a university it could be because they are extremely interested in a particular subject and want to be taught by the people who are at the cutting edge of defining that subject.

- The new universities generally sprang from the old polytechnics. The polytechnic mission was to take higher education to the broader mass of people, either because there was a need for highly educated people in the professions – such as engineering – or from a more ideological position of believing that the education system actually disadvantaged many people who had the ability to benefit from higher education but were not enabled to do so. In 1992 the government opened the university charter such that the old polytechnics could apply for university status. These new universities were expected to widen their research base but at the same time keep some form of 'widening participation' agenda and concomitantly have a commitment to supportive teaching and learning environments. If students choose to go to a new university it might be because such an institution offers exactly the right course, because they want a more mixed student body or because they think that they might find more supportive teaching and learning strategies helpful.

- Who goes to university? In the past only 5 to 7% of the population went to university at all. It was expected that the brightest and the best – the elite – would go to the Russell Group of universities and eventually emerge as social leaders in business and politics. Critics might argue that this was a system predicated upon educational inequality,[1] designed to exclude the mass both from higher education and from social status.

- Widening participation: over the years – partly because of the polytechnic mission, partly because of access programmes and even partly due to high levels of unemployment – more and more people have chosen to enter HE. Further, the government, at the time of writing this book, has expressed a commitment to having 50% (not five) of 18–30 year-olds in or through HE by 2010. Arguably therefore the nature of HE is changing as those that embrace it move from the elite to the majority.

- What university should I choose? Your students should take note of the information on universities and status, of research agendas and links with business, of postgraduate opportunities and links with forms of employment other than business – NGOs, charities, social services, etc. Students should reflect on their own interests and commitment to their chosen subject, and on whether or not they want to attend a high-status monocultural institution or an institution perhaps with lower status but that has a more mixed culture or perhaps a more supportive teaching and learning environment. Basically students should undertake much more research into the university that they should choose than they typically do at the moment. Further, even if for them there is no real choice as to which university they choose to attend, they should still research the institution at which they will be studying. They should discover its strengths and weaknesses, and they should have a clear awareness of just what they want to do while they are there – and when they leave!

● **Tip:** If helping students prepare for university, make the time to support their research – including reviewing university websites. It may also be useful to prepare your students for what will be expected of them at university. (See also Resource 5.2, 'Places to go, people to meet ...', Resource 5.3 'For study success think SOCCER' and Resource 5.4 'Teaching and learning at university demystified'.)

- 'OK, I've been accepted – what do I do now?' Whether you are a sixth-form tutor or an FE lecturer preparing students for university – or a university lecturer receiving students into your institution – it is useful to inform students as to useful activities in which to engage before and immediately when they reach the university door in September or October. Things to flag up might be: summer reading, summer programmes, induction and enrolment sessions and HE orientation. Further, all students should be made aware of what attending university will entail in terms of, perhaps, support systems (see Resource 5.2), joining academic communities and teaching and learning strategies (see Resources 5.3 and 5.4).

Supporting HE orientation

The summer activities sheet (Resource 5.1) and the 'Places to go, people to meet and things to do at university' handout (Resource 5.2) both help orientate your students to the HE environment, but there is more that the preparatory sixth-form and FE college and the receiving HE institution can do.

Sixth-form and FE tutors and institutions

Your institution might prepare students for their transition to HE with certain forms of HE orientation activities. Things that we have seen work in FE include:

- **Study skills programmes:** focusing particularly on active note-making and a thorough introduction to the academic essay.

- **Tip:** Discuss the sorts of study skills approach you should adopt with the institution to which many of your students will progress. Have a continuity of approach.

- **Research project:** Set a specific task that requires students to research the university of their choice – in terms of courses offered, teaching and learning practices, awards of credits and class of degree, work placement and postgraduate opportunities. Students can write a report or deliver a presentation on their findings.

- **History of (Western) Ideas lecture programme:** We have seen such programmes work both in further and higher education. Typically these might consist of a series of lectures covering the history, science and technology, literature and the arts from the mediaeval period to the present day. Such a programme not only prepares students for the lecture process it also allows the introduction of the key themes and narratives that have shaped society as a whole and that underpin the majority of subjects or disciplines.

- **Taster sessions at university:** Something else that we have seen work well is to offer students sessions at university. Whether this takes the form of whole units or modules or just a few lectures in topics useful to the A levels that students are taking, this can prove a very valuable introduction to the university teaching and learning system.

HE tutors/institutions

It may be that your university does more than offer **summer pro-grammes** for prospective students – for example, you may have a specific unit or module or even the whole first year that acts as an HE orientation process (see also Chapter 15 on How to promote overall success). Perhaps you have a thread of modules or courses running through whole degree programmes that move students from an awareness of HE practices and culture to an understanding of the demands of postgraduate study and/or work. Whatever your particular institution engages in, it is useful for you as a tutor to help your students understand the what, why and how of these activities. Do clearly explain 'what' the students will be doing, 'why' your university offers the specific activities and programmes that you do and 'how' the student can make the most of these opportunities – in both the short and the long term. Where appropriate, explain how your particular unit, module or course plays its part in this process.

HE orientation – some things to consider

In Chapter 15 we outline the HE orientation module that we have operated for many years now. We have also run something very similar to this course in FE – mainly on access programmes – to help students prepare for university. Typically at their most basic level such HE orientation modules help students to learn how to learn, study and communicate effectively in the academic environment. We typically focus on things like making a commitment to your studies – emphasised by the good and bad learning exercise and the learning contract. We then offer students the opportunity to rehearse and refine the techniques that are suggested in the other parts of this book: note-making, research and reading, presentations and seminars, group work, essays and reports, learning styles, revision and exam techniques. These can be encapsulated in the following mnemonic: 'For study success think SOCCER' and Resource 5.3 provides a photocopiable handout for you that sums up study tips for your students.

More orientation: academic communities, teaching and learning practices and cultural capital

Of course it is not enough just to hand out Resource 5.3 and expect your students to change overnight. Students will need the opportunity to practise their study and academic skills in safe spaces in order to rehearse and refine them. They will also benefit from receiving feedback on their various study and academic skills and practices if they are to take control of themselves as active learners and successful students.

Moreover, all students, as part of the formation of their emergent student identities (Holmes, 2002), will need to grasp the fact that they have joined specific academic communities with habits and practices all of their own – and with which they will have to become familiar. Thus students will need to adapt generic information on, say, note-making or research and reading strategies to the note-making or research needs of their particular subject. They will have to adapt information on the academic essay to the requirements of a history or biology essay. The more subject tutors can make clear and overt the nature of the forms and processes of research and enquiry of their discipline, the more they will help students to understand exactly what is required of them.

In Resource 5.4 'Teaching and learning demystified' we have put together a summary of some of the key information that it might be useful to impart to your students about teaching and learning in the academic community of the university. You may wish to give a talk to your students on the material covered in these pages, tailoring it to the particular practices of your university – and the way your subject is taught at that institution. Alternatively you might like to photocopy the pages as handouts for your students. If taking the latter course, you might consider asking your students to give short presentations on their hopes and fears about studying a particular subject at university in the light of what they have gained from their reading of the handouts.

Cultural capital

As well as understanding how universities operate, including developing an awareness of the epistemological practices and the key players of the particular disciplines in which they are engaged, students will benefit from an introduction to the sorts of grand narratives or key movements that have informed the subjects that they will be studying. Hence it may be that at your institution, alongside an HE orientation programme that introduces students to key study and academic skills and practices, you also run some form of **'cultural capital'** programme – as with the 'History of (Western) Ideas' programme described briefly above.

Tutor tips: Useful things to do with students

When helping students make the transition to university – and when helping them to realise what is expected of them both as university students and as students of particular subjects or disciplines – we can take nothing for granted. Simple expressions for us such as 'make notes on this', 'read around the subject', 'write a short paper', 'prepare a literature review' and so forth may have little or no meaning for your students. Hence if we really want to help students succeed, we have to think about how we can make our meanings clear. Here are a few tips that might help.

Motivation: Do not assume that all students want to get A grades. Some have too many work or family commitments to make that a realistic option, still others have very low expectations of themselves. Ask students to complete a learning contract like the one below for your unit, module or course to take a temperature reading of the expectations and motivation levels of your students.

The Learning Contract:
What do I want from this course?
What will I have to do to achieve my goals?
What might stop me?
What's in it for me?

Organisation and time management: Typically students have no concept at all of the amount of time that studying requires. Moreover, they do not realise that they are in fact working on their final assignment from the moment a course starts. Chapters 7 on organisation and time management, 11 on writing and 15 on overall success give many suggestions that can be brought into seminar practice to raise student awareness of how they must negotiate a course and manage their time more effectively.

● **Tip:** Give students a seminar workbook that contains staged formative activities: brainstorm – action plan – present notes on the lecture – present notes on three different sources – write one essay paragraph, etc. This can help students to use their time more productively.

Grades: While we might understand what the different grades that we award mean, students tend not to. Take the time to explain how marks are awarded for your course and what the different grades indicate. Discuss the implications of assessment criteria. Show students where to get additional help.

● **Tip:** Get students to grade anonymous sample essays. Discuss the grades that they award – and the ones that you did. Discuss why they have marked higher or lower than you.

Course booklets/handbooks: You may have written the perfect course booklet that clearly explains the what, why and how of your course: aims and learning outcomes, the syllabus, the reading list, the assignment, the assessment criteria and the meaning of the different grades awarded. Two points:

1 Do not expect students to read it! Many students are too frightened to really scrutinise such information fearing that it will just reveal their inadequacy.

2 Even if they do read it, it may mean nothing to them.

● **Tip: You could talk through the booklet and explain clearly what it all means for the student in terms of the work that you will do and the effort that is expected of them. An alternative, suggested by Ed Foster (Nottingham Trent University) is to allow the students to interview you closely on the course. Give students a few moments to browse through a course booklet, and then in pairs to devise questions to ask you. This will indicate to you whether or not they are asking the 'right' questions and what additional information they might require.**

Aims and learning outcomes: Some people do object to writing aims and outcomes for their students. For many of these perhaps there is the feeling that 'education' is slightly unknowable and unpredictable – it cannot be classified, and what can be written up and measured in this way will be the least valuable part of education (Noble, 2002). However, many of us have to write aims and outcomes – and students can benefit from them. If writing aims and outcomes, clearly spell out what the course is trying to achieve – and exactly what the student will have to do and learn to pass that course. But, as with the general advice above on the course booklet, do not just expect students to read or understand aims and outcomes information. Take students through it and explain the ramifications for them in terms of what work they will have to do and the sorts of things that will have to appear in their final assignment.

Learning development or support: Typically learning development or support people do not see themselves as offering a remedial service – nor do they see their students as deficit. They do tend to acknowledge that some students may be less academically inducted than others and that the role of learning development therefore is to make transparent the forms and processes of HE so that students can be empowered to succeed more swiftly.

● **Tip: Find out what learning development or support facilities operate at your university in terms of what they offer both staff and students. If possible, introduce your students positively to these facilities.**

Dyslexia and disability: As with learning development above, the dyslexia and disability people will not see their students as the problem – and the law concurs. We must make reasonable adjustments for students with disabilities, including dyslexia, ensuring that we do not disadvantage such students by offering them a worse service than all other students. For example, materials that we utilise in our teaching practice must be capable of being produced for visually impaired students, see SENDA – Special Educational Needs and Disability Act 2001.

● **Tip: As this is a new Act, with new implications, it is worth getting advice from the disability staff at your university to discover how the Act will impact on you and what sort of technical assistance the university offers you to this end.**

Careers: Many students will not visit careers till just before they leave the university – this is not a successful or useful strategy. It can help students if tutors indicate career opportunities as part of their teaching practice – and if they introduce their students to careers staff as part of this. This does 'break the ice' and facilitate a fruitful relationship between students and careers staff. Further, given that many universities will be moving to PDPs (Personal Development Portfolios) with a concomitant requirement to build Key, Employability, Capability or Graduate Skills and Attributes overtly into units, modules or courses, it could be even more useful to collaborate with careers staff (see also Chapter 14 on reflective practice and PDPs).

HE orientation: We have written elsewhere in this chapter on this topic, so to briefly reiterate here – do not expect students to just be able to make notes, to research and read academically, or even to write what you might call an essay. It can help if you make explicit what you want from the students and to give seminar time to some of the following activities:

■ With note-making from lectures, you might help students by showing an example of the notes that might have been made on one of your lectures. You could produce skeleton lecture notes that students have to complete either during the lecture or immediately afterwards, possibly in pairs. You can make clear to students the sorts of activities in which you expect them to engage before, during and after your lecture – revising their notes, reading a couple of chapters, discovering a journal article by the person that you have just mentioned. (See also Chapter 9 on note-making.)

■ When it comes to undertaking that reading, stress that we read not only to excavate ideas but also to discover models for writing. Ask students to discuss their strengths and weaknesses as academic readers. Ask for tips from the class to improve reading strategies. Get students to form reading groups and to give presentations on their reading in your seminar programme. Offer chapters or journal articles such that students can practise reading and note-making from reading. (See also Chapters 9 on note-making and 8 on research and reading.)

■ With the writing that you want students to undertake, make explicit what you mean by an essay, report or paper – with examples (see also Resources 10.1, p. 243, 11.1, p. 246 and 11.3, p. 248). Bring in sample essays or reports for students to grade and comment upon. Discuss the marks that you would have awarded and why. Stress that writing gets easier with practice and allow students some time – even weekly – to write short pieces such that they start to realise the truth of that statement for themselves.

Conclusion

In this chapter we have flagged up that being a student these days may be a much more stressful time than it was for us (older) lecturers. We have argued that it will be useful for students to research and understand the different sorts of universities that they might choose to attend – Russell Group, campus, old or new university. We have indicated that it can help students to make an effective transition to university if we problematise or distanciate some of our own practices – rather than problematise the student. We suggest adopting a transparent pedagogical practice that makes explicit the forms and processes of HE, and of our own subjects or disciplines.

We have included several resource handouts that detail the implications of joining such academic communities and you can either photocopy and distribute to students or use them to seed your lectures or discussions with your students. We paid particular attention to positive activities like summer reading or programmes (Resource 5.1). We also looked in some detail at HE orientation and at ways this could operate before the transition to, or while at, university. Here we also considered making explicit to students the support systems that will be in place for them (Resource 5.2) and the teaching and learning practices with which they will be expected to become familiar once they are at university (Resources 5.3 and 5.4). As always we stressed that just presenting students with this information will not be enough. Typically we have suggested that tutors facilitate student understanding of this material by specific seminar activities (see especially Tutor tips).

Resources

5.1   Ok – I've been accepted – what do I do now?
5.2   Places to go, people to meet and things to do at university
5.3   For study success think SOCCER
5.4   Teaching and learning in university demystified

Note

1 Radical educational theory asserts that in England from 1870 with the Elementary Education Act specific classed and gendered curricula have been developed for children of 'the labouring poor' (Sutherland, 1971: 3) – see Burn and Finnegan (2003), Swift (2003), Thompson (2000).

Bibliography and further reading

Anie, A. (2001) *Widening Participation – Graduate Employability Project*. University of North London (now London Metropolitan University).

Burn, E. and Finnigan, F. (2003) 'I've made it more academic by adding some snob words from the thesaurus', in Satterthwaite, J., Atkinson, E. and Gale, K. (eds), *Discourse, Power, Resistance: Challenging the Rhetoric of Contemporary Education*. Stoke-on-Trent: Trentham Books.

Burns, T. and Sinfield, S. (2003) *Essential Study Skills: The complete guide to success @ university*. London: Sage.

Cottrell, S. (2001) *Teaching Study Skills and Supporting Learning*. Basingstoke: Palgrave.

Holmes, L. (2002) Available from: *www.re-skill.org.uk/thesis/*, accessed February 2002. (See also: *www.re-skill.org.uk*; *www.graduate-employability.org.uk*; *www.odysseygroup.org.uk*.)

Jeffers, S. (1987) *Feel the Fear and Do It Anyway*. Chatham: Century.

LDHEN (2003) Learning Development in Higher Education Network discussion at: *http://www.jiscmail.ac.uk/lists/LDHEN.html*.

Leathwood, C. (2004) 'A critique of institutional inequalities in higher education (or an alternative to hypocrisy for higher education policy)' paper accepted for publication in *Theory and Research in Education*, 2 (1).

Leathwood, C. and O'Connell, P. (2003) ' "*It's a struggle": the construction of the "new student" in higher education*', in *Journal of Educational Policy*, 18 (6).

Lillis, T. (2001) *Student Writing, Access, Regulation, Desire*. London: Routledge.

Noble, D. (2002) *Digital Diploma Mills: The Automation of Higher Education*. New York: Education Monthly Review Press.

Northedge, A. (1991) *The Good Study Guide*. Milton Keynes: Open University.

Sinfield, S. (2003) 'Teaching older learners: an opportunity not a problem', in *Investigations (in Teaching and Learning in Higher Education)*, 1 (1): 35–40.

Sinfield, S., Burns, T. and Holley, D. (2004) 'Outsiders looking in or insiders looking out?', in Satterthwaite, J. et al. (eds), *The Disciplining of Education: New Languages of Power and Resistance*. Stoke-on-Trent: Trentham Books.

Sutherland, G. (1971) *Elementary Education in the Nineteenth Century*. London: Historical Association.

Swift, A. (2003) *How Not to Be a Hypocrite: School Choice for the Morally Perplexed Parent*. London: Routledge.

Thompson, J. (ed.) (2000) *Stretching the Academy: The Politics and Practice of Widening Participation in Higher Education*. Leicester: NIACE.

Warren, D. (2002) 'Curriculum design in a context of widening participation in higher education', *Arts and Humanities in Higher Education*, 1 (1): 85–99.

6 How to promote student self-confidence

Introduction

It is impossible to overestimate the fear and lack of self-confidence of students, especially that of non-traditional students. All the students with whom we work express their lack of faith in themselves in some form or other in that they are not clever enough, that they have no potential, that they are out of place, that they are impostors soon to be discovered – generally that they are not good enough. These negative opinions are only reinforced by the way that the widening participation debate has been conducted in Britain in the early twenty-first century. There is constant talk of lowering standards and dumbing down – and 'Mickey Mouse students for whom Mickey Mouse degrees are quite appropriate'. Margaret Hodge when Minister for Lifelong Learning (2002–03) underscored this with the reassurance that many of the new students would not be entering professions or industries requiring traditional degrees but would rather undertake vocational programmes (Hodge, 2002).

HE institutions can exacerbate student lack of self-esteem in the way that they implicitly view and explicitly treat their students. If lecturers do view the new students as a pollution of the ivory environment, this will very quickly communicate itself to the student and reinforce the negative self-perception already extant. Further, if the HE institution makes no attempt to bridge the gap between the student and the forms and practices of HE, or if the HE orientation bridge that the university builds is one that overtly or covertly defines the student as deficit, where perhaps:

> Student language is made visible and problematised but the language of discourse and the pedagogical practices in which they are embedded . . . remain invisible, taken as 'given' (Lillis, 2001: 22)

this will help confirm a negative notion of the (non-traditional) student in both staff and students.

In this chapter we explore the affective position of the student entering higher education, with a special focus on the thoughts and feelings of the non-traditional student. We move on to consider how we in learning development attempt to build student self-confidence and promote self-esteem.

Caught on the cultural cusp

At our institution Anie (2001) in an employability study that explored the employment outcomes of our students and Leathwood (2003) drawing on a longitudinal study that followed a cohort of 600 students through their whole degree process both spoke of the lack of self-confidence experienced by non-traditional students and how this initial low self-esteem was exacerbated by the cumulative and interlocking struggles of HE – struggles with finance, struggles with the reality that their degree would be worth less in the job market (Archer, 2002), struggles with not being able to take up postgraduate study opportunities and struggles with the occult and mysterious practices of HE itself.

Leathwood (2003), citing Kuhn (1995) and Reay (1998), speaks of the pervasiveness of the 'shame' inherent in gender, race and class, where to be working class is to experience the constant fear of never getting it right. For Leathwood these feelings are not personal failings but rather she relates them to the pathologising of the 'other' within the 'systems of oppression' of an unequal society, exacerbated by the myths of meritoc-racy and classlessness that pervade all social systems, including our education system. As Tett, citing Bourdieu and Passeron (1979) describes it: 'Education could be the royal road to the democratization of culture if it did not consecrate the initial cultural inequalities by ignoring them' (Tett, 2000: 190).

The non-traditional student in HE

> Those triumphalist celebrations of fluidity always overlook the fact
> that being unfixed, mobile, in-between, can distress as much as it
> liberates. So one's sense of class identity is uncertain, torn and
> oscillating – caught on a cultural cusp. (Medhurst, in Munt, 2000: 20)

The transition into HE is often a painful one for our students. And
indeed the students that we have interviewed and with whom we speak
always tell of their fear, anxiety and apprehension. There is the terror of
walking into the building, of that first lecture where it seems like
everybody is looking at 'me' (some lecture theatres hold 300 or more
people – that is the size of some secondary schools, or it may be the year
size of a student from a comprehensive). Students speak of 'words
swimming before their eyes', of the terror in a seminar when they can't
understand a word that is being said. Students break down when trying
to read a complex academic article (Sinfield, 2003; Sinfield et al., 2004).

We detail this not to confirm tutors in negative impressions of
non-traditional students, but to argue that widening participation repre-
sents an opportunity for all our institutions to evolve. As we argue
elsewhere in this text, adapting to mass higher education need not
involve any lowering or levelling down of standards, but that in positively
recognising difference and devising empowering curricula, or spaces
within curricula and within our institutions, we will be facilitating the
success of all our students (Warren, 2002). For, yes, student self-
confidence does change if the student is welcomed into the academic
environment – and the forms and processes of education itself are
demystified. Given opportunities to learn, rehearse and refine academic
skills and practices – without stigma – the success of all students is
promoted.

Arguably all the work that is undertaken under the aegis of study and
academic skills or learning development operates to improve student
understanding of and performance within the academic environment –
and thus promotes the building of a self-confidence and self-esteem based
on perceived improvements in performance. Further, our students have
also indicated that they have valued the opportunity to directly discuss
issues of self-confidence, self-esteem and positive thinking. While this
latter does draw on some elements of pop psychology and may be
dismissed as psycho-babble, we can only say that after such sessions
students report back that they not only feel better in college/university
but they have also felt enabled to speak up at work, change jobs, pass
driving tests, actually do that presentation and so forth.

How we do it

Welcoming practice

As indicated above, we start this process by valuing the non-traditional student and the qualities that they do bring to the HE environment. We make our learning development space as friendly and welcoming as we can, for you cannot downplay the impact of a friendly face! We remember that while our students may have experienced the world in powerful ways before they have entered college or university, typically they will have had unsuccessful or traumatising previous educational experience. We work to demonstrate that we value our students, and attempt to help them to value the skills, aptitudes and experiences that they bring with them. We stress that there is no shame in not automatically knowing how to study, learn and communicate effectively but that these things can be learned. We stress how we really like working with such motivated and keen students.

Tackling positive thinking

Our interactions with students take place one-to-one in workshops, in small group work and with a whole class in our study and academic skills programme. When directly addressing positive thinking in our study and academic skills programme, we typically do so when we tackle presentation theory and practice for often that is the academic practice that students fear the most. When lecturing on positive thinking, we explore fear and where it originates, the impact of fear and low self-esteem on study, and then suggest steps to take to build self-confidence. Below is the gist of our session upon 'Fear, self-esteem and positive thinking', including a summary of the contents of the 'lecture' that we normally give preceded by the preliminary activities that may be undertaken. Please feel free to use something similar with your students.

⬤ **Tutor tip:** You may not initially feel comfortable giving a lecture on this topic – we certainly did not. It does not feel academic perhaps or it feels like something that only certain sections of an audience might appreciate. We can only report that this has worked for us – even in mixed groups of students: male and female, young and old, home and international, first-year and postgraduate.

Fear, self-esteem and positive thinking – preliminary discussion and activities

We often start by asking students whether or not low self-esteem affects student performance. To illustrate we ask the class to consider the sportsperson, asking who will win the race, the runner who believes in him- or herself or the one that is loping along thinking that they can't possibly win? When looking at sport it is obvious that the mind can have a strong impact on how the body will perform – we argue that this is also true for academic study. We illustrate how low self-esteem has force in education, not least because it can lead to stress – and the release of the stress hormones cortisol and adrenalin (see also Chapter 10 on presentations) which reduce short-term memory and bring about the tunnel vision and focus necessary for safety – but which is counter-productive in education. For example, if a building is burning, you do not want to stop and wonder from whence the fire originated and whether or not there is an arsonist at work – you just need to flee the building. However, in academic study the 'from whence' and 'I wonder if' questions are essential.

Activity tip

Utilise an illustrative activity (Jeffers, 1987): ask for a volunteer and get them to extend their stronger arm. Tell the student that they must think negative thoughts such as 'I am a failure' and 'I am weak' as they resist you pushing down their arm. Typically the arm is very easy to push down. Now try again, but this time the student must think, 'I am powerful' and 'I am strong'. Typically the second time it really is more difficult to push down the student's arm.

Student activity: The difficult sentence

Find for yourself a typically obscure academic sentence from your discipline, or use the one below. Write it on an overhead or on the board. Ask students to read the sentence and then write down their *reaction* to it.

Go round the room asking students for their reactions. Take a few moments to discuss these, possibly indicating that while there are no necessarily right or wrong reactions, there were different ones. Further, say that noting that different reactions are possible should make students realise that their own reactions are neither necessary nor inevitable – they are learned. Once learned, they may be unlearned – or at least reflected upon.

Sample sentence:

'It is in order to return at this point to Jameson's "loss of referent" theme, because it is precisely this phenomenology of the everyday that Jameson's work both lacks and consciously relegates to the ethnographic sidelines' (Feather, H.,

2000, *Inter-subjectivity and Contemporary Social Theory*. Aldershot/Avebury – a really useful book by the way!).

Here are some responses gathered from our students (see *ESS*, pp. 146–7):

■ I got really angry! Why on earth do they have to write like that? It's stupid.

■ This is strange and scary, but it's where I've got to get to.

■ I read it several times to try to make sense of it.

■ I used my dictionary of literary terms and tried to make sense of it piece by piece.

■ It made me feel like giving up, it's obvious that I'm not welcome here.

■ Well I just laughed and laughed. They've got to be joking haven't they?

Ask students: What did you make of the different reactions to that sentence? Were you surprised? What effect will this have on you?

Potential discussion: It can help to reassure students about their personal responses to the sentence. Negative responses typically reveal how unconfident the student is feeling, but this situation can change. Further, remind them that as there are different responses recorded from the group, no one response is inevitable, it has been learned. Students can work to learn a different response to academic language and situations.

Fear and positive thinking – lecture notes

Study impacts upon the whole person for the human being is made up of mind and body, of effect and affect. Often 'affect' feels inappropriate in the academic, primarily cognitive, context and thus students feel that they ought to ignore or repress their feelings, especially negative ones. Obviously in terms of affect, we hope that students will feel excited, stimulated and challenged – but we must be aware that they might be horrified, terrified and demotivated. Ironically, the push for the repression of negative feelings can lead to an increase in their power rather than a decrease, in students becoming more subject to the occult practices of education rather than in mastering them. In this discussion we are going to cover fear and what we fear, why we experience low self-esteem and fear and what can be done to overcome our fears.

Fear and what we fear

● **Tutor tip:** You can ask students for fears (not phobias) before speaking on the topic if you wish.

We are frightened of many things. We are frightened of ageing, disease and death, typically we are all frightened of change, of the new. Change makes us uncomfortable – and it is not just major change that discomforts. Students are often frightened of entering the library, of reading an academic text, of giving that first presentation. We can be frightened of anything and everything, and while fear may be perfectly natural and normal, it can make life – especially student life – really difficult. For while there might be some things in life that you can choose to avoid – you really do not have to bungee jump if you are frightened of heights – the majority of things that we fear as students **do** have to be engaged with.

Why we experience fear and low self-esteem

It can be argued that the fear response is the body's way of telling us that something is not for us, that there are too many risks involved – after all, it is rather silly to bungee jump. But if people avoided everything that they feared they would undertake nothing at all. Remember, to become a student is actually to embrace change, and change does involve risk – risk to one's sense of self, to one's identity – as well as fear of failure, of looking, sounding and feeling like a fool. While nobody actually enjoys these feelings, in an educational context if you avoid what you fear as a student, then you definitely will not succeed. It can help if we try to understand how low self-esteem and fear originate or operate in our society.

Sociologists might argue that in an unequal society members of underprivileged groups suffer low self-esteem as part of social conditioning; it is an internalisation of the views that society holds of them. Further, fear and low self-esteem can have an inhibiting effect on the 'lower orders' that serves the interests of the ruling class, for it is easier to oppress people with low aspiration and who you can despise for their own sense of inferiority (Leathwood, 2003).

Evolutionary psychologists (such as Baron-Cohen, 1997) argue that fear, anxiety and even depression are a legacy of evolution. When an animal is on unfamiliar territory it is in danger of its life, hence a fear response is a survival mechanism. Unfortunately, as human beings we also have consciousness and consequently an awareness of our own fear that can inhibit us in ways that would never be true of an animal.

Popular psychologists (Jeffers, 1987) argue that fear and low self-esteem are taught to us by our primary caregivers – 'mind how you go', 'be careful', 'don't do that, it's dangerous'. When people say these things to us they are often just expressing their fears ('I don't want anything bad to happen to you') but what we hear and internalise is that they do not have faith in us, that they think we are inadequate. Once internalised this negative self-perception can be extremely inhibiting preventing us from undertaking challenges or embracing risk.

Even economists have a say in this area – the non-stop pushing of pensions and insurance policies implies that there are ways of eliminating risk and making the world a totally safe and controllable space. But to be human is to constantly move into unfamiliar territory, to embrace risk. The more we focus on avoiding risk the more we are dehumanising ourselves. And the more we listen to our fears, the more we will focus on our inadequacies – and the less we are likely to do. This can be especially negative for the student who has so many new things to face, so many new challenges to embrace. If these changes are only viewed as problems and opportunities to fail then it becomes even more difficult to positively embrace education. This has a further consequence when studying if we consider the role of 'mistakes' in the learning process.

The learning environment may also play a part in the fear factor. Human beings do learn by trial and error. If the learning environment feels over-threatening, the student will not want to make mistakes and open themselves up to criticism: they may give up rather than reveal their mistakes to hostile scrutiny. The lesson we can learn as academics is to make the learning environment a safe one for **all** our students: a space for trial and error, for learning from mistakes – and we must reassure students that we have done so. The students have to realise that they will get things wrong – quite often – but if they work to learn from these experiences they will learn more.

What can be done to overcome fear and build self-confidence?

We have argued that fear, while often uncomfortable, is a perfectly natural and normal response to life and to new and unfamiliar experiences. We are now going to take a leaf out of the self-help book in order to argue that it is possible to reframe fear and thus change our response to it. We will move on to discuss how to take responsibility for our lives, change a negative vocabulary, make positive friends and utilise affirmations.

Reframing fear

Kipling said that the only thing to fear was fear itself. We argue that fear is unavoidable – what we can change is our response to fear. Here are some new ways to look at fear – see if they help (**you and**) your students.

■ **Fear is good:** Fear is a wonderful indicator that we are doing new things, moving into new areas and undertaking new challenges. In this way fear is a good thing, it means that we are still growing, we are still alive. Arguably, if we are not experiencing some element of fear it means that we are stagnating – we are dying inside. Try to see fear as an indicator of growth and welcome it – celebrate the fact that life still holds opportunity for you.

- **Fear affects everyone:** One problem for students is that they tend to think that everyone else is OK, that they are the only ones feeling frightened and looking foolish. Obviously this is not true: if Cohen is to be believed, everyone feels fear when embracing the new. Sometimes just realising that everyone else is also frightened can take the stigma out of our fear. Instead of a fear response proving once and for all that we are either inadequate or a coward we can relax in the realisation that it just means that we are as human as everybody else.

- **The only way to get rid of the fear of something is to do it – quickly:** Most people know this cliché to be true. The only way to overcome a fear is to do that which we fear – and the quicker the better. Students can spend months worrying about that presentation – and then it is over in five minutes. The months of worry have just served to make the task harder.

- **It's easier to face fear than to live with fear:** It really is easier to deal with fear rather than to live with it. Every time we allow fear to prevent us from undertaking something it is as if we are conspiring against ourselves to make the world a worse place. So if engaging in something that you fear, tell yourself you have actually chosen the easier option.

- **It takes practice:** Reframing fear in the ways detailed above may not come naturally to your students. However, they will find that with practice they will be able to face fear differently, and this will help them embrace the challenges of being a student.

Taking responsibility for our lives

We have argued above that students can experience lack of self-confidence and low self-esteem as a result of an unequal society and the social pressures under which they operate. While this is true, this can be read as a way of disempowering students and confirming them in a victim status. This is not a helpful place for anyone to be. While neither nature nor society are fair, it is not enough for the student to sit back and say well it's not my fault. To be able to move forward the student must be able to look at any situation in which they find themselves and work out just how they can take control of it – or how they can move forward. For if they just think 'it's not my fault' they stay trapped – if it is their responsibility then they can make things happen.

As a student, it may not be their fault that they are not as academically inducted as the Oxbridge undergraduate, it may not be their fault that their professor thinks of them as a Mickey Mouse student . . . but there will be something that they can do to improve their own chances within the situation in which they find themselves if they get used to thinking of themselves as in charge of:

- their decisions
- their actions
- their state of mind
- the amount of effort that they put in
- getting work in on time
- getting good grades . . . etc.

If those things matter, students can take steps to make them happen. Of course we as academics can facilitate this by making our forms, processes and criteria clear. We can operate successful and empowering induction and HE orientation programmes, we can scaffold student learning in our seminars and we can operate and work with learning development facilities.

A positive vocabulary can help

The difficult sentence exercise above can reveal to people just how they normally respond to (academic) challenges. When first responses to situations tend to the negative this will often be reflected in the language typically used. Work is always hard, tough and difficult – metaphors of struggle, tunnelling, searching and suffering might all be used. If such a student thinks about an assignment it will be in terms of the amount of effort they will have to put in and the unending struggle that they will have to endure rather than in terms of the excitement, the challenge – the glorious frisson of fear.

It can help if we suggest that students start using language differently:

- A problem becomes an opportunity. (To solve a problem we must make something different happen – this is an opportunity for change.)

- A disaster becomes a learning experience. (Well, if a problem is an opportunity, a disaster must be a real opportunity – if we can reflect upon it.)

- 'If only' becomes 'next time'. (We will make mistakes – and instead of lamenting them we can learn from them and note what could be done differently next time.)

- Should becomes choice. (So it's not 'I should do that essay' but 'I choose to do it' or not.)

● **Tip:** Remind students that each choice they make – to do or not to do something – will have a price attached. This is another part of being human, our choices have prices – it is best to accept this joyfully and move on.

Each of these vocabulary shifts is easy to mock but they all embrace a shift in consciousness that will help the student face academic life more positively. Obviously no one can make people shift their perspective – but if the student does want to change, practising using this different language will make a difference.

Positive friends

One thing that may occur for the 'changing' student is that they will encounter derision or resistance from peers and family members. Young students may find that they do not enjoy people viewing them as a swot – and that a studious mien is neither 'buff' nor 'cool'. Older students may find that when inputting effort into their studies they will be expecting family members to help more with chores – this does not always meet with approval. Young and old students may find that they no longer have time for everybody else's woes and they will not always be at the end of a telephone or ready to stop everything for a chat.

If the student wants to retain contact with friends and family throughout their time as a student they will have to negotiate this change as diplomatically as possible. It is not usually a good thing just to confront everyone around you with the new, positive, in-your-face and self-interested person! Gently does it.

Further, it may be useful for students to start making new, positive friends to help them maintain their positive outlook and their energy levels. Negative people drain energy – positive people can excite and stimulate. Encourage students to make positive study partners and to form a positive study group. When encouraging group work in students yourself, you might let them choose their own groups so that they can work with people with whom they feel compatible – suggest that when making this choice they choose someone as positive and motivated as themselves – that is suitably ambiguous.

Affirmations

Typically we find that this is the topic with which the average academic has the most difficulty. Affirmations are short positive statements that students can use to overcome stress, to build their self-confidence and to generally help themselves.

The initial idea behind the affirmation is to drown out the internalised negative voice that we have grown up with. The 'you'll be sorry – you're too old, too stupid, too fat, too lumpen . . .' voice that lives in the heart, head and ear of many of us – and the majority of our students. This voice has to be replaced with a positive one of which the most basic is the 'I can handle it' (Jeffers, 1987). If students say 'I can handle it' whenever they face a difficult situation or when they feel a wave of insecurity or self-doubt flood over them, they will calm down and be able to face things.

From the basic 'I can cope' statement, students can move on to develop their own set of affirmations, ones that address the other functions of the affirmation, to energise and boost the self-confidence of the individual. Remind students that affirmations should always be in the present tense and always in the positive, the present tense so that the goal of the affirmation becomes rooted in the now rather than remaining distant and unobtainable, in the positive to emphasise that which is desired rather than that which is being left behind. For example, it would be 'I am brave' rather than 'I will not be afraid.'

It is useful if people write out their affirmations and stick them up around their homes so that the first thing they see in the morning could be 'it's a great day'. When brushing their teeth it could be 'I am wonderful' and so forth. If encouraging students to use this technique do warn them that it is one that requires maintenance. People find that they use this technique, feel great, decide they don't need it anymore – and sink back into negative thinking and behaviour. Remind them that they will have had many, many years of practising their bad habits – they need to give the new, positive ones the same chance.

● **Tip:** As a light-hearted follow-up to a session like this, ask students to bring in their affirmations to share and discuss with the group.

Of course students will have to put in the academic work and effort as well – they cannot just sit confidently chanting affirmations in a corner and expect an essay to write itself. But thinking positively about their ability to write that essay can lead them to discover the steps that need to be taken to research and write an essay – and they may be able to give themselves the time that they need to do the work required. Thus a better essay will be written.

Conclusion

When concluding this session with your students as well as the reiteration of the lecture as a whole: 'We have looked at fear and the effect that this has on the student, we have considered from where fear has arisen and some things that we can do to overcome our fears ...' **do** reassure them that if they are currently feeling more frightened – all that power and responsibility can be quite intimidating – they just need to feel the fear and do it anyway.

Also: If you deliver a lecture based on the above with conviction and enthusiasm, do not be surprised if you get a round of applause! Students really do enjoy this one.

Practising it

■ When using 'learning logs' with your students do stress the value of the 'reaction' section (see also Chapter 14 on reflective practice). Honest personal reactions (especially when not penalised by the tutor) can help students discover aspects of the education process that affect them positively or negatively.

■ Have a session where students bring in affirmations to share with the seminar group – risk sharing some of your own.

Extension

■ Arguably all the activities that you use with students to help them become more aware of the forms and processes of education will extend their self-confidence.

Overall conclusion

In this chapter we have considered the factors that tend to promote a lack of self-confidence and self-esteem in the non-traditional student. We have argued that academia has an affective as well as an effective dimension – and that it is important to point this out to students and to acknowledge it for ourselves. Finally we looked at how we cover this topic in learning development, typically in a lecture on positive thinking looking at self-esteem and fear, and what we can do to overcome fear and build self-confidence. We do hope that you have found this an interesting chapter and that you find it easy to use this 'lecture' with your students.

Bibliography and further reading

Anie, A. (2001) *Widening Participation – Graduate Employability Project*. University of North London (now London Metropolitan University).

Archer, L. (2002) 'Access elite', *Times Higher Education Supplement*, 18 January.

Baron-Cohen, S. (1997) *The Maladapted Mind*. Hove, East Sussex: Psychology Press.

Bourdieu, P. and Passeron, J.-C. (1979) *Reproduction in Education, Society and Culture*. London: Sage.

Burns, T. and Sinfield, S. (2003) *Essential Study Skills: The complete guide to success @ university*. London: Sage.

Hodge, Margaret, Secretary of State for Education (2002) Keynote speech: *What Is College and University Education for?* Ecclestone Church House, Westminster, Education Conference, 24 January.

Holmes, L. (2001) 'Reconsidering graduate employability: the "graduate identity" approach', *Quality in Higher Education*, 7 (2): 111–19.

Holmes, L. (2002) Available at: *www.re-skill.org.uk/thesis/*, accessed February 2002. (See also: *www.re-skill.org.uk*; *www.graduate-employability.org.uk*; *www.odysseygroup.org.uk*.)

Jeffers, S. (1987) *Feel the Fear and Do It Anyway*. London: Century.

Kuhn, A. (1995) *Family Secrets: Acts of Memory and Imagination*. London: Verso.

Leathwood, C. and O'Connell, P. (2003) ' "It's a struggle": the construction of the "new student" in higher education', *Journal of Educational Policy*, 18 (6).

Lillis, T. (2001) *Student Writing, Access, Regulation, Desire*. London: Routledge.

Medhurst, A. (2000) 'If anywhere: class identifications and cultural studies academics', in Munt, S. (ed.), *Cultural Studies and the Working Class*. London: Cassell.

Munt, S. (ed.) (2000) *Cultural Studies and the Working Class*. London: Cassell.

Reay, D. (1998) *Class Work*. London: UCL Press.

Sinfield, S. (2003) 'Teaching older learners: an opportunity not a problem', *Investigations in teaching and learning in Higher Education*, 1 (1): 35–40.

Sinfield, S., Burns, T. and Holley, D. (2004) 'Outsiders looking in or insiders looking out?', in *The Disciplining of Education: New Languages of Power and Resistance*. Stoke-on-Trent: Trentham Books.

Tett, L. (2000) 'I'm working class and proud of it – gendered experiences of non-traditional participants in higher education', *Gender and Education*, 1 (2): 183–94.

Thompson, J. (ed.) (2000) *Stretching the Academy: The Politics and Practice of Widening Participation in Higher Education*. Leicester: NIACE.

Warren, D. (2002) 'Curriculum design in a context of widening participation in higher education', *Arts and Humanities in Higher Education*, 1 (1): 85–99.

7 How to promote effective organisation and time management

Introduction

While undoubtedly having to work and study concurrently has a negative effect leaving students little time for independent study, and while some students will remain disorganised no matter what, we have found that many students appear to have poor organisation and time management skills because they have no idea of the amount of work that is involved in HE per se nor of the work that is involved in producing a good assignment. Typically these students are unaware of the steps that they will have to take, and the processes with which they will have to engage to plan, draft and produce a finished piece of academic work. This problem can be exacerbated where a student's self-confidence with respect to academic study is so low that they have a thousand and one displacement activities with which to engage rather than settling down to their studies. The impact of this is demonstrated by the number of students who rush in to learning development workshop with an essay draft crying, 'Could you give me some feedback on this – but it will have to be quick I have to hand it in, in half an hour!'

Given the importance and need for organisation and time management it is a topic that we address ourselves in our own study and academic skills programme – and one that we recommend that subject tutors address in any HE orientation programme that they design and deliver. Further, this is a topic that also very easily fits into subject teaching especially in seminar programmes or academic tutorial sessions.

In this chapter we explore some possible student attitudes towards organisation and time management, moving on to give an overview of how we approach this topic in learning development.

Tutor tip: Use a workbook

Devise a seminar handbook to support the lecture programme. Make space in the handbook for students to write a learning contract (see p. 40), to write out and analyse the assignment question, to write out a study 'action plan', to write lecture notes, to write notes from journals and other texts and so forth. Such a handbook with such staged activities can reveal to students the constituent academic skills and practices necessary for academic study. If the handbook is used over time it not only models good organisation and time management practice for students, it also has other academic benefits, for example:

■ It underscores the amount – and types – of academic work that must go into producing a good assignment.

■ It emphasises that you can think about an assignment question even before you have a chance of answering it.

■ It reveals that academic endeavour is not necessarily about knowing the answers, but it can be about knowing the questions to ask.

■ It can help students realise the links between different parts of a unit, module or programme and the final assessment. (This is something that, while obvious to the tutor, is not always clear to the student. We have found students who have no idea that course material is supposed to be engaged with or that the assignment is supposed to be related to that course in some way.)

▓ It can help students take more information from lectures and seminars because they are focused in completely new ways.

▓ Further, with seminar activities based around different elements of an assignment question, the student can be rehearsed in good academic practice as they are helped to engage with and understand new ideas and concepts.

Some student attitudes to time

▓ **The deadline junkie:** As with many lecturers perhaps, there are students who feel unable to start work unless operating under the pressure of a deadline. If the student is already reasonably academically inducted, they can sometimes muddle through with this technique for quite some time. However, they are not operating to their best advantage – especially with respect to the plan, draft and review processes necessary for good oral and written work. However, if the student is not academically inducted, such that they are not drawing information from lectures and seminars nor are they reading successfully, this is a dramatically dangerous technique.

▓ **It's all too much:** There are many students, especially those who are the first in their families through HE, who become overwhelmed by the sheer amount that they feel they do not know – and hence the sheer amount of work that they must do. For them walking into a university library is one of the most demoralising experiences in the world – there are hundreds, thousands, perhaps millions of books that they have not read! They feel completely unequal to the task and just cannot start work.

▓ **If I don't look it can't hurt me:** Some students are so lacking in self-confidence and so terrified of the HE process that they are frightened to look at an assignment question or to investigate possible upcoming exam questions. They really do seem to believe that if they don't look it can't hurt – but if they do look they will have to acknowledge the total futility of their being in education.

▓ **Displacement king or queen:** Other students have realised that academic work – research, learning and producing assignments – happens over time. They acknowledge that if they could sit down and do a little bit of work every day they would feel better, they would enjoy their studies, they would learn more and get better grades, and so forth. Unfortunately they just cannot do it. Every time it is that time – the time to do some work – they start dusting or cleaning the fridge. They cook something or rebuild the car engine. They pick up the phone or rush in relief to answer it because someone has called. This may be because these students do not have successful strategies at their fingertips, maybe they do not have a well-organised study space or maybe they do just have blocks to starting work.

- **But I don't feel inspired:** Still others seem to be waiting for inspiration to strike before they can start work. This harks back to images of the creative artist needing to be struck by the muse, rather than, say, the notion of the playwright, the writer or student as craftsperson.

These categories are not necessarily separate or mutually exclusive. For some subjects a student might bury their head and not look, for others they feel confident, but require the urgency of a deadline to get started on the assignment, for others they may wish for inspiration to strike. Arguably, however, all these students can be helped by seminar activities that gradually take them through assignment preparation processes.

How we do it

While typically it is difficult to tackle this issue with students, we have built the topic into our own study and academic skills programmes and our own HE orientation module (see Chapter 15); in these we cover 'when, where and how to study' as a way into this topic. This can be delivered as a lecture, or students can be taken through group discussion activities on when, where and how to study across a teaching/learning session. The tutor can feed in supplementary information from the material below if it feels appropriate to do so.

Note that this can be a liberating experience for students, for underscoring the importance of developing good time management techniques can reveal that there is no shame or stigma attached to the non-traditional student in not knowing successful practices. Further, when good techniques are taught, rehearsed and learned, it can be the mature student, with experience of juggling home and work commitments, who might be the one that adapts most easily to the multi-tasking demands of HE.

Organisation and time management – preliminary activities

■ Ask students how they find academic work – what they do well, what they do badly, when they work, why they do not. The pyramid discussion (as described below) also works very well here – students can jot down thoughts initially on their own, then in pairs and finally in a plenary session where solutions can be suggested for the various problems raised and good ideas or tips can be highlighted.

■ Introduce students to the different descriptions of student avoidance techniques above, and ask them what sort of student they think they are. Ask them to SWOT their own approach to study. Then ask them to find solutions for their own weaknesses/threats.

■ The good and bad learning exercise (below) is another good way into this topic.

● **Tutor tip:** If you have never taken part in the good and bad learning activity, it might help if you do so either alongside a group of students or on your own. If you can realise the things that help and hinder you, it might increase your empathy for your students.

Student activity: The good and bad learning exercise – pyramid discussion

Resources: flip chart paper and pens sufficient for student groups formed.

1 Students individually:
 – Jot down any previous bad learning experience – what was it? Why did no learning take place? (2 minutes)
 – Jot down any previous successful learning activity/experience – what was it? Why was it successful? (2 minutes)

2 Students in pairs: compare your previous good and bad experiences. Notice similarities and differences. (10 minutes)

3 Students in fours with flip chart paper and pens: briefly refer to each other's good and bad experiences, reflect, extrapolate – what factors appear to facilitate learning? What factors hinder learning? (10–20 minutes)

4 Plenary session, tutor to make notes on the board: draw one factor that promotes learning from each student group in turn until all the ideas are given up. Discuss the implications of what they raise – for the institution, for you as the tutor and for them as students (on your course). Note: typically

factors that impede learning are just the opposite of the facilitating factors but do give students the opportunity to call out really burning issues. *(10–20 minutes)*

When, where and how to study – lecture/discussion notes

Once you have introduced students to the topic of organisation and time management via the above activities or a preferred one of your own, you might like to give a lecture based on the following sections on when, where and how to study.

Introductory content

Studying is really hard work and this is something that we do have to acknowledge, but hopefully not in a way that increases student stress and fear levels and decreases motivation and energy. While education may be viewed as the route to personal fulfilment and freedom, the student may just be seeing all the notes that they will have to make, the books that they will have to read and all the writing that they will have to do. Rather than being fun and exciting this can be daunting, even frightening, especially to the student who is working 20 hours a week, raising a family and knows neither the rules nor the ropes of education. Here we are going to explore aspects of 'when, where and how to study' as an introduction to good organisation and time management practice.

When to study

Studying is hard and typically students will not leap out of bed in the morning carolling 'Today's the day I tackle that massive assignment!' Typically students will benefit from having some form of study plan in operation whereby they do a little work every day: reflecting on a lecture or seminar they have just attended; reading a chapter or journal article; revising their notes; planning an assignment; drafting just one essay paragraph – and so forth. Ask students if they already work in this way. Typically they will not. When talking to students about how they organise their time, you might like to encourage them to consider the following:

- **Whether they are morning or night people:** A morning person who has internalised the stereotype that the good student is up all night toiling over a hot hard drive feels even more stressed. Typically students should be encouraged to think about their own preferences in terms of study times – when do they have the most energy? When do they have the least? Will it be possible to work at optimum energy times?

■ **Overall available time:** Typically students have to divide their time between work, family, friends, domestic chores and so forth. There is no point in us just telling students to do more work if they really cannot. Each student has to make a realistic inventory of their time commitments and then reflect on how much studying is possible in the time they have left. In some cases students might need to drop from full- to part-time study if they are over-committed in other areas of their lives.

■ **Time for rest and relaxation:** As we have said, studying is hard work, and as well as making time for that work, students have to make time for themselves where they consciously relax and do not feel guilty about other commitments or people. Moreover, if students build stress relief activities into their programmes from the beginning, they can draw on them when the stress levels increase, around exam time for example.

● **Tips for students:** Build yoga, meditation, running or gym activities into their lives. Have a timetable with time for study – but also with time for guilt-free rest.

Student activities: When to study – timetables

I Give students two 24/7 timetables (Resource 7.1). Get students to complete one timetable quite early in your programme – putting in time for sleep, work, family commitments, rest and relaxation, etc. They must include times of lectures and seminars – and then some time for independent study.

● **Tip:** Students should think of working in one-hour blocks.

2 After some real time has elapsed ask students to reflect on their 24/7: how far have they been able to keep to it? What is working for them? What is not? Ask them to complete a second 24/7 with respect to their real experiences and in the light of their goals for themselves as students (are they A, B, C or D students? What do they want to be?) and in the light of the amount of work they have discovered that they have to put in to achieve their goals.

3 Give students an events and deadlines timetable (Resource 7.2) – ask them to photocopy it. They should complete such a timetable for each term/semester during their time at university.

4 Give students a weekly term/semester planner (Resource 7.3). Again, ask students to photocopy and then complete one for each term/semester through their time at university.

5 Optional extras:
  – Collect in the completed timetables and discuss in tutorial.
  – Ask students to submit completed timetables as part of their portfolio work – plus or minus a written reflection.
  – Ask students to complete a written reflection – perhaps as a section in a personal learning log or as a self-assessment activity – wherein they comment on their own organisation and time management strategies, making specific reference to the previous activities.

Where to study

As Virginia Woolf argued, everyone deserves a room of their own; however, for the majority of our students life is not so convenient. Many of our students will not have a study space let alone a study, yet it will help students to work better if they can organise their homes such that they do have a place that is theirs, in which they can lay out their work, put out their books and pin up their notes. Not only does a study space facilitate academic work in terms of having materials and resources to hand, it can also be a part of getting mentally prepared for study. Students should be encouraged to develop a positive state of mind whenever they work in their study space: I am really looking forward to this, I do enjoy this topic, rather than I can't do this, I don't know what to do.

Things for the student to consider:

- A good study space should have the optimum light and noise conditions for the student. Work on learning styles stresses how different people work better with bright or shaded light, with some or no noise. The student has to discover what their optimum conditions are.

- Students will need space to lay out their work and pin up timetables, assignment deadlines and notes. It will help if they can have textbooks and journals to hand. All these things are useful in themselves – and they can also help the student to feel like a student. Further, negotiating a study space with family or flatmates is a useful way of helping those around acknowledge that the student is a student.

- Students will typically need access to a whole range of resources while they study alongside the textbooks. They will need paper, pens, pencils, highlighters, Post its, Tippex, etc. Again all these things are useful and they help one to feel like a student. Fresh stationery can also help inject a little motivation when a task has otherwise gone stale.

■ A computer is rapidly becoming an essential study tool. Dyslexic students with psychologist statements can get financial assistance to get a personal computer, but all students should be encouraged to utilise a computer to prepare work (we tutors do tend to privilege work that looks neat, cared for and well-presented). Some students open research folders in their computers. Here they might immediately type in references and quotes – fully accredited – as they read for an assignment. This can make their writing much easier. Further, if the student also has Internet access, they will be able to conduct library searches and access on-line journals and course materials from home.

■ Students can be encouraged to purchase files for each subject that they undertake, and they can be encouraged to file notes from lectures, seminars and reading in those files. Again, this is something that is glaringly obvious to the tutor but is not necessarily so for the student. Some tutors, especially on HE orientation modules, do provide students with a starter file – neatly sectioned off week by week – as a model of good practice.

■ Other study spaces: study does not just take place in the student's home study space. Students can be encouraged to experiment with both the quiet and noisy sections of the library (if you have such facilities) and even on the bus, tube or train. We had a student who was achieving really well on a programme and enjoying it so much he moved nearer to the institution to facilitate his work. Suddenly he was not achieving so well, he finally realised that losing ten hours commuting each week had eaten into his study time and he had to compensate for this.

■ Opportunities and threats: having a study space can be emotionally complicated for the student and their families. Some students report that they only have to sit down to work and their family members, especially their children, suddenly demand attention. Others can be intimidated by their study space – yes they now felt like a student, but there was no hiding place!

● **Tutor tip:** Get students to speak about their preferred study spaces – what works for them and why. Ask them what problems they have encountered in setting up a space and what their solutions have been.

How to study

This whole handbook is designed to help tutors facilitate student learning and study. In this brief section we will outline a few quick study tips to help get your students started with successful study practices.

▓ **Want it:** Students should want to do well. If we do not want to learn something, then we will not – but study is facilitated if we are interested and motivated, if we want to do well.

● **Tutor tip:** Get your students to complete a learning contract (p. 40) for your programme. This is especially useful after you have conducted the good and bad learning exercise – and after you have explained the aims, outcomes, syllabus, reading list and assessment mechanisms for your programme.

▓ **The right course:** Students should have chosen the right course for their needs, and they should know why they have undertaken a specific course, even a specific module. We can help students with their choices if we give clear information on the what, why and how of our programmes (aims, learning outcomes, epistemological practices, syllabus, assessment and assessment criteria – see also Chapter 3).

▓ **Motivation and positive thinking:** Linked to the points above, the student who is motivated and can practise positive thinking stands a better chance of success than the unmotivated student who could not care less. At the same time, students are not uniform, and while we might like to think that everyone we teach is striving for a first this may not be true of everyone. (Where it is true, it is our responsibility to help students to know what it would take to do well – Chapter 3 again.)

▓ **Organisation and time management:** It is not enough for students to complete study timetables as empty exercises, it will help students if they can manage their time effectively. We can help if we can build timed activities into their programmes.

Time tips for students

▓ Lose stereotypes about working for hours and hours on end – work for an hour and take a break

▓ Research indicates that we concentrate best in 15-minute bursts, so students should be prepared to regularly recharge their batteries within a study hour and between study periods. This can be achieved by:
   – taking a short rest;
   – changing what we do;
   – making the task very important;
   – making the task interesting, stimulating or more difficult.

- **Using time:** We have mentioned above that students can use displacement activities to avoid work – cleaning, cooking, answering the phone. Students can also use mini-displacement activities when they settle down to work – getting out the pens, paper and lucky gonk, rearranging their notes and books, deciding against one assignment and deciding on another, putting one set of books away, getting another assignment out and so forth. Suddenly an hour has passed and they can stop work – but nothing has been done. Obviously this is to be avoided

- **Too many worries:** Sometimes this vacillation between one assignment and another is not a displacement activity but rather a symptom of an overloaded brain, of not knowing what to worry about first. Here the student might try to work on something but they cannot because worry about all their other assignments swamps them. Here we tell students that they will have to practise concentrating on one worry at a time: to learn the art of putting tasks on mental shelves – taking down one assignment and concentrating on it then putting it back ready to start on something else another time. Not only does practice help here, this is supplemented by good organisation and time management. If the student can tell themselves that it is OK, they will work on that tomorrow and that other thing two days after that, then they will be able to focus on one thing at a time.

- **Goal setting:** Students should never just sit down and start reading – neither should they just drift into a lecture or seminar . . . Before any study activity, independent or tutor led, the student should know what they are doing and why – they should have an idea about how the activity fits into the programme as a whole, how it will help with their learning and their assignment and so forth. We can help students develop this technique by goal-setting activities before seminars and lectures. Here we can ask students to say or write one thing that they want to take away from a session or one thing that they expect the session to give them in relation to a course aim, a learning outcome or one aspect of the assignment.

- **Active learning:** Clear goal setting can help students become active learners. They also need to read actively, make active notes when reading or in lectures and actively engage in group discussions or other activities.

- **Tutor tip:** Help students with good reading preparation (see also Chapter 8).

- **Quick tips:** when reading students should be asking – what does this mean? How does it connect with what I already know on this topic? Do I agree or disagree – and why? What has the tutor said about this? Which bit of my assignment will it help me with?

▓ **Study partners or groups:** Students may not react positively to the group activities that we set them (see Chapter 13). However, having a study partner or setting up a study group can be an invaluable part of active learning, of enjoyment and of study success. Unfortunately the need for students to work – and even the modular system – can militate against students being able to create their own study networks. If there is anything that you can do to facilitate this, we do encourage you to stress how important it can be. Typically we give examples from our own study experiences when trying to encourage students to get a study partner or set up a study group.

▓ **Do not end on a sour note:** Students should be encouraged not to finish a study session on a sour note. If working independently and encountering a real problem, a student should phone a study partner or make a note of the issue rather than just give up in a dispirited fashion. Similarly if you can see that students have reached the end of your session and they are obviously unsettled or unhappy, try to do something about it. It can help just to call them to order for a few minutes and either sort the problem out or promise to tackle it next time (making sure that you do not forget to do so). Ending on a sour note always makes it harder to start again, and the impact can be greater with students who do not have confidence in their own abilities in the first place.

▓ **Review, review, review:** Students can be encouraged to conclude a study session with a few moments reflection along the lines of: what have I done? Why? What have I learned? How has this helped me? What will I need to do now? A few moments reflection can help to make learning conscious – which can dramatically improve both the quantity and quality of that learning.

● **Tip:** We can facilitate this process if we conclude a session by asking students for one thing that they feel they have gained from the session. We can get students to say this or collect it on Post its for display and/or to help us plan future sessions. See also Chapter 14 on reflective practice, where we explore this in greater detail, especially in the learning diary.

Lecture conclusion

If delivering the above as a lecture, you might like to draw it to a close by reiterating your main points and emphasising those you think to be the most important. It might help to dispense the timetables after this whole lecture and give students some time to complete them in class – and even to discuss them with each other.

Practising it

In order to build student awareness of the value of good organisation and time management strategies the following activities can be undertaken:

- Seminar workbook with staged activities (pp. 40, 61/62)
- Good and bad learning exercise (p. 64)
- Learning contract (p. 40)
- 'Timetable' exercises (pp. 66, 67)
- Brainstorming at session beginnings – reviewing at session conclusions (p. 4)
- Learning log (pp. 261, 262)

Extension

- Ask students to reflect on the effectiveness of their time management strategies as part of their summative assessment.

Overall conclusion

In this chapter we have raised some issues with respect to organisation and time management. We have said that in our experience, while students are typically more time stressed than ever before, they either ignore this area or actively set themselves against this form of study management. We covered the 'when, where and how to study' information that we give students in our study and academic skills programme. What is encouraging is that while the notion of having a session on this topic is resisted by students, once you do cover the ground with them, they do tend to find it liberating. Further, if you engage in the activities that we have suggested above, students do very quickly start to make some changes to their practice – and this can have a dramatic impact on the way that they feel about themselves as students and about the quality of their work.

Resources

7.1 Blank 24/7 timetable
7.2 Events and deadlines timetable
7.3 Term/semester plan
7.4 Weekly timetable

Further reading

Burns, T. and Sinfield, S. (2003) *Essential Study Skills: The complete guide to success @ university*. London: Sage.

Cottrell, S. (1999) *The Study Skills Handbook*. Basingstoke: Palgrave.

Northedge, A. (1991) *The Good Study Guide*. Milton Keynes: Open University Press.

8 How to promote effective research and reading strategies

Targeted research and active reading – and the reflexive student

Students at British universities have the opportunity to plug into the best research in the world and to emerge from undergraduate study with cutting-edge knowledge, skills and aptitude that they can take with them into the world of work or further formal study. But given the complex nature of HE with which students have to get to grips, and given that our university lecturers are typically not teachers but rather researchers who may teach well, adopting targeted research and active reading strategies may be a very useful way to start developing as an active, reflexive student. Reflexivity in the student is of paramount importance not just to obtain good grades but also to foster the conscious development of a graduate identity (Holmes, 2001). This does require the student to be critical not only of the course material but also of themselves. This is a difficult task for any student, but for the non-traditional student this can be more threatening. Within our HE system the non-traditional student often feels more criticised than criticising, and hence feels poorly placed to critique the material with which we expect them to engage.

Research in a changing assessment environment

Students today are assessed across a broader range of skills and knowledge than ever before. Presentations, group work, reports, journal articles, reflective logs or diaries, portfolios, etc., are some but not all that a student will be assessed upon. For the student who is chasing a good degree, or is just trying to stay sane and not fail, these tasks are daunting. Although tutors now typically reveal assessment criteria, individual lecturers may assess differently: where one will give a pass mark another will fail, where one will give a 2:1 another may give a 2:2 or even a third. With many students in paid employment and student debt accruing, obtaining a high quality degree is important, while to fail is demoralising – and to re-sit expensive. Moreover, one bad mark in one assignment can drag down a whole degree once that mark has been aggregated. Further, not only does success have to be achieved in 12-week modules, students may at the same time be getting to grips with HE orientation while struggling with the knowledge content of their study programmes.

But surely they know how to read?

Research and academic reading seem so obvious to the university lecturer – surely our students know how to read, and they must obviously understand what we mean when we tell them to 'read around the subject' or undertake their own research. However, our students come from many places with many different attitudes towards research and reading. Some mature, non-traditional students may not have had recent experience of hard academic reading, some, perhaps international, students will come from cultures where research is practically supposed to involve 'cutting and pasting' other people's ideas into their own writing, some perhaps younger A level students may not understand just how self-directed and motivated they have to be with respect to their reading and research, nor how widely we will expect them to read in order to do well in their assignments. Further, even where students do have a grasp of what is required of them in HE, evidence is emerging (Leathwood and O'Connell, 2003) of the impact of paid work on student lives which is revealing the negative effect this has with respect to the ability of (particularly working-class) students to undertake the reading that we feel is necessary.

While there might be a case to reevaluate the notion of fees, loans and grants in terms of the effect that they have on the whole concept of a university education, this chapter will take a pragmatic approach to helping current students in the current climate be more successful with the academic research that they do undertake. As always, our argument is that we can help all our students succeed if we work to make explicit just what it is we expect of them and if we give them safe spaces in which to practice some of the skills that we wish to foster in them. We begin by discussing student attitudes to academic reading and research. We move on to consider 'how we do it' in terms of suggesting some activities in which to engage that foreground student reading experiences, progressing to a detailed consideration of our active research and reading system.

Tutor tips: Approaching research and reading

■ If you choose to tackle academic research with your students, it is here that you could discuss the purpose of reading, raising issues of moving from novice to initiate and the notion of knowledge-claim, argument and evidence. You can be quite detailed in your information – from how you put your reading list together to how many sources are expected in an assignment bibliography.

■ Explain the difference between primary and secondary sources as they relate to your subject. If appropriate discuss quantitative and qualitative research methodologies – and direct students to cogent material that discusses the strengths and weaknesses of the same.

■ As time is so tight for our students, provide students with photocopies of key articles and chapters rather than expecting them to search them out. Give seminar time for research and reading activities.

■ Typically, alongside an introduction to academic research per se, your students will require some form of general orientation/induction to your library and a specific introduction to electronic information systems – electronic catalogues, online journals and dictionaries and information on and access to useful websites.

Student attitudes to research and reading

'One student just sat there and cried – I didn't know what to do!'

Typically students are stressed by academic reading and while they might not all sit and cry, there may be those who disappear from our courses because they just cannot cope with the reading that we expect them to undertake. While we cannot, and perhaps should not, remove all the stress associated with academic endeavour, we argue that students can be supported in their engagement with complex academic practices such as research and reading, and that when this is consciously undertaken over time, the student's reflexive, critical graduate identity can emerge.

How we do it

Typically we find that students are very apprehensive about academic reading. This fear can lead them to hardly read at all, to read extremely passively with little engagement, interrogation or understanding, and/or to read without really understanding how to effectively utilise the data they collect in their learning or in their assignments. We find that it helps to get students to articulate their thoughts and fears about reading as some form of brainstorming activity. We then move on to tackle these fears proactively by introducing our students to an active reading system. Finally, we allow them to practise the system in a safe and supportive space.

Student preliminary activities

- Using books
- Structured brainstorm

Using books

Resources: Take a box of useful textbooks to your seminar – make sure that there is more than one per student.

Activity: Students will have to select a book, spend two minutes with the book and then describe the book, either to the whole class or to a partner. In a plenary ask students how they gained their overview/picture of what the book was about and of how useful it might be to them as students.

Things that students might mention as useful:

- Whether or not the book they selected was on the reading list
- Title and author – and whether or not recognised

■ Date – recent or not

■ Blurb – useful or not

■ Contents pages – referring to course content/assignment or not

■ Index pages – referring to useful pages or not.

Discussion: While students often do have negative attitudes towards academic reading, they often underestimate their own approaches to reading. This activity allows students to make conscious their own active scanning and selection techniques. Here students can be encouraged to make links between an academic research system and the ones they employ elsewhere in their lives, for example when station hopping with the television remote control or by their approach to newspapers, or the amount of information that can be gleaned from the first few bars of a song. Students can decide if a television programme is worth watching by knowing the genre, actors and production values, or by the television channel and a programme's place in its schedule. Newspapers can be read backwards, sport first or avoided altogether. Two bars of the wrong song and students channel hop till they find something they prefer. For students not only know what they like, they also know what they do not: they can argue critically for or against a certain programme, paper or song. It can be useful here to point out to students that they should not forget what they have already learned when they cross the threshold of the lecture theatre or classroom. This can begin to break the fear of academic reading by being a positive and even an amusing experience, particularly with older students.

Structured brainstorm

As a preamble to the structured brainstorm, we might say something like this: As a university student you will be expected to read continually and extensively. However, many of us are unclear as to why we are reading at all, we might be unsure as to what to read, and we do not really know how to read academically other than thinking that it will either be 'really hard' or completely different from anything else that we have ever done. So before we move into exploring our active reading system let us ask you:

■ Why do we read?

■ How do you know what to read?

■ How much should you read for one assignment?

■ How easy or difficult do you find academic reading?

Allow students five minutes to jot down some responses on these questions, then take responses from the group and elaborate upon them as

you think fit. Typical responses to each question above are given below. If appropriate elaborate as required.

Why do we read?

■ **Experts:** You might like to discuss how people become the recognised experts or leaders in your subject. You might like to introduce students to the people that you will be expecting them to read over the next few weeks, months and years, emphasising that typically students will return again and again to the same experts and that each return will bring a more mature mind to the reading task. Discuss the notion of moving from novice to initiate and of reading often being most difficult when we know the least but getting easier as we gather new information to add to or challenge what we have already understood.

■ **Assignments:** Discuss the difference between 'fact' and knowledge-claim. Discuss notions of argument and evidence. Discuss the range of evidence you will expect students to look for and use. Mention that 'the experts' do not write in answer to our assignment questions – hence we have to **use** references and quotes somehow in our writing. Talk about how to use the data that we gather in our writing. Perhaps discuss the difference between temperate or equivocal writing as opposed to polemics.

■ **Understanding:** Reiterate the notion of a process leading from novice to initiate. Admit that, yes, early reading is difficult, but provide reassurance that it really does get easier, even while the material might get more difficult in content. Mention how note-making can aid understanding but point out that if notes are made too soon, they will be too passive (and long) because that understanding is missing. Mention that starting with simpler texts holds no shame but can facilitate a speedier development of understanding. Mention, for example, the Writers and Readers series *Beginners Guide to ...* and subject dictionaries and dictionaries of scientific terms, of literature, sociology, psychology, etc.

How do we know what to read?

■ **Reading lists:** Often reading lists are very long and intimidating – at first! When introduced to an active research and reading strategy students might discover that they might read less in terms of quantity (never a whole book again) but more in terms of quality (obtaining more from any reading).

● **Tutor tip:** Students often feel very uncomfortable with the notion of 'dipping into' texts rather than reading from cover to cover. This often feels like cheating, or they fear they will miss something. We typically mention that time constraints may impose this system and that, while change is uncomfortable, such uncomfortable feelings do pass. Tell students how you put your reading list together – what informs your choices and why some texts might be marked 'essential reading' while others are not. Discuss the implications of these terms for your students. Tell students just what use you would expect them to make of your reading list, and how you would judge whether or not they had made that use in their writing.

- ▪ **Tutor:** Yes, the tutor can direct students to useful reading – this is the purpose of the reading list. However, the tutor also indicates further reading in the lecture or in the seminar! Students have to notice the names that lecturers mention and look for these people in the library catalogue or see if they have recently written a journal article.

- ● **Tutor tip:** Write names up for students – they cannot research effectively if they do not know how to spell the names correctly and they may be too embarrassed to ask.

- ▪ **Subject librarian:** The subject librarian is an expert in their own right and can direct students to useful sources of information – especially if asked politely!

- ● **Tutor tip:** Speak to your subject librarian and see what sort of induction they are prepared to give your students. We know librarians who are prepared to visit students in lectures to discuss what services they offer, or who will take students through the electronic catalogue system and Internet searching in a student training suite.

- ▪ **Searches:** Key words from an assignment question can be used to seed researches in the university electronic catalogue – this will take students to useful books. Students can index surf these to discover which parts of the book covers the topic they are researching. Students will also need to find out how to do key word searches in the online journals and quality press.

- ● **Tutor tip:** Maybe your subject librarian will show your students how to undertake journal and other searches.

- ▪ **Other students:** Other students can help with reading choices in that your students can ask them directly what books they recommend, but also student dissertations or projects are often kept by the university behind the library counter or in a department. Students can explore past dissertations on a topic similar to the one in which they are interested. Not only might the paper be useful in itself and may act as a useful model of good student academic writing, a recent thesis should have a bibliography containing the most useful and up-to-date sources of information. Students should note the bibliography and look for the texts cited there.

How much should we read for one assignment?

Typically here students do underestimate what is required of them. Tell students how many sources you would expect to see at the end of a D, C, B or A assignment. (We normally state that anecdotal feedback leads us to think that tutors expect to see upwards of eight sources in an average piece of work – and upwards of 15 in an A piece.)

How easy or difficult do you find academic reading?

▨ **Comparatively easy – I have always liked to read:** Obviously if students already find reading easy they do have a slight advantage. Stress how the system to which you are about to introduce them will only make the task easier – and more effective.

▨ **Really difficult – I never read:** Typically this is the more common response with respect to academic reading. Here students do need to be reassured that help is at hand in terms of the lecture you are about to give and the follow-up practice session that will take place. If you notice that a large proportion of your group are indicating that reading is difficult for them, it may be that you will have to reassure students that you will be including additional sessions on practical reading techniques (see extension activities below) – tell them when these will take place. Perhaps suggest that finding a study partner or forming a reading group will help.

Once you have finished discussing the brainstorm, announce that you are moving onto the lecture proper – and make sure that students know that they are to make notes.

Make a meal of your reading – use the QOOQRRR (pronounced 'cooker'): lecture notes – adapt as necessary

It is clear that you are already aware that you will be required to read – and that you are also aware that academic reading might prove challenging to you. Indeed academic research involves much more than working through your reading list, plodding through each text from cover to painful cover, and academic reading involves much more than copying out huge chunks of text to quote in your essays. It is definitely much more than finding an article online and cutting and pasting it directly into your assignments – this is considered plagiarism, which is a serious academic offence and we have ways of discovering if you have done that!

Academic reading is about carefully selecting what to read, knowing why you are reading it, and then reading in an interactive and interrogatory manner. We are going to look at an active reading system called QOOQRRR – which stands for question, overview, overview, question, read, re-read and review – and we are going to look at each of these processes in turn.

Question – why am I reading, or reading with a purpose

There is no one reason to read academically – there are many:

- We can read because we are a novice in a subject, we are just starting to study a topic and learn about it and we need an overview to aid our understanding.

- We may be reading because we have a basic understanding of a subject, we feel initiated into it, and now we want to explore the more controversial arguments or knowledge-claims – we are no longer happy sticking to the basic texts.

- We may be reading because the lecturer has mentioned someone who sounds interesting and we want to see what that person has to say.

- On the other hand, we may have read from the reading list and followed up the people that the lecturer has mentioned in class and now we want to find someone who no one else has mentioned at all.

- We may be reading extensively to find a whole series of quotes or references for a whole essay or reading to find one quote to finish off an already good paragraph.

These are all valid reasons for reading but they will all require a slightly different reading approach and should be accompanied by different note-making techniques. It is ridiculous to make detailed notes on a whole chapter if we are only looking for one quote, for example. But similarly just jotting down a couple of quotes will be no use if we have no understanding of the subject at all – and we are really reading to initiate our understanding of a completely new topic. Knowing why you are reading will help you become an active and successful academic reader.

Overview – reading with a context

Academic research is difficult. Shout this at students. It usually involves a very intense form of reading wherein we are searching for information to aid our understanding of what we are studying: we read within a CONTEXT and we must understand that context to target our research and make sense of our reading. This is an opportunity to encourage students to make visible what they are going to attempt. Tell students:

- To photocopy their syllabus and stick it on a wall, preferably one that is going to be viewed often.

- To stick the reading list underneath.

- To paste up module aims, learning outcomes and assessment criteria and exam questions from past papers.

- That specific assignment questions should be stuck on this wall.

All these give the reading context and indicate the information that needs to be researched, read and synthesised.

● **Tutor tips:**

- **Reading lists:** You may wish to point out to students that reading lists vary. Some may have essential reading some may just record every text that a tutor thinks might be useful. Some may offer a time line, or an attempt at contextualising the epistemology of the subject; others may offer a theory line. This information may itself overwhelm some students depending on where they are in their course.

- **Exam preparation:** You may wish to remind students that even where they are reading for coursework, they are also preparing for their exams, and further, that feedback on coursework can indicate areas to improve in preparation for those exams. Hence when students eventually get to their exams they will find that they are using material that has been tested three times: in research and discussion, in coursework and feedback and in extension and revision. Revision and exam technique starts first week of term.

- **The tutor:** For the most part coursework is going to be marked by a tutor. Discovering what a tutor thinks, feels and believes – and about what they have written or in which they have a special interest – can help drive productive research and can play an important role in obtaining a high grade.

What we are trying to engage students in is a proactive, creative and reflexive approach to studying. It is great if students can try this in their first year and practice it. For it is this approach that radically alters a student's experience of higher education – and it can punch up grades.

Overview – choosing what to read and knowing what you are reading

Once you know why you are reading – that is you have an understanding of your own broad goals (to gather an overview/general understanding, argument, contrary argument, quotes, references, etc.) matched against the course context (aims, outcomes and assignment) – you should be in a position to start the process of deciding what to read. Here you move through another series of overviewing processes:

- overview all that the library – or the Internet – has to offer on (one of the key words of) your topic;

- overview a book or journal;

- overview a chapter or article;

- overview each paragraph.

● **Tutor tip:** See Resources 8.1 and 8.2, pp. 233–6.

That is, typically you will want to overview the following sources of information in order to select what to read:

- Library catalogue – which can lead you to key texts or journals.

- *First decision time* – Make decisions about how many books and journals you are going to dip into for your assignment. Pace this reading over several weeks.

- With a book – scan the index to search for assignment 'words' on particular pages – and the contents pages to see if there are whole chapters on your topic.

- With a chapter (or a journal article) – read the introduction (first paragraph) and the conclusion (last paragraph) first. These summarise the whole chapter. Think, what is this about? Do I need to read it? Why will I read it?

- Paragraphs – read the first line of every paragraph. These topic sentences or paragraph introductions tell you what the paragraph is about. Think about that too.

- Once you have read the intro, the conclusion and the topic sentences you should have a very clear outline of a whole chapter (or journal article). This leads to your –

- *Second decision time* – you must choose exactly **what** you are going to read: you need to decide which bits to read in-depth and which bits to scan.

● **Tip:** This active scanning device is really useful for summary and précis work.

Question – and question again

So we have looked at Q for question in terms reading with a purpose and O for overview in terms of reading with a context and of choosing and understanding what we are reading. It is time to question and question again.

Why am I reading this, now?

Make clear to yourself exactly why you are reading what you have decided to read. Here a targeted brainstorm will help. Ask yourself:

- What key word am I reading around?
- What do I already know on this topic?
- What do I need to find out?
- Which bit of my assignment will it help me with?
- Which learning outcome does it meet?
- Where will I use this information?

This brainstorm really tunes your brain into the reading that you are about to do. When you read in this manner you get more from your reading than if you just passively start reading something not quite knowing what, why or how it will help you.

The second questioning is to read actively, asking more questions as you go, which we will cover next.

Read

While this academic reading is the reading that does seem to intimidate many students, it is something that does get easier with practice. Typically this reading is more successful if undertaken in manageable chunks – usually a paragraph at a time – and if reading is active and interactive. Active in that you should read asking a series of questions as you go. Interactive in that you really do need to get physical with texts when reading – you need to underline, highlight, make margin notes and comments (but only if they are your texts). If working with library resources you should photocopy them first and get physical with the photocopy – you should never mark up or annotate someone else's book!

Manageable chunks

- Put paper markers or paper clips in your book to mark off the section that you intend to read. This helps the brain to relax – I can manage that much! Otherwise you can look at a huge textbook and think 'I can never manage all that!'

- Take it a paragraph at a time. Each academic paragraph is often like a mini-essay with a proposition, an argument, evidence, discussion and final point. Thus each paragraph deserves detailed consideration before you move on to the next. Read one paragraph at a time, asking the following questions as you go.

Reading questions

- What is the main idea? The main topic of the paragraph is usually revealed in the introductory sentence. Read that. Underline/highlight the key word – or summarise the topic for yourself and write your key word in the margin.

- What is the author's argument? Decide what the author is saying about the topic. Are they for it or against it? Make a margin note.

- Where is the author coming from? Here you should be looking for the author's position on the topic – are they on the left or the right? Are they a Marxist or a postmodernist? Is this distinction important in your subject? (This is typically more important in the arts and social sciences – and even in business, computing, leisure and tourism – than in some areas of science or engineering, but it never hurts to notice.) Again, make a note.

- Have I encountered similar arguments before? Where? Relate your reading to what you have heard in lectures and seminars – and to what you have encountered in other texts. Write the names of people who agree with this in the margin.

- Have I encountered different arguments from this? Again this means relating this reading to other ideas that you have encountered and actively noticing that people disagree with each other, that different arguments will be offered on the same topic. You have to note the people who think one way and the ones that think differently. Write the names of people who might disagree with this author – perhaps in different coloured ink from the names of people who might support the view that you are reading.

- What evidence is being offered? Obviously we are looking for argument rather than assertion so evidence should be offered to back up the argument being made – look for it and highlight it.

● **Tip:** Some people highlight the different parts of the paragraph in different colours – argument in blue, evidence in green, author's position in yellow, etc. Think of a system for yourself.

- Is the evidence valid? Why do I think it is or is not valid? This is definitely something that gets easier with practice. Remember, things are not true just because they are in print. You will need to get used to looking for and then judging the evidence that is being offered.

■ Do I agree or disagree with what I am reading? And why? Again, this is another thing that gets easier with practice. Often when we just start studying a subject we may not feel qualified to judge what we are reading ... but it is the nature of the British education system that we read interrogatively, and that we get used to judging argument, evidence and knowledge-claims for ourselves.

● **Tip:** It is often easy to know why we disagree with someone – you have to find reasons for agreeing also!

■ What is the author's final point? Often an academic paragraph has an actual or an implied 'therefore' or 'this means that ...' – often near the end or actually in the very last sentence. Look for these points.

● **Tip:** When doing this first read through, only make notes on the text itself – do not make your 'take away' notes yet. Notes made too soon tend to be too long and detailed – much too passive. Think and annotate now – make notes later.

Reading resources

As this is such an interactive reading strategy, it does help to have plenty of resources to hand when you read. Things to think about:

■ Strips of paper or paper clips to mark off sections for reading.

■ Highlighters to colour and emphasise key parts of the text.

■ Pencils and pens for underlining key points and writing key words – your annotations and marginalia.

■ A ruler to guide your eye down the page. The human eye is constantly on the move – when we read our eyes tend to dart all round and not stay with the line or the words that we are reading. If we place a ruler under the line that we are reading we can always bring our eyes back to the right place on the page – a simple trick that can actually save much time.

Once you have read one manageable chunk or paragraph in the way we have suggested using all your resources, move on to read the next and the next – annotating as you go.

Note that this active, interactive reading system may appear slow and cumbersome at first but:

1 It will get easier with practice.

2 It also gets easier when you are adding to information (becoming an initiate) as opposed to just starting out (being a novice), where everything is new – and noteworthy.

3 Actively selecting what to read allows us to read less in quantity but more in quality. That is, when reading, you should know which bits to scan and skip and which bits to read in depth. And, when reading in this way, you are understanding as you go rather than hoping that understanding will follow at a later date.

Re-read

As said, it is not advisable to make notes on your first read through something. It is always tempting to do so – we always think that we can save time if we just start making notes immediately – but it is usually a costly thing to do. Typically notes that are made too soon are too passive and too long. Work through your text thinking and annotating, then re-read your own annotations and marginalia, note what you have underlined or highlighted . . . then go back to your original reading goals. What were you reading for and why? Ask yourself whether or not your annotations, marginalia and highlighting captured all that you wanted from the text. Do you understand it all? If the answer to these questions is yes then you are ready to use your annotations to create your own set of notes on that text. If the answer to the first question was no you are missing bits of information – go through and mark up some more. If you do not understand what you have read discuss it with your study partner, your tutor (if possible) or with the learning development people. We do learn more when we understand what we are trying to learn.

Note-making from reading – some strategies

1 **Staged notes:** Sometimes it is difficult to make key word notes on a new topic.

● **Tip:** Divide your paper in half. Label the top of one half 'summary', label the other 'key words' (see Resource 8.3). When you go over your annotations and marginalia write a summary of good points in the summary column. Once you have completed your summary writing go through your own summaries – condense these to keywords in the key word column. If you wish, make a set of pattern notes from your key words.

2 **Cornell notes:** Again divide your note-making sheet in two – label one-half 'notes' and the other 'course'. Make notes in one column. Afterwards, go through your notes and in the 'course' column, relate the points in your notes to specific aims, learning outcomes or parts of your assignment. This is a very active note-making/reflecting strategy that aids understanding – and should tell you how useful your notes really are.

3 Pattern notes: Whether you start with staged notes, Cornell notes or just the annotations on the text, it is really useful to form a set of unique pattern notes with the key words gathered from your reading. Illustrate your notes with memory triggers, using colour, highlighting and illustrations to make the notes interesting and even more memorable. Again, this is an active system, one that allows you to 'play with ideas' and helps you to take control of your learning.

4 Paragraph patterns: Often we are making notes in order to write assignments. It may be that key words from your assignment question will eventually seed individual paragraphs in your final piece of writing. Get really large sheets of paper – A1 rather than A4. Write one key word or phrase from your question in the centre of each A1 sheet. Add (sourced) notes from one piece of reading to a paragraph sheet. Read something else on the same topic and add the notes from this to the same sheet, maybe in different coloured ink. Continue adding notes from reading to your paragraph sheets. Each time that you record new information start to notice which arguments and evidence start to go together and which start to form an opposing set of arguments.

5 Always source notes: For the Harvard system record: author, date, title, publisher, town. For the British Standard System record: author, title, publisher, date.

● **Tutor tip:** Have a handout ready that illustrates the referencing system that you want your students to use.

If you copy out small pieces to use as quotes, copy them out exactly. If you cut words out put in an ellipsis (dot, dot, dot) and if you change a word indicate this with square brackets. Always put the page number. You will need all this information if you use the data in your writing.

6 Index cards – comments and quotes: As well as recording sources in your notes, consider starting an index card record of all your reading. For each useful text/source that you read, keep information on an index card: author, date, title, publisher and town – but also jot a few words describing the book or article and how useful it was. Make a note of key words or useful quotes. File alphabetically by author surname.

● **Tip:** When studying on other units, modules or courses go to your own card index system to kick-start your own reading . . .

7 Plagiarism: Plagiarism is a very serious academic offence that can fail you a unit, module or course or that can cost you your whole degree. Literally plagiarism means kidnapping, and we take it to mean that you are passing off someone else's work or ideas as your own. While plagiarism does therefore refer to copying a fellow student's work, more often it is where you copy out material from a text – online or otherwise – without crediting your sources. It also means where you refer to or use certain ideas without citing your sources.

8 **'Well, I've read it, I agree with it – and I've put it into my own words. It's mine now isn't it?'** No. This still counts as plagiarism. When you draw on ideas from other people, even where you do not copy them exactly but put the ideas in your own words, this is plagiarism unless you give the source. On a positive note, referring to sources by putting the key points in your own words and writing, for example, 'Buzan (1997) argues …' shows a confident and mature academic practice.

9 **How many sources?** If you have not already mentioned this, as a rule of thumb first-year assignments should have between eight and 15 sources in a bibliography.

10 **A bibliography or booklist:** This comes at the end of an assignment and is a list of all the sources upon which you have drawn in your assignment. It has to be in the correct format … and in the correct place: with written assignments the bibliography comes literally at the end; with reports the bibliography comes at the end of the report but before the appendices; with oral assignments a bibliography may have to be handed in with a presentation.

● **Tutor tip:** As with reference systems, it can help if you have a student handout that models the bibliography style that you actually want.

Review

The final part of this active and interactive academic reading system is the review. This is where you, the student, have to look over the notes that you have made, judging for yourself whether or not they are useful, useable and effective. It is vital that you begin the habit of checking the quality of your own work as soon as possible. Do not rely on other people, even tutors, to tell you whether or not you are doing a good job. Start deciding for yourself.

Note review – questions and actions

■ Are my notes sourced and cited in the correct manner – Harvard, British Standard, other?

■ Are my quotes accurate and sourced (page numbers!)?

- Do my notes do what I want? Have they answered my questions? Do they meet my goals? That is, can you do what you wanted from reading that piece of writing?

- **Scan:** Quickly scan both notes and sources to see if anything is missing.

- **Goal setting:** Once you have read one thing you have to decide what else to read. So ask yourself: what else will I read – when?

- **Stop reading:** At some point the reading/thinking bit has to stop and the thinking/writing bit has to start.

- **Tip:** Beware of using reading as a way of putting off writing. Sample or rough paragraphs can be written very early on in a term or semester, even before your reading has finished, and then be improved.

- **Index surfing and other tricks:** Once you have a rough draft of a paragraph or even of a whole essay, index surf on your paragraph topics. See if your work can be improved by additional quotes or references that you glean from a very quick reading session.

When you are happy with your notes move on to additional reading – or to drafting your writing!

Concluding the lecture

We have looked at the QOOQRRR system – in particular we have focused on how active a reader you have to be in terms of reading with a purpose and a context – which involves questioning why you are reading and of having an overview of the course for which you are reading. It also involves scanning all the sources of information at your disposal. We recommended an active and interactive reading strategy that requires you to ask questions of your reading as you go, and to mark up and annotate your texts – stressing that they must be *your* texts! We recommend that the only notes that you make on a first read through are those annotations on the text itself and that afterwards you re-read these in order to structure your own notes. Finally we stressed that you have to take control of your own work – and that includes judging whether or not your notes are useful, useable and effective. One thing that we emphasised here is that notes be adequately and accurately sourced. We made recommendations as to key word notes, paragraph patterns and building up an index card collection from the very beginning of your time as a student.

Any questions . . .?

Take questions and answer. Inform students as to what, if any, follow-up activities in which you will engage and when.

For an example of a student's notes made on the lecture in this chapter see Resource 8.4. For this same student's notes made when putting the reading theory outlined here into practice on a text by Tony Buzan, see Resource 8.5.

Extension activity 1: QOOQRRR practice

Once you have introduced students to the theory of active reading, it is beneficial to let them practise this system and to reflect on the parts of it they understand and the areas where they are encountering problems.

Resources

Have several copies of different, short but useful articles. It helps if the articles are related to your assignment question or, for the more astute students, are related more obliquely to aspects of the course aims and outcomes. Initially articles should be short so that students can work on them in a seminar period and still make useful notes.

Time

Try to choose pieces that will allow students to make notes and then actively reflect on the notes in the seminar period you are using. Typically a one-page A4 piece from the quality press can take students 20–30 minutes to read.

Activity: note-making from reading

Tell students that they will be choosing an article to read and make notes upon.

Remind students to apply their QOOQRRR strategy to choose and then read the piece and to make effective notes upon it. You could possibly set different groups of students a different note-making strategy – staged, Cornell or pattern notes.

Consider writing on the board:

■ **Question:** Purpose – why am I reading now? Am I looking for a general understanding, a standard opinion, a contrary opinion, a set of useful references or quotes, one key quote, other?

■ **Overview:** Context – what are the aims, learning outcomes, assignment parameters for this course? What am I focusing on today?

■ **Overview:** What are these different articles on? Which one is the most useful to my immediate goals for today?

■ **Question:** So what am I reading now and what am I looking for? What do I already know on this topic? What do I need to find out? Where will I be using the information I am gathering?

■ **Read:** Actively and interactively, asking and answering questions, and marking up as you go.

■ **Re-read** your underlinings, highlighting and marginalia – check your understanding and the quality of your annotations. Make your own key word notes – in stages, using the Cornell system, in patterns.

■ **Review** notes to check accuracy, quality, sourcing . . .: Note immediate thoughts about additional reading required.

● **Tutor tip:** Sometimes students just sit unmoving, unwilling or unable to start. If this happens we might comfort those in extreme distress if appropriate, or prompt them to work with a partner. Sometimes we just announce to the room that if they are having trouble they should pair up and work with someone else who has chosen the same article.

In pairs

Get students to show notes to other students and to discuss notes in terms of form and content.

Plenary

Consider having a plenary to discuss reading and notes, pleasures and pains, strengths and weaknesses . . .

● **Tutor tip:** Alternatively, give all students the same article and use the plenary to build one set of pattern notes on the board, drawing on student suggestions.

Inform students of what additional work you will be doing on this – if any.

Extension activity 2: Writing about reading – using notes in writing

A useful follow-up activity to the note-making from reading is to set students the task of using a specific set of notes in their writing. Thus this activity can act as an extension to the one above.

Resources

Tell students that they must bring their articles and their notes to the requisite seminar session.

Activity

Tell students that they must now write a paragraph drawing upon the notes that they made upon their article. You will want students to quote and refer to the article – tell them how many quotes and references that you actually want them to make.

Once they have written their paragraphs, first get students in pairs to read and review each other's writing and to comment positively upon it.

Collect the work in at the end and check that students are citing accurately and in the system that you require.

Further extension activities

■ Give students journal articles from which you have removed the abstract. Ask them to read the papers and write an appropriate abstract.

■ Give students journal articles and ask them to critically evaluate an article in terms of its methodology, findings and conclusions.

Overall conclusion

In this chapter we linked targeted research and active, interrogative reading strategies to the development of the reflexive student identity. We have stressed just how emotional an experience reading can be for some students, and we indicated that different students may have very different approaches to their academic reading which need not stem from lack of ability, but from lack of practice, from cultural differences – or even because active reading systems can feel like 'cheating'. We suggested practical ways of helping students to approach their research and overcome their fears of reading – and to become informed, competent and effective academic readers: the using books activity, the targeted brainstorm and the lecture. We also suggested follow-up activities wherein students could both practise their reading and note-making and their use of their reading notes in their writing. We have found that these activities do promote understanding in students of all ages and abilities and at every stage of their student life.

We have found the information and activities beneficial with very timid foundation students and with very intelligent and motivated, but perhaps not academically inducted, third-year and even postgraduate students. Sometimes it is as though scales fall from the eyes and students are liberated to study effectively. We hope that you find some or all of these activities useful in your own practice.

Resources

8.1 Library worksheet
8.2 Overview: choose what to read – know what you are reading
8.3 How to move to pattern notes from your reading
8.4 Student notes on QOOQRRR: targeted research and active reading
8.5 Student notes on Tony Buzan: QOOQRRR theory into practice

Further reading

Buzan, B. and Buzan, T. (1999) *The Mind Map Book*. London: BBC Publications.
Holmes, L. (2001) 'Reconsidering graduate employability: the "graduate ident-ity" approach', *Quality in Higher Education*, 7 (2): 111–19.
Leathwood, C. and O'Connell, P. (2003) ' "It's a struggle": the construction of the "new student" in higher education', *Journal of Educational Policy*, 18 (6).

9 How to promote effective note-making

Introduction

Most lecturers want their students to take and use notes and students often realise that they will be required to make notes of some sort. However, students can experience confusion as to the sort of notes they should take, how notes are supposed to help them to study and what to do with notes once they have been made. In this chapter we will link note-making strategies to active and creative learning techniques. We will then consider how we in learning development prepare our students for note-making strategies that help them engage with rather than merely record information.

Before moving on, if you have not really thought about note-making before, it might help if you take some time to consider the questions in the Activity box below.

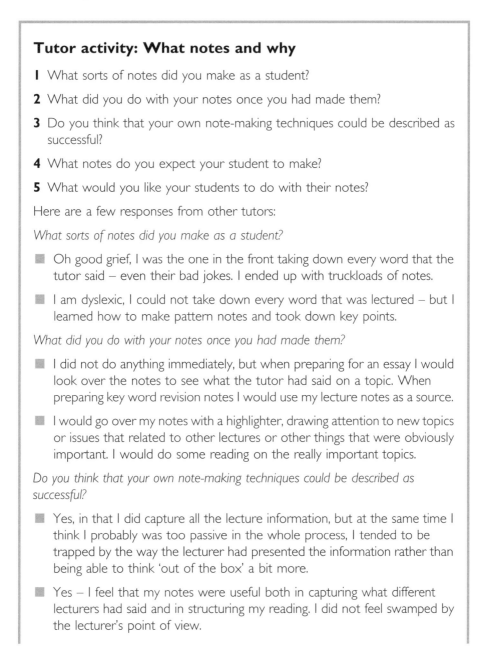

Tutor activity: What notes and why

1 What sorts of notes did you make as a student?

2 What did you do with your notes once you had made them?

3 Do you think that your own note-making techniques could be described as successful?

4 What notes do you expect your student to make?

5 What would you like your students to do with their notes?

Here are a few responses from other tutors:

What sorts of notes did you make as a student?

■ Oh good grief, I was the one in the front taking down every word that the tutor said – even their bad jokes. I ended up with truckloads of notes.

■ I am dyslexic, I could not take down every word that was lectured – but I learned how to make pattern notes and took down key points.

What did you do with your notes once you had made them?

■ I did not do anything immediately, but when preparing for an essay I would look over the notes to see what the tutor had said on a topic. When preparing key word revision notes I would use my lecture notes as a source.

■ I would go over my notes with a highlighter, drawing attention to new topics or issues that related to other lectures or other things that were obviously important. I would do some reading on the really important topics.

Do you think that your own note-making techniques could be described as successful?

■ Yes, in that I did capture all the lecture information, but at the same time I think I probably was too passive in the whole process, I tended to be trapped by the way the lecturer had presented the information rather than being able to think 'out of the box' a bit more.

■ Yes – I feel that my notes were useful both in capturing what different lecturers had said and in structuring my reading. I did not feel swamped by the lecturer's point of view.

What notes do you expect your students to make?

- I would like my students to make key word notes that highlight all the important areas of the topic that I cover in my lecture. I want them to note key names and dates that I mention – and to use these notes to seed their own research.

- I would like my students to make key word pattern notes and to use them to structure their research and help but not limit their thinking.

What would you like your students to do with their notes?

- I would like students to go over their notes immediately after the lecture, writing a shorter version of the notes (cutting out my bad jokes!). I would like them to reflect on how the information in the notes takes their learning forward. I want them to read up on the people that I mention in my lectures – and to discover some people to read that I have not mentioned. I would like them to surprise me in their assignments.

- I tell my students to stick their notes on their walls – to immerse themselves in the information, especially if it is new to them. I want to see the key information being worked on in their assignments and in the exam answers – not just passively parroted back to me. I want the notes to be the starting point for their own research, not the only information they bother to get on the topic.

Query: Were any of these replies similar to your own? In what ways were your points different to these? Does this tell you anything about your expectations of your students?

Discussion: One thing that these replies tell us is that we often have very high expectations of our students, sometimes expecting them to perform to a higher standard than maybe we did ourselves.

We appear to want students to operate in ways that require high levels of motivation and commitment and in ways that implicitly embody an awareness of the practices and discourses of academia and that rely on an understanding of the workings of short- and long-term memory.

While it is admirable to have high expectations of our students, we have found that if we want students to perform to the high standards that we have of them we do have to support and scaffold their learning in some ways. With note-making, we have found that we have to teach them how to make and use their notes and we have to allow them many safe spaces in which to practise and refine their note-making skills.

Notes and creative learning

We have noticed a change over time from the student who tries to write down everything and the new student who may write down nothing at all in a lecture. Neither of these strategies is necessarily very helpful to the student. Recent research (Sutherland et al., 2002) indicates that while students will make notes to help them pass exams, many do not reflect on their notes or use them to seed their research. Similarly, while we believe that notes should be an active and creative part of a student's learning process we feel that this does not necessarily happen. To address this we locate our note-making advice in the companion text to this handbook, *Essential Study Skills*, within Chapter 6: How to learn creatively. Here we look at note-making as part of the active learning process, and we also link it to other creative learning techniques such as brainstorming and question matrixing. We stress that students have to prepare to make notes, that they should endeavour to make active and creative notes, and that they must do something with their notes once they have made them. We have found that this prompts the student to engage more with their material and, by utilising an active revision cycle, to take steps to learn that which is important.

Before we move on to consider how we cover note-making proper with our students, we shall briefly consider here some of the arguments that we put to students when encouraging them to employ creative techniques in their learning.

Why be creative?

Buzan's argument for adopting creative techniques is that we need to encourage whole- rather than half-brain learning. Put at its most basic, Buzan argues that we need to utilise both the logical left and the creative right sides of the brain when we engage in an active learning activity. Traditional linear types of note-making strategies, he argues, only utilise the logical left side of the brain and consequently are passive and monotonous, actually militating against active learning. Key word notes that are mapped out non-hierarchically in a pattern of some sort allow more space for the student's active engagement. If this is coupled with the building of mnemonic triggers into notes and combined with an ongoing revision process, the student is likely to learn more.

We also refer to Graham Gibbs and the notion that knowledge means to have sport with ideas – to be able to play with them. As academics I think that we can see that engaging with possibly new and challenging information in a playful way actually requires a maturity and confidence that many of our students may lack. We have found that encouraging a pattern note-making system can inject an element of play into the learning process as a way of initiating the process of having sport with ideas. Further, as students are rearranging the data that they gather to create their own note patterns, they are being encouraged to rework data and take control of it for themselves rather than remaining trapped by the way that data has been presented to them.

Finally we stress the common-sense argument that if they only give back to the tutor that which the tutor gave to them they will never move beyond the attainment of an average grade. In this way, even if their whole approach to learning is utilitarian, they will benefit from being creative in their learning for it will improve their chances of getting a good grade for their work. Thus even the most assessment-driven and pragmatic student can be encouraged to more actively and creatively engage with their learning – and in the process shift from surface to deep learning practices.

... and significant learning

Drawing on the work on Carl Rogers and the facilitation of significant learning, we also stress to students that if they want to learn, they must be reaching out for what they want and need from a course in general – and specifically from their lectures and reading. We encourage students to gain an awareness of the overall aims and outcomes of a particular unit, module or programme – and then stress that they use this awareness to generate the questions that they ask of lectures and texts. That is, we encourage students to see lectures and texts as sources of useful information, and to understand that they can usefully excavate this information once they know what they are looking for. This in turn makes their note-making more effective and productive.

How we do it

In this section we are going to cover how we in learning development tackle note-making with our students. We have found that these activities work best with groups of students – from 12 to 30 in number – rather than with individuals.

Preliminary activities

- Structured brainstorm

- Discussion of linear and non-linear notes

- Discussion of the characteristics of successful notes

Structured brainstorm

Before moving into note-making proper we normally engage in a structured brainstorm on note-making with the class. This models the good practice that we emphasise throughout this text: that students need to prepare for study. A brainstorm allows students to recall what they know on a topic and encourages them to identify gaps in their knowledge, hence indicating what they want and need from their efforts. Further, such a brainstorm helps the student to tune into and focus on their work.

The structured brainstorm

On the board start a pattern note by writing 'notes' in the centre of the board. Draw three lines from the centre, labelling them 'Why (do we make notes)?', 'When and where (do we make notes)?' and 'How (do you make notes)?'

Give the group a couple of minutes to think about the subject then take answers from the class, writing up key words under the appropriate headings. You can discuss points raised as you write on the board – usually in affirmative ways.

Typically you will draw in answers thus:

Why?

- To remember key points
- To use information in assignments
- To follow up in some way
- To understand the topic

When and where do we make notes?

- At work, in meetings
- In lectures
- When I'm reading
- In discussion – group work, seminars, tutorials, etc.
- On the bus – when I remember key points or have a brain wave
- Etc.

How do you make notes?

- Badly – I can never read my writing
- Badly – I forget what they mean

■ I take down too much/too little information

■ I make a rough draft and do a shorter version later

■ Etc.

After the brainstorm you may like to remind students that such an activity does prove that they already have ideas on the subject. Remind them to use their own ideas as a starting point for any note-making that they do – in lectures and with their reading – and in the note-making practice that is to follow. In particular they should know what they want to learn about note-making from the practice exercise that you are about to take them through.

Linear and non-linear notes

As a lead-in to the lecture proper you may find it useful to briefly discuss linear and pattern notes as follows.

Linear notes

Taking down information line by line is known as linear note-making. If a student can write really fast, linear notes can be quite information packed and this can give a really comforting feeling. However, there can be some problems with attempting to capture everything the tutor says. And there can be problems with linear notes – especially if you are trying to become a more active or creative learner. Problems with linear notes can include the following:

■ You can take down so much information you feel swamped by it.

■ You take so many notes you never have the time to read them again.

■ If you cannot write really fast you lose your place and may start to panic and miss more information.

■ If you leave things out you can feel like a failure.

■ All the information looks the same, it is difficult to focus on specific points.

■ Although you have not thought about the information, the notes already have a top-down hierarchy imposed.

■ You can be trapped by the way that the lecturer has presented the information – you might find it difficult to think about the topic in any other way.

■ It is a very passive form of note-making – you do not have to think to write these notes, but you do have to think to learn.

▓ It only utilises half the brain (in Tony Buzan's terms left-brain logical rather than right-brain creative). As such it is monotone – monotonous and even boring. It does not excite.

How to improve linear notes

Cornell University in the USA utilises an active linear note-making system whereby students link notes to specific course aims, outcomes and assessment criteria. In practice this involves note-making paper with a central dividing line. One side of the page is labelled 'course aims and assignment' and the other is labelled 'notes'.

When listening to a lecture (or when reading), students jot notes down on the note-making side – in key word form if possible, but putting in longer sentences where necessary. After the lecture, students review their notes, highlighting key words and further reading suggestions. They then work on the 'course aims and assignment' column, noting where a lecture item relates to particular course aims and learning outcomes, and where points relate to specific parts of the assignment.

Although this appears to be a very pragmatic, even surface, approach to note-making, it actually encourages reflective learning as students work to understand how the learning has been structured over a programme. In the process students begin to take a more in-depth, proactive approach to their studies – and they are encouraged to take more control of their own learning activities.

Pattern notes

If appropriate, you might like to point out to students that you have not used a linear system yourself, but that you have created different notes on the board – diagrammatic key word notes. You may have drawn a pattern:

▓ to defer ordering and prioritising information;

▓ to encourage short notes;

▓ to create distinctive notes;

▓ or in order to utilise the whole brain – logical left and creative right.

Obviously a key word system is useful whichever note-making strategy students eventually decide to adopt, as are the use of memory triggers – symbols, pictures, colour and highlighting. All these make notes more distinctive, interesting and memorable. However, there are some specific advantages to *pattern* notes and you could stress the following to your students:

Pattern notes have the following advantages:

■ They encourage a key word system.

■ You actively reduce information to key words as you go (or as you subsequently revise notes). This means that you have to think about your notes – you have to engage.

■ Such notes are short and therefore more useable.

■ You do not need to be able to write quickly – you just have to learn to think on your seat.

■ Notes are not hierarchically ordered – you can think about them for yourself.

■ Each set of notes looks distinct from other sets of notes, making them more memorable.

■ Information is more easily located within these notes.

■ Buzan would argue that this is an active, creative note-making system that utilises the whole brain and thus prompts more learning.

You may wish to conclude this preparatory activity by taking a moment to decide as a class the sort of information that should be present in a successful set of notes. Hopefully you will collect something like the following. (For a useful handout on pattern notes for your students see Resource 9.1.)

Successful notes should have the following:

■ Source – if lecture: title, lecturer's name, date; if text: author, date, title, town, publisher.

■ Headings – capturing key sections.

■ Key words – key points, examples, illustrations, names, new ideas.

■ Some structure – things that make the notes easy to read: patterns, numbering, arrows, highlighting, etc.; things that link the notes to the course aims, outcomes and assignment.

■ Mnemonic triggers – things that make the notes memorable: cartoons, colour, illustrations (the Von Rostorff effect – we remember that which is bizarre, funny or bawdy (in Palmer and Pope, 1984)).

■ Further reading – names highlighted in the notes or gathered in a specific place.

Note: If students mention that notes should be understandable or easy to read, etc. indicate how the above facilitates this.

Once these preliminary activities have been completed you can decide how much of the following lecture to use with your students in order to get them to consolidate their thinking around note-making by putting the ideas suggested into practice.

The practice lecture – note-making from lectures

Typically after the preliminary activities described above, we move on to give students a practice lecture followed by some note revision guidance and practice. This gives students the opportunity to practise their note-making in a safe space. Obviously this can be undertaken with any lecture – it does not have to be the one that we give here. Our lecture is entitled 'Note-making from lectures' and we usually encourage students to attempt pattern notes – and we stress that while this advice is hinged around the academic lecture the same processes promote note-making from reading.

If you are utilising this exercise yourself you might like to tell students to turn their paper sideways, landscape fashion. They should write the title of the lecture, the lecturer's name and the date somewhere on the paper – this is useful source information. Students should attempt just to note key words or phrases and if possible to jot them down in a rough pattern – or if using the Cornell system, only in the 'notes' column.

Reassure students that they will be acting on the information after the lecture, so there will be time to plug any gaps – they do not need to panic if they miss something as you speak. Typically you should try to lecture at a reasonable speed – do not be tempted to give a dictation, and students should not attempt to write down every word that you say.

Note-making from lectures – lecture notes

Introduction

In this lecture I am going to look at active and passive learning, why we make notes and why universities utilise lectures. I will move on to discuss how to make notes from your lectures, focusing on what to do before, during and after a lecture.

NOW STOP.

At this point we usually stop and ask students what they have done with what has just been said, that is what use have they made of the lecture introduction/agenda. Some students will have made no use of it at all. Others will have dotted the words around their note-making paper, others might have captured the key words in some other way. It is useful to stress that if a lecturer gives an introduction/agenda to their lecture (and it really is good practice to do so) then students should use this lecture overview productively. One tip that we share with students is that they could draw a margin (a second margin if they are utilising the Cornell system) and quickly jot down the key words. This will help them to structure their notes as they go, and they can also use this margin to capture key names (the further reading) – and it will tell them which topics the lecturer did not cover if you all run out of time.

● **Tutor tips:**
● Do tell your students the purpose of your lecture, what they are expected to get from the lecture, and what you want them to do during and after the lecture.
● Write your lecture agenda on the board at the beginning of every class. Help students to learn to write down the topics before you start to lecture. Eventually students use the writing of the agenda as their own focusing/settling down activity.
● After saying your introduction/agenda, get students to brainstorm for two minutes on the lecture topic.
● Before you start a lecture ask students to say or write down one thing that they would like to take away from your lecture.
● After a lecture get students to say or write down one new thing that they can take away from your lecture.

Once students are aware that they should utilise your introduction/ agenda, you might like to start the lecture again, perhaps modelling good practice by writing down the lecture key words (learning – active – passive; why? why lectures? how?) down the 'margin' of the board.

Note-making from lectures – the lecture

Introduction

In this lecture I am going to look at active and passive learning, why we make notes and why universities utilise lectures. I will move on to discuss how to make notes from your lectures, focusing on what to do before, during and after a lecture.

Active versus passive learning

Passive learning is where we take no responsibility for, nor any active part in, our own learning processes. We may neither know nor care how a programme has been put together, what to do to gain the most from that programme, or what our own reasons for taking the course were. We just drift through a course as if it is was all happening to someone else. We may briefly memorise a few names, dates and facts – but we make no effort to understand their significance. We stay on the surface of the course rather than probing beneath – and ultimately we remain un-changed by what we see, hear and do.

Active learning is where we not only make conscious our own reasons for undertaking a course, we also attempt to determine how the course has been put together and why. When encountering new ideas or other information we strive to understand their significance – what it means, what it tells us and what else we will have to discover. In taking active control of a course in this way we not only enjoy it more, we also move from surface to deep learning, and we engage in a learning process that can radically alter us as human beings. In this process we are taking as a starting point a definition of learning that argues that true learning must be witting and conscious and it must bring about a permanent change in the learner.

Why make notes?

We not only make notes to record key pieces of information, we make notes as part of our own active engagement with that information. Our notes become the arena wherein we work to select and then understand data. Notes are our record of important information and they are what we use to seed our thinking and our research. Notes become source material for our discussions and for our writing. In this way our notes become a key part of our active learning process.

Why lectures?

The lecturing system in universities has been criticised for promoting passive learning in students. In such a passive learning experience the lecturer speaks and the student either writes or does not write down some notes. The notes may hit the page without actually passing through the brain of the student – and may hit the bottom of the birdcage rather than ever being used again. Obviously this was not the original purpose of the lecture.

Since Socrates there has been a tradition of the student engaging with the words of the wise person. The learner was supposed to reflect on what was being said and utilise the information in his or her own philosophical development. There is a historical tradition of the wise person speaking and the student reflecting upon that which has been said.

And in Britain since mediaeval times, when manuscripts were rare and expensive commodities and as such not available to the majority of students, there has been a lecturing tradition. There are other economic factors to the lecturing system: one lecturer can address hundreds of students in this way while other teaching/learning activities tend to require different staff:student ratios.

In the modern British university, the lecture is supposed to give students access to the work of a researcher, a leader in the field. The lecture allows the student a short cut to intense and significant information, although not 'all they need to know' on the subject. Typically the lecture is supposed to seed student thinking and student research on the lecture topic. If students engage actively with lectures they are powerful vehicles of information, as well as being epistemological – thinking – models.

That is, the lecturer is using the discourse of the subject – the language, the arguments and the evidence that apply in their own subject. Students should mine the lecture not only to excavate data but also to explore how to think about a topic and how to construct arguments and use evidence within a particular discipline.

● **Tutor tip:** It may be appropriate to give an example of how this is true in your own discipline.

How to make notes

In this final section of this lecture I am going to briefly cover what to do before, during and after a lecture. Remember, it is useful to engage in these activities before, during and after your reading, also.

Before

The essence of good note-making is preparation. Students should prepare by exploring the aims, learning outcomes and overall syllabus of the programme. They should examine the assignment in detail and pause to think – how does this lecture fit into all this?

Immediately before the lecture the student should recall the programme as a whole and then brainstorm: 'What do I already know on this topic? What do I need to find out?' (as we all did in the structured brainstorm and discussion that took place before this lecture – and which is now helping you to make better notes than you would previously have done!).

During the lecture

After active preparation, you should remain actively in tune with the lecture. Listen for new ideas and information. Select key points and write them down as briefly as possible – using key words if you can. If the lecturer mentions research evidence or further reading, note down names.

● **Tutor tip:** Write names on the board for students – they may not know how to spell them.

If you remember something previously heard or read note that also. If you react positively or negatively to what you hear perhaps put in a question mark or an exclamation mark to remind yourself.

● **Tip:** Perhaps record these interventions/comments in a different coloured ink to separate them out from the lecture proper.

If this process appears difficult, remind yourself that it will get easier with practice. When you first engage with a topic everything is new and potentially disorientating. But after a while you will start to recognise the information, and the names and dates that are being mentioned. It will then be that much easier to make your notes – and often this is when it will be easier to jot down key word notes rather than writing down everything that you hear (or read).

After a lecture – do something!

Revise: After every lecture the active student should do something with their notes. Tony Buzan argues that unless we do something we will forget 98% of what we have heard in just three weeks! Typically we might take a few minutes to draw up a much shorter version of our notes, replacing phrases and sentences with those key words. Remember you do not need to panic about forgetting the significance of these – not only will you be able to retain your longer notes if you wish, this active revision will increase both your understanding of the material and your ability to remember it.

● **Tip:** Use the revision cycle:
● Always treat lecture notes as a first or rough draft – then:
● Ten minutes after a lecture spend ten minutes doing a shorter, more dynamic version of your notes. Remember the tips for successful notes: source the notes, organise them effectively, connect key points and identify further reading; build in memory triggers – make the notes good to look at, easy to understand and memorable.
● A day later spend two minutes actively redrawing your notes and plugging the gaps.
● Repeat this process a week, a month and six months later. In this way you will be actively transferring information from your short- to your long-term memory. In fact you are actively creating your memories in this way.

Discuss: Another simple and really effective active learning technique is to discuss the lecture with someone else, maybe comparing your notes at the same time. If there is information in the notes that you do not understand, definitely discuss this. Talking about your learning is the simplest and most enjoyable way of promoting understanding and actively revising material. Further, knowing that you intend to do this can reduce the stress of a lecture – it is not so terrible to miss something as your study partner will most probably have gathered it up. This is a very active learning process.

Connect – and goal set: After these revision processes, use the Cornell system, that is make connections between the information in your notes and your course as a whole. Highlight topics that will be useful in your final assignment. Make a note of key topic areas and, hence, information that you will need to research further. Take a few moments to decide what you will now read or what you will now do for you may be ready to undertake some writing as well as follow-up reading. Note in your study timetable just *when* you will undertake follow-up activities – if you do not make a date for it, it will not happen.

● **Tip:** Do not leave all your writing till you have finished reading. Write a little bit every week – writing promotes learning and gets easier with practice.

Conclusion

So we have looked at active learning and linked that to deep and significant learning, and we have linked all of that to active note-making. We looked at the role of the lecture in the university, that the lecturer is a practitioner of your subject, probably engaged in research, who will give you a short cut to information and who will model the language, arguments and evidence of your subject for you. They will help familiarise you with the epistemological practices of your discipline. We emphasised that you will need to do something after the lecture in terms of working to understand, revise and learn the material – and to extend your learning by further research. To use a sporting analogy – the brainstorm before the lecture is the warm-up, the lecture is the training, but it is what you do afterwards – your research, reading, thinking, talking and writing – that is actually the event. They are what being a student is all about. This will be facilitated if you work to understand how the course as a whole has been put together – and if you discuss the material with a study partner.

Do you have any questions?

Obviously – it is useful to pause and to take and answer student queries at this point.

Practising it – the next step

As you have just told students that it is beneficial to revise notes, it is useful to now give students at least ten minutes to revise their notes – possibly in pairs. You could hand out paper and coloured pens to facilitate their making the notes more visually interesting and memorable.

Move around the room and encourage students as they work. Think about giving students a handout of a key word version of this lecture (see Resource 9.2) or you could draw a copy of the notes on the board.

Encourage students to move around the room and see what notes other people have made and to see what sort of devices they would like to adopt in their own practice. This is useful because it does reveal that there is no one correct way to produce memorable and useful notes.

At the end of the session consider giving students the opportunity to discuss how they have found the whole exercise, and what they will do next to continue to develop as successful note-makers.

Practising it further

▓ Tips: encourage students to make key word pattern notes of television and radio programmes or to visit lectures that are not vital to their success. It will be easier to practise this technique in situations that do not feel critical to their success or failure as students.

▓ Encourage students to make pattern notes of all your lectures.

● **Tutor tips:**

● Build pattern notes of your lectures as you lecture – on the board or on an overhead.

● Rather than lengthy handouts that students rarely read, prepare one-page pattern notes of your lectures which you can hand out in advance so that students can add to them as they listen to you or immediately after your lecture.

● Vary this by giving out your notes after rather than before the lecture.

Extension activities

▓ Get students to bring lecture notes to seminar sessions. Ask students to review notes in pairs. Show your own notes.

▓ Encourage students to build one huge pattern of your whole course, adding to it week by week.

▓ Encourage students to build pattern notes of each potential paragraph of the assignment essay. Using A1 paper get different groups of students to focus on different parts of an assignment. Each group should add to their key word or phrase, appropriate lecture notes, then notes from one reading source, then another, etc.

▓ Get students to build course notes and or assignment notes week by week in seminars in pairs or groups.

Resources

9.1 Beginner's guide to pattern notes
9.2 Student notes on the lecture 'Note-making from lectures'

Bibliography and further reading

Buzan, B. and Buzan, T. (1999) *The Mind Map Book*. London: BBC Publications.

Buzan, T. (1989) *Use Your Head*. London: BBC Publications.

Gibbs, G. and Habeshaw, T. (1992) *53 Interesting Things to Do in Your Lectures*. Bristol: Arrowsmith.

Palmer, R. and Pope, C. (1984) *Brain Train: Studying for Success*. London: Spon.

Rogers, C. (1992) *Freedom to learn*. Upper Saddle River, NJ: Merrill.

Rose, C. and Goll, L. (1992) *Accelerate Your Learning*. Aylesbury, Bucks: Accelerated Learning Systems.

Sutherland, P., Badger, R. and White, G. (2002) 'How new students take notes in lectures', *Journal of Further and Higher Education*, 26 (4): 377–88.

10 How to promote effective presentations and seminars

Why oral assignments?

There are many assessment mechanisms in higher education that promote active learning in the process while providing a product for assessment – see also Chapter 3 on how to assess (and Chapters 7 on time management, 8 on research and reading, 9 on note-making, 11 on academic writing, 12 on revision and exam techniques, 13 on group work and 14 on reflective practice). Of these arguably the presentation – and by association the formal seminar with its presentation component – is the one that appears to present the student with the most feared academic event: public speaking. It is perhaps ironic that this is the case, for in learning development we hear lecturers repeatedly say that they will use the presentation as an 'equal opportunities' assessment device in the assumption that this will privilege the non-traditional student in some way. That is, it is argued that because academic writing is so incredibly difficult and stressful and because students, especially the widening participation student, are typically much better at speaking than they are at writing then oral assessments should perhaps be used to shift the balance a little more towards the non-traditional student.

There are several problems with this. Not only does it embody an implicitly deficit notion of the non-traditional student, it also ignores the fact that a presentation of sufficient academic depth and breadth to merit a high grade requires very similar processes and endeavour to those necessary for the generation of an academic essay. It also completely ignores the fear factor.

This is not to say that we should not utilise oral assessments in our programmes – they can be extremely useful assessment tools, especially once a student has learned to deal with the concomitant fear. However, we should acknowledge that a good presentation can be as challenging to prepare as a good essay – and that the delivery of a successful presentation is a remarkable feat in its own right.

In this chapter we will explore some tutor attitudes towards the setting of presentations, moving on to detail how we approach presentations, and then seminars, in learning development.

Tutor activity: Why set a presentation?

Take a few moments to answer the questions below and consider how your answers will help you to better utilise the presentation with students in the future.

1 Have you set a presentation as an assessment mechanism before?

2 How did you assess the presentations?

3 What are the strengths of a presentation?

4 What are the weaknesses?

5 What opportunities did it present for you or your students?

6 What threats did it present for you or your students?

7 How did you prepare students for presentations?

8 What would you do differently next time?

Some responses from other members of staff:

Have you set a presentation as an assessment mechanism before?

▣ Yes, I have used both presentations and the more formal seminar in my programmes.

▣ No, I have never known how to mark presentations so I have always avoided them.

▣ I think that I have only used them for the 'wrong' reasons, not because I didn't really think that my students were up to an essay yet, I hope, but I did think that a presentation would be easier than an essay.

How did you assess the presentations?

▣ I have developed an assessment form. I give one to each student, so that they know what I will be looking for in advance – also so that they can use the pro forma to assess themselves. In fact, I refuse to give students my grade until they have assessed themselves first.

▣ I set group presentations in my Maths Culture module. I have a set of assessment criteria, which I do give to the students in advance. When it comes to the presentations themselves, as well as marking the presentations myself, each group marks every other, but not their own, across four areas: answering the question, use of mathematics, interest and relevance, and presentation skills including use of visual aids.

What are the strengths of this form of assessment?

▣ Because I do know that presentation giving is so horrifying to students, I set them to build student self-confidence. Once students have given two presentations for me – one individual and one group – they do tend to report back that they feel much better about themselves as students.

▣ I think that presentations really help students to understand the material. I don't think they can write about a topic if they have not spoken about it first – and now that students are often raising families and working alongside undertaking their studies, sometimes the presentation feels like the only space they get to really talk through the ideas that they are learning.

What are the weaknesses of presentations?

▣ I think that the fear is a factor here, but if you prepare students well, then you can overcome it to an extent.

▣ Ill-prepared presentations – in terms of form or content – can make the whole experience excruciating, not only for the presenter but also for the whole group.

What are the opportunities?

■ This is a selfish one, but the first opportunity came for me in the improvement of my own lecturing technique. It was not till I introduced students to good presentation technique that I realised how bad my lectures were!

■ One opportunity is that I give students the chance to give a presentation on the assignment topic before they hand in their written assignment. I check their thinking, prompt them to further research or steer them back to the question if they seem to be losing sight of it.

What are the threats?

■ One threat does come with a really large group. I want to give everyone the opportunity to listen to everybody else's presentation – one problem is the sheer length of time this can take – another problem is the boredom factor ... Hour after hour of poor presentations can really lose a class.

■ Some people believe that practice makes perfect – but it is only perfect practice that makes perfect. If bad technique is not tackled early on it only gets reinforced over a student's life as a presenter.

How do you prepare students for presentations?

■ I invite the learning development person in to talk to my students about presentation technique – I then invite her back to help with the evaluations. Not only does this illustrate to my class how seriously I am taking their assignment, it also helps the students to make a real and positive connection with learning development, one that they will hopefully utilise for other areas of their studies.

■ I tell the students exactly what I will be looking for in terms of form and content. With form, I detail the shape and structure of a good presentation. In terms of content, I refer students to the module aims and learning outcomes, as well as the presentation topic itself. I also encourage the students to practise before their presentation proper.

What would you do differently next time?

■ I will definitely decide exactly what I will be assessing in the presentation – form, content, etc. – and I will reveal that to the students in advance.

■ I will try to build in the opportunity for a practice presentation where I will give feedback, before I set a formally assessed presentation. Time is a factor here, especially as the groups get larger.

Query: Were any of these responses like your own? Even if these responses were completely different from yours, they can give you something to think about the next time you set a presentation.

How we do it

In our practice in learning development we often help students prepare for their formal academic presentations. We can do this one to one with students in a workshop, in our study and academic skills programme where students choose to come to prepare themselves for their oral assignments or, by invitation, in subject sessions, where a tutor wants us to help students succeed in this assessment activity.

When preparing students for presentations, as with preparation for other mechanisms of assessment, we tend to make transparent both the form and process of this academic practice. Typically this would involve an introduction to the 'what, why and how' of the presentation (or seminar), ideally coupled with the opportunity for presentation practice in a safe space prior to the delivery of the formal, assessed presentation itself. Additionally, in recognition of the stress levels related to presentations, we will typically also include a session on positive thinking when preparing students for academic presentations – for more on this, see Chapter 6: How to promote self-confidence.

Below we detail the presentation information that we give to students – from access to foundation level, from year one to postgraduate. You can give the information just as it is or adapt it to suit your own students, taking into account your own teaching and learning goals and assessment criteria as well as the students' previous presentation experience.

● **Tutor tips:**
● Obviously students do not become proficient in presentation practice, nor with engaging with any academic form or convention, via one information-packed introduction to the topic. Students will benefit from having many opportunities to rehearse presentation preparation and delivery, in a variety of contexts and at a variety of levels, in order to mature in this teaching/learning process.
● In Chapter 11 we will be looking at the strategies useful in the preparation of written assignments – there is obviously much overlap between preparing for a written and preparing for an oral assignment and it could be useful to point this out to students to encourage their development of an awareness of the transferability of academic skills. In particular you might like to give students the handout 'Ten steps to assignment success' (Resource 11.2), when preparing your students for their presentations.
● If talking through the presentation structure with your students, it can help to give out the presentation structure handout (Resource 10.1) and the paragraph question handout (Resource 10.2) before you do so. Students can annotate the handouts as you talk through the points you make (this can also reinforce good note-making practice).

Lecture notes: the academic presentation – what, why and how

Introduction

Typically we preface the session with mention of the specific presentation for which students are preparing. We explain that we are going to cover the what, why and how of presentation preparation and practice and that this information can help them to prepare better presentations in the future:

- 'what' because if students know what is expected in terms of the form itself, they can stop worrying about that and instead put their energy into fruitful planning, research and drafting activities;

- 'why'' because if a student can accept the logic of an activity it can at the very least prevent their resentment and rejection of it, and more positively it can help them to embrace the activity with gusto;

- 'how' because there are some techniques that can be used to help students prepare better oral assignments.

What is a presentation?

There are several 'whats' to the academic presentation – formal talk, performance, interactive communication and formal convention. Further the *viva* and job interview can both have elements of the presentation. Typically we tell students the different 'whats' of the presentation and stress that they must reflect on how knowing that information will help them to prepare a better presentation in the future.

Formal talk

At its most basic a presentation is a formal talk of a set length on a set topic and delivered to a set audience: when preparing their presentations students have to take all these factors into consideration.

Set length: As with a word limit in a written assignment, a presentation time limit can be a pass/fail factor, or it can impact on student grades in other ways. It helps to stress that students must fit the topic into the time limit set, and that, yes, this will mean thinking clearly about what to include and exclude from their final product. Here it is useful for you to think just how strictly you will monitor the time factor. Students become very angry when they have tailored their talk to a time limit and someone else is allowed to run over time – especially if that other person then gets a higher mark for their work. Typically we feel that it can be helpful to be slightly flexible with time in a practice presentation and then to subsequently be strict with time. But everyone – tutor and student – must be aware of the particular time rules that will pertain.

Set topic: Again as with a written assignment, when giving a presentation, the student does have to answer the question set, not just say all they know on the topic. Answering the question is always a challenge and there is more advice on this in the section on written assignments in Chapter 11. Typical problems with presentations, as also with writing, is that even when students are tackling the question, they may be too descriptive or chronological in their presentations. They may be neither creative nor discursive. They do not challenge, they just recount. Of course we can tell students not to be descriptive, chronological ... or boring, but just telling them does not necessarily make a difference. Devising a marking scheme that guides the student in the right direction can play an important role here, but even so, it may be that some students will have to learn through painful experience that such narrative techniques are typically not enough.

Set audience: The difference between the written assignment, specifically the essay, and the presentation is often the notion of audience. Typically with the essay, especially for first-year undergraduates, while the student knows that they are writing for a particular tutor, we encourage them to write impersonally, in the abstract, with no one reader in mind (sometimes we may describe this rather unhelpfully as writing 'as if for an interested member of the public'). A successful presentation, as with a written report, should always be tailored for its actual audience. Students can be encouraged to think about their audience. Who are they? What can they be expected to know about the topic before the presentation? What would the presenter like them to understand about the topic after they have finished speaking (the aims of the presentation)? What language, examples and visual aids would help a particular real-life audience both follow the presentation and understand it? This advice can be refined further; for example, they can be asked to consider whether or not they will be presenting an audience with frightening, challenging or controversial material and, if so, what they will have to do to mitigate that. Thus tone and style become important factors to consider, alongside language, when students are putting presentations together.

Performance

Many academics distinguish between the academic presentation and other forms of public speaking. We have not found this a helpful separation, especially in that it is a distinction that tends not to offer helpful survival tactics. Typically we will instead urge students to think of the presentation as a performance. As performers students do not need to be really enjoying either the event or the material, neither do they need to be interested in it, but they must *act* as if they are, for if they are not interested, then why would an audience be? We also stress that it is the presenter's job to make the audience feel comfortable, so standing radiating fear and indecision is not a good tactic. Thus the overall advice to students here is to act like you are having a good time and you really enjoy the topic – pretend to be interested, confident and in control. Use positive body language to convey this to the audience – stand or sit facing the audience. Do not face the board, or hold anything in front of your face – people need to see and hear you. Do smile and draw people into your presentation with friendly gestures. Do not fold your arms in front of your body or clench your fists, tap your foot or make nervous chopping movements – it just cries out fear. Do 'dress for success' in clothes that are comfortable and promote strength. In a group presentation do not all sit in different parts of the room looking like you all hate each other, but do act like a strong, cooperative team. If students start to use this advice they will start to enjoy the presentation experience.

Interactive communication

Many students become so conscious of presentations as 'assessment' that they forget about the communication aspect of the presentation. We stress that the presenter's job is to help an audience follow and understand what they have to say. Further, as a performer, the student will have to build a rapport, a relationship, with their audience. This means that students do have to make eye contact with everybody in the audience – not just the tutor. It is not helpful to tell students to look at the ceiling at the back of the room – while this might work in an auditorium with an audience of hundreds it is not appropriate in a small group. The presenter really does have to look at the audience to draw them in, to see whether or not they are being understood and whether or not they need to repeat themselves, for example do they have to give a second example of something because everyone still looks blank?

Of course this means that a presenter must never, ever read from a script! A presentation is recreated from notes, in front of an audience. Not only does a script become a literal barrier between presenter and audience, but also typically when people read their voices go dead and they deliver the topic in an ill-paced monotone that has the average audience losing interest after about the second sentence. If we are marking for successful communication, then an audience must be listening to and following a presentation. To this end, we typically stress that students will definitely lose marks if they read from a script whereas they will receive marks when using prompts of some kind – notes on cue cards perhaps.

Formal convention

As with other academic genres, an effective presentation has a specific form – put simply the presentation consists of introduction (plus agenda), body, conclusion and question and answer structure, plus audio-visual aids (AVA) – see Resource 10.1.

● **Tutor tips:**
● It is not enough just to explain the presentation structure to students; they will need to learn the purpose of that structure through practice. However, we do feel that students will need some explanation of the structure at some point in their development as presenters.
● Students find the linearity of the structure problematic. That is, because the introduction comes first, many students want to write it first, while having nothing to introduce: stress that introductions, as with conclusions, should be written last.
● Some things that you might like to point out could be aspects of the different parts of the presentation:

The body: This *is* the presentation proper. It is where you answer the question set in a chain of arguments. As with writing an essay, think of making one point at a time. Introduce each point, give an example, discuss your example and possibly illustrate it with a reference or quote which you discuss.

● **Tip:** Use the paragraph questions to help shape each part of your presentation for your audience – see Resource 10.2.

The introduction plus agenda: Once you have the first draft of your presentation written, you might like to draft an introduction for it. In the introduction you have to hook the audience in. Why should they listen to you? Will you be interesting or useful? Will you be amusing or stimulating? Will you be tackling a significant part of the prospective assignment? Will you be introducing a new topic or will you be revising a familiar one? Touching on things such as these are all useful hooks. It is really helpful in the introduction to give the overview of the presentation as a whole – this is also called the **agenda** of the presentation. For example, 'I am going to discuss XXX. In particular I will look at blah, then blah and finally I will discuss blah.' A good introduction tells people why they have to listen to your presentation; a clear agenda helps them to follow that presentation.

Conclusion: As with the conclusion in an academic essay, the presentation conclusion is where you draw the whole presentation together –

revisiting your main arguments and restating your main points. The emphasis here is on the 're-', that is, you have to have made arguments before, you have to have made points before.

● **Tip:** Many students feel that introductions and conclusions are unnecessary and therefore omit them from their presentations. They often leave out the introduction plus agenda because they know what they are going to say and assume that because it is self-evident to them it does not need saying. They leave out the conclusion for they have said it all already and repetition feels foolish – and they do not want to appear foolish. If you want students to give good introductions and make pithy concluding remarks, you will have to stress that these are important – and why. Further, you will have to award or subtract marks around these features.

Audi-visual aids: Audi-visual aids are an essential part of oral communication. We use AVA typically in three ways:

1 To help audiences understand the presentation itself. For example, writing up the agenda of the talk on the board or as a handout will help an audience follow the structure of the presentation itself.

2 To emphasise different parts of the presentation. Here we might underscore a key word or point by capturing it on an OHT or PowerPoint slide, by giving a supporting quote or reference or by producing a illustrative image or object.

3 To take the pressure off the speaker. For a brief while all eyes are on something else for a moment. This is a good thing.

● **Tips:** Presenters should not write out whole essays or even long quotes for the audience. Using too detailed an illustration – whether on a handout, overhead transparency or a PowerPoint slide – just encourages an audience to start reading and stop listening. Key words should be written in a large and clear font such that everyone would be able to read the AVA. Presenters should not pass material around the room for people to look at – this will just start off a 'Mexican wave' of disturbance around the room and the presenter will have sabotaged their own presentation. Presenters should always have back-up AVA in place – if using overheads or PowerPoint slides, allowances should be made for technical failure and there should be paper handouts in reserve.

The question and answer session: Typically an academic presentation will conclude with a few moments where the audience can ask questions of the presenter. Here it is useful for the presenter to anticipate possible questions – and either address them pre-emptively in the presentation, or prepare answers in advance.

● **Tips:** Because presentations tend to be adrenalin driven events, there is a tendency for fight or flight reactions to the Q&A session. Students should be encouraged to take deep breaths before answering questions, to keep answers short and light and to be good humoured. Remind students that questions should be taken in order of hand raised. Answers should be brief. If unable to answer, a question can be passed back to the class. The whole Q&A session should be tightly managed and brought to a firm conclusion.

Concluding the 'what': As you can see there is a significant amount of information to cover just detailing the 'what' of the presentation. You might even want to say more than this, for example requesting that students submit a bibliography *with their presentation.*

What we have tried to do here is illustrate what we feel is important about the presentation structure – if you do feel these things are important also, do make sure that your marking scheme takes account of them. If you wish, you can move on to convince students of why *you are asking them to prepare and deliver presentations.*

Why do we set presentations?

There are many advantages to undertaking oral assignments.

▨ One factor that we have already touched on above is that the presentation offers an alternative assessment mechanism. It is spoken instead of written, and just offering this variety is a potentially good thing.

▨ As with other assignments, we argue that the presentation process is designed to be a heuristic one. As the student plans, prepares, practises, delivers and finally reflects upon a presentation they will have engaged in a very active learning process which can promote critical and analytical thinking and the selection, evaluation and use of appropriate arguments and evidence, etc.

▨ Further, as there is a very real and physical audience to be considered, the presentation can really underscore the need for effective communication. Hopefully these can be transferred to written assignments.

▨ As well as modelling good academic practice for students which can be transferred to their written assignments, another positive of the effective presentation is that it does prepare students for *viva* examinations – and for job interviews, especially if you draw attention to this transferable 'skill', practice or process. If you are using the presentation process formatively in relation to a final assessment, do stress how this is supposed to happen.

▦ Finally the presentation process can be really useful in building student confidence: once students realise that they can succeed in this most challenging of academic processes, their self-confidence can be enormously boosted. Increasing student self-confidence is arguably a good thing in and of itself; however, there is also a strong physiological case to be made for increasing student self-confidence with respect to academic study. If the student is over-stressed by lack of self-confidence and fear, there is a constant overload of adrenalin and cortisol – the stress hormones. Cortisol shrinks the cortex and hence reduces the effectiveness even of the short-term memory; adrenalin, as the fight/flight hormone, encourages the tunnel vision and focus necessary to escape from danger – but which are anathema to the depth and breadth required for academic study. Hence promoting student self-confidence is designed to reduce stress levels and promote the physiological conditions necessary for successful academic study.

How to prepare successful presentations

In conjunction with the 'Ten steps to assignment success' handout (Resource 11.2), you might like to take your students through the four Ps of successful presentation preparation – plan, prepare, practise and present – which we will cover here in brief and which you can elaborate as you think fit. The detail that you give to students might depend on how academically inducted you feel that they are and perhaps on what you are emphasising in the particular assignment for which you are preparing them. For example, if you are focusing on research strategies, you may want to emphasize the activities in Chapter 8 on promoting successful research strategies and so forth. You might like to say the following:

Here we will be looking at the four Ps of presentation preparation: plan, prepare, practise and present.

Plan

When getting ready for a successful presentation, students should plan early and undertake the following:

▦ Open a research folder (*see also Chapter 11 on written assignments*).

▦ Analyse the assignment question.

▦ Compare the question with module aims and learning outcomes (*see also Chapter 5 on the effective transition to HE*).

▦ Brainstorm the question (*see also Chapter 8 on research strategies*).

■ Think about the topic, time limit and audience. Students can ask themselves:

– **Topic:** What do I know on this topic already? Where have I covered this in the module? What do I need to find out? Where will I find this information?

– **Time limit:** How much of this area can I cover in the time allowed? What will I include? What will I leave out?

– **Audience:** What can I expect my audience to know on this topic before I start? Where will I take them? How? (This can prompt the student to think of a possible structure for their presentation.) What language, tone and style will be appropriate for my audience? What AVA will they respond to? How will my audience react to this topic? What can I do to optimise their reactions? What questions might they be expected to ask?

■ **Action plan:** Make a list of all the things that need to be done and made to get the presentation ready. Note when each task will be undertaken and, if in a group, by whom. Things to think about include key words that require research and AVA that will need to be found and/or made.

Prepare

Once the student has an action plan, it is necessary for them to follow it. Here they would be expected to:

■ undertake targeted research and active reading (*see also Chapter 8*);

■ make key word notes (*see also Chapter 9 on note-making*);

■ review findings;

■ plan the body of the presentation;

■ prepare the first draft of the presentation;

■ prepare the first set of prompts;

■ put the presentation aside for a while (*see also Chapter 11 – here we argue that the brain requires closure, and leaving gaps in one's work and then a space in time allows the brain to work on the rough draft and close the gaps*);

■ review, revise and edit first draft – decide on a 'good enough' draft of the presentation (destroy your script! If you keep it you might read from it);

■ decide on the AVA that will be useful;

■ prepare the 'good enough' set of prompts – cue cards, pattern notes, key points on a paper list, on OHTs or on PowerPoint slides.

Practise

Once a student has prepared a presentation they must rehearse. Not to rehearse is not an option. It helps if you can stress the importance of rehearsal to your students, and subsequently if you remember the amount of work that has to be undertaken to produce a successful presentation for you (see box below).

Tutor tip: It does not come naturally!

Student M came to a workshop desperate for help with her first ever presentation. Not only was English an additional language for her, but she was the first in her family to enter HE and she was generally unconfident and specifically terrified of having to prepare and deliver a presentation.

We worked with student M on the what, why and how of the presentation. We explored positive thinking strategies and helped her devise an action plan.

When M had a first draft of her presentation together we gave critical feedback on her strengths and weaknesses. Specifically we indicated here that she had created a chronology and that she could do something more interesting than that with the material.

M refined her draft, prepared her cue cards and rehearsed her presentation. Overall, M worked for many weeks both with us and independently on this presentation.

After the presentation, which did receive a high grade, the tutor told M that she must be a 'natural' when it came to oral assignments.

We feel that this tutor underestimated the effort required to prepare and deliver a successful presentation and, by calling this a 'natural' gift, worked to undercut and undervalue the effort that this student had to put in to produce a successful presentation.

Rehearse, rehearse and rehearse: Presentation rehearsal is necessary partly as an editorial tool and partly to learn the material. As an editorial tool, students can rehearse in front of a 'critical friend' to see which bits of the presentation are clear and in good order and which are not. In this way the 'good enough' draft can undergo another 'review, revise and edit' process.

● **Tips:** Tips that we give students at this point include:
● Do not rehearse in front of your children – they can be an overly critical audience that helps you lose your confidence.

● Do listen to the feedback that a critical friend gives – if they cannot follow you then you are doing something wrong, so change your 'good enough' version until you have a version that works and with which you are happy.

Once the presentation is in its final shape, it will be necessary to practise the delivery of the presentation from prompts. Students must rehearse until they really know the presentation and can deliver it with confidence. Then they must rehearse some more so that they can deliver the presentation each time as though for the very first time!

Present

We have a very difficult balance to strike when preparing students for the stressful event that is a presentation. It can help if we acknowledge student fears but not in such a way as to exacerbate them out of all proportion.

● **Tutor tip:** Remember your very first time in front of a lecture theatre full of students and do realise that even an unmarked practice presentation can be that terrifying for your students.

Tips for students – before, during and after the presentation

Before:

▨ Practise positive thinking: I can handle it; this is a great presentation, etc. (*See also Chapter 6 on how to promote self-confidence.*)

▨ Get there early! Do not make a stressful event worse by dashing in late, out of breath and trailing AVA down the corridor.

▨ Organise the seating: audiences can be in semicircles, in rows or on the floor – take control.

● **Tip:** Stand behind a lectern or desk – this small barrier between speaker and audience can make the presenter feel in control.

▨ Check that equipment is working – and run through the presentation using the equipment.

▨ If going first, write the agenda on the board.

▨ If highly stressed:
  – Stop.
  – Sigh.
  – Drop your shoulders (we hold them up when stressed and this increases the tension in our muscles).
  – Wriggle your toes (similarly clenched feet increase blood pressure).

    – Unclench fists (a typical fear/anger reaction – let it go).
    – Take a few deep slow breaths (deep quick ones and people do pass out).
    – Start again more slowly.

During:

▨ Introduce yourself and your topic.

▨ Give a brief introduction and *speak* an agenda even if written.

▨ Speak slowly and clearly – let the audience hear and follow the presentation.

▨ If panicking or if the mind goes blank (and it does), stop, pause, find your place and carry on.

▨ Make good eye contact with everyone in the room.

▨ Remember the linguistic markers: 'we have looked at . . .', 'we are moving on to . . .' (Tell people where they are!)

▨ Use AVA with confidence.

● **Tips: Stop speaking, let people see the AVA, take it away, move on.**

▨ Remember to give the conclusion, draw the presentation to a firm close and ask for questions.

▨ Chair the Q&A fairly, keep answers brief and bring that also to a firm conclusion, thanking your audience again.

After:

Review the presentation:

▨ Immediately after presentations students should be very kind to themselves. Was I not brave? Was I not interesting? Good for me! It is all too easy to focus on what went wrong, and that can make it that much harder to undertake future presentations.

▨ After a while students should conduct a more thorough personal review, asking themselves: What went well? Why was that? What did not go so well? Why was that? What can I do about it?

Note: It is all too easy for students to forget that they did anything well at all. Not only does this make being a student (or a human being) that much harder and more stressful – it can also mean that they can forget to repeat good strategies. They might repair their faults, but make mistakes that they did not make first time round, and that is silly.

● **Tips: Self- and peer-evaluation can be a part of the assessment of a presentation. Furthermore, students can be encouraged to note what they have learned about presentation techniques from observing their peers.**

Concluding the what, why and how of the presentation

When drawing this lecture to a close, we will reiterate the main what, why and how points covered in the lecture. With 'what' we emphasise especially notions of audience and academic convention; with 'why' we look again at heuristic function and self-confidence; and with 'how' we quickly refer to plan, prepare, practise and present – with a strong underscoring of the importance of rehearsal. We then say, 'That was a conclusion, it really is that simple!'

In conclusion

So we have looked at the basic 'what, why and how of the presentation' information that we cover with our students. As said this material can be used just as it is with your students or by editing as appropriate for your target group. Below we cover the seminar in brief. As a seminar contains both oral and written elements, the trick with seminar preparation is to make links with presentation information and with information on the written element that you will be assessing, and to clearly demonstrate to students where the marks are.

Practising presentations

The three-minute presentation

If students are preparing for their first ever academic presentation it helps if they are allowed to practise by first giving a three-minute presentation on a topic of their own choice. Here students can either choose a topic in which they are very interested or a topic with which they are very familiar. With the former their interest can give a relevance and energy to the task – with the latter they can relax about the content and worry instead about their handling of this academic form. Feedback on this first activity can stress the students tackling of the presentation as a specific academic form, with minor guidance as to how they could better use argument and evidence in the future.

● **Tip:** Use the assessment pro forma (Resource 10.3). Give students a copy of the resource before they prepare their presentations and encourage them to mark themselves before you give your own assessment.

Extension activities

Once students are familiar with preparing for and delivering presentations you can:

■ Set students the task of preparing and delivering a group presentation on the unit, module or course assignment.

■ Set students – either individually or in groups – the task of preparing a formal seminar (see below) on an assignment topic.

How to promote effective seminars

The academic seminar is often used as a formative assessment tool designed to help students prepare an important academic paper. As such seminars are often utilised in PhD preparation. However, as the seminar captures the academic paradigm so beautifully, we have found that it is a useful activity to build into any level of a student's academic experience from access programme to third-year undergraduate. If setting a seminar activity for your students, do decide how you will mark the various parts of the seminar – and do encourage your students to embrace the opportunity that is the seminar. Here we will quickly explore the sorts of 'what, why and how' advice that may help students prepare for their seminars with you.

What is a seminar?

The academic seminar is typically a four-part form consisting of paper, presentation, discussion and overall conclusion – see box below.

The academic seminar

Typically a seminar is made up of the following:

1 **The paper:** Typically a draft essay or report is compiled by the seminar giver and delivered in advance so that it can be read before the seminar proper by the tutor and members of the audience. Advice on written assignments (see Chapter 11) is useful here.

● **Tutor tips:** The seminar paper can take any shape that you wish. Here it helps if you decide whether you want the student to prepare a formal essay or report or whether you would like something more creative. We once had a student prepare an aged scroll detailing formal charges of witchcraft for a seminar on that topic; another student prepared a fragmented poem to capture the way that an autistic child could view the world. Contrarily you can ask students to prepare something more basic, like bullet points of key topics and/or an annotated bibliography. The trick is to be clear about what you expect and communicate clearly just what you will be evaluating.

2 **The presentation:** The seminar giver or givers deliver the presentation part of the seminar. Advice on the 'what' of the presentation given above is useful here. Typically we stress that the presentation is not the paper read

---

aloud. That would be a redundant activity, especially in that with a good seminar the audience should have received and read the paper in advance. A successful seminar presentation could capture the key points of the accompanying paper. It could touch on the problems encountered in researching the topic and the solutions discovered. Again, be clear in your mind what you would like the student to undertake – and indicate this in your instructions and in your marking scheme.

3 **The discussion:** Not only is there the possibility for a Q&A at the end of a seminar presentation, there should also be an orchestrated discussion of some sort. Typically the idea is that the seminar giver should have some unanswered questions with respect to their research or areas of interest that they would like discussed by their audience. These questions could be flagged up in the paper that the audience received in advance of the seminar proper, so that everyone has a chance to prepare for the discussion.

● **Student tips:** When running the discussion typically it is not fruitful if the speaker just asks questions of the audience – the result is often silence. So, divide the audience into groups of three to five. Give each group a topic to discuss (one per group or everyone with the same one) and five or so minutes in which to do so. Have a report back at the end.

● **Tutor tip:** Marks in this section of the seminar can be awarded on pertinence of questions set and ability to engage all the audience in the discussion.

4 **Overall conclusion:** After the presentation and the seminar, the seminar giver should draw the event to a close via an overall conclusion that restates the main points from the paper, the presentation and the orchestrated discussion, indicating which avenues of further research they will now follow. Typically, if you are offering marks for the overall conclusion, these will be the easiest marks for the student to gain, or the easiest for them to throw away. Where the seminar is being used formatively, it is really important to encourage the student to use the conclusion process to help shape their final paper, hence it can be very important to award significant marks here.

Marking schemes: When marking seminars, we usually divide available marks equally across the four parts of the seminar – thus 25% each for paper, presentation, discussion and conclusion. This stresses the importance of the latter two parts of the process, which are otherwise often undervalued by the student. This in turn, hopefully, stresses the formative nature of the seminar process. Obviously tutors can decide for themselves how and where they will award marks and, by communicating the marking scheme clearly to students, they can effectively guide students through the seminar process.

Why engage in seminars?

When preparing students for seminars we do underline how the seminar captures the Platonic academic paradigm. That is, we emphasise how academic endeavour can be an exercise in hypothesis generation, in the gathering and shaping of research data and in the value of discussion with peers for the raising of further research topics and in the resolving of particular problems encountered. If a seminar is the formative part of a summative assessment, we stress how a final paper should be dramatically improved if the seminar is harnessed positively. And, as indicated above, we find that tutors can help bring about awareness of this by devising marking schemes that indicate the value of each part of the seminar process.

How to engage in seminars

Preparing students for seminars can depend on their current familiarity with the constitutive parts of the seminar – written, oral and group discussion. If students need extra guidance on the preparation of the paper, advice can be given from Chapter 11 on written assignments. If students appear unfamiliar with the presentation, advice above on that practice can be delivered. If it is group work with which students are unfamiliar do draw on Chapter 13 on group work. If the overall conclusion – and its role in preparing students for a better summative paper – is the key for you, remember to stress that importance and to accord marks for that activity.

Practising this

■ Either individually or in groups set students the task of preparing and delivering a seminar in advance of their summative assessment.

Extension

■ Set and grade the task of peer assessment of seminars. Award marks for the cogency of the written feedback that students give, and with reference to how well students have utilised course aims and learning outcomes as part of their feedback.

Overall conclusion

In this chapter we have considered the formative and summative nature of oral assessments and considered the role of oral assignments in the current HE climate. In looking at oral assessments we described how we in learning development would introduce students to presentations then seminars. We have detailed the what, why and how of the presentation in greater depth than that of the seminar but stress the links between the two as well as indicating links with other parts of the handbook. We do hope that you have found this chapter useful and that not only will it help you to better prepare students for presentations and seminars in the future, we hope that we have also made a case for further utilising these oral assessments in your own practice.

Resources

10.1   The structure of an academic presentation
10.2   Using the paragraph questions for presentations
10.3   Assessment pro forma: the presentation

See also from Chapter 11:

11.2   Ten steps to assignment success

II How to promote effective writing

Introduction

In this chapter we will explore ways of developing students' ability to produce better written assignments, noting that nowhere in the university system is the debate about the 'crisis' in education and the 'lowering of standards' (Lillis, 2001) more intense than in the arena of student writing. Alongside other colleagues in the SEN and the LDHEN[1] we have heard lecturers say such things as, 'the trouble with students these days is that they cannot write an essay!' (Mitchell, 2003[2]). In fact lecturers often condemn students for not being able to write grammatical English or to formulate syntactically correct sentences, and frequently send such students to learning development to be 'fixed'. In this chapter we will offer an alternative approach to the issue of student writing, suggesting ways of approaching writing as part of a more transparent emancipatory pedagogical process, we shall also detail how we tackle student writing in learning development.

Changes in the HE environment

Elsewhere in this text (see also Chapter 3 on how to assess) we argue that the increased participation of students in paid employment and the move to modularisation can both negatively affect student performance in assessment – and typically this means in respect of their written assignments. Given that students, including the less academically inducted student, have to engage with new material, complex epistemological practice and often a bewildering range of assessment engines in very brief spaces of time, it is arguably no surprise that student writing is as it is. We argue that students learn by actively engaging with their material – including by engaging in frequent, short, formative writing tasks or exercises. At the same time, we acknowledge a tension between the need for formative activities that do develop student ability to think about and engage with epistemological practice, academic discourse and key concepts, and over-assessing students, especially where **all** the (formative) work that second- and third-year students generate contributes towards degree classification.

Writing and learning development

We often do see students who are having problems with their writing in learning development. Typically students tend to focus on their issues with the bewildering array of academic forms with which they have to engage:

- 'Tell us what you mean by a case study!'
- 'What on earth is a paper?'
- 'If only they all meant the same thing when they talk about an essay.'

And so on.

And, when we work with students on their assignments, we will input information on academic genres or forms and we will help students to restructure their written work. Often we just have to prompt students to be less concise or condensed in their written expression: sometimes very small interventions can make an enormous difference to a student's ability to express themselves effectively in writing.

However, we do find that it is where students are writing about insufficiently understood concepts that they have the most problem, and that this problem is exacerbated by the sheer quantity of assessed work that students have to generate. In effect students are producing summative pieces of work about inadequately comprehended material again and again: a vicious cycle of fear and failure is being set up for many students, module after module.

Rather than agreeing that the trouble with students is that they cannot write, we would argue that the problem for students is that they are unable to write effectively because they are inadequately inducted into the epistemology, the discourse and the key concepts of their disciplines. It is not that students need fixing, but that pedagogical practice needs to shift so that the forms and processes of academic discourse are revealed. In this way student writing can be developed by offering many opportunities to think about key concepts, including the opportunity to express this thinking in frequent, short writing exercises. If good pedagogical practice is to mean anything, it must generate improved outcomes for students.

Embedding learning development – again

Throughout this guide we argue that the success of university students, including the non-traditional student, is the responsibility of all professional staff. The first locus for student success will always be within subject teaching, and while learning and teaching development units will have a role to play in terms of generating resources, promoting the sharing of good practice and offering staff development initiatives, such units cannot 'fix' students. Arguably it will be within subject teaching at its best that students engage with 'transparent' pedagogy. And it will be a pedagogical practice that utilises active learning approaches, including an emphasis on writing to learn rather than learning to write, that will fundamentally change the HE experience for students. Below we detail 'how we do it' in learning development in terms of the information that we give to students with regards to academic forms or genres and the 'ten steps to success' strategy that we encourage students to adopt when approaching their assignments.

How we do it

In learning development we tend to adopt a 'what, why and how' approach to teaching students how to succeed in their assignments. The 'what' allows us to disclose the rules about academic forms, genres and conventions – and given the level of stress that students experience about these, the value of offering models of academic forms cannot be overestimated. With 'why', we stress the heuristic nature of engaging in activities that lead to the production of items for assessment, and with respect to written assessments, we argue that students write to learn, rather than learn to write. We try to reduce the negative impact of the fear of being judged that impedes student thought and we attempt to defuse issues around the 'struggle to write', for all writing is difficult and academic writing is very difficult, especially if the writer is insufficiently inducted into academic discourse and content. We also stress that effective writing is about communication, that good writing takes note of prospective readers. With 'how' we detail a ten-step plan, for the prepare, draft and review process that encourages good practice. Below we will apply the ten-step programme to the academic essay followed by a brief examination of the academic report.

How to support essay writing: preliminary activities:

- Ask students what they currently like or dislike about their writing strategies.

- Ask students to qualify what would constitute a successful essay.

- Explore generic assessment criteria (those associated with grade descriptors perhaps – for example, such phrases as: 'Analytical writing that utilises sufficient sources which are used appropriately and critically' etc.).

● **Tutor tips:**
● You may like to give students the essay structure diagram (Resource 11.1) and the 'Ten steps to assignment success' handout (Resource 11.2) prior to discussing the component parts of the essay.
● It is possible to cover essay writing in an intensive 'Writing Week'. Here you can:
- open the week with the preliminary activities suggested above
- cover the 'what, why and how' lecture;
- take a group of students through the ten-step process with respect to a specific essay assignment.

The academic essay: what, why and how – lecture notes

When conducting a session on academic writing we can discuss all the writing with which students will have to engage – learning logs, summaries or abstracts, literature reviews, reading records, essays, reports, projects, dissertations, papers – or we can focus on one particular genre in a session. In this 'lecture' we are going to cover the 'what, why and how' of the essay with the caveat that, with slight amendments – especially with respect to the specific formal conventions attached to the various academic genres – the information is typically applicable to most assignments.

What is an essay?

There are several 'whats' to an academic essay. They are all important – the trick will be for the students to consider how knowing the following will help them produce better essays.

The legal precedent

The word 'essay' is said to derive from the Latin *exagium*, the presentation of a case. Thus, when writing essays, students have to think about 'making a case', i.e. constructing arguments and utilising evidence rather than making assertions. It may help students to think about the legal precedent. That is, lawyers do not just prosecute or defend in a vacuum – both prosecution and defence must take account of the case the other side is going to make, and they must strive to gather and offer better evidence than their opponent.

Formal writing – set length

An essay is a continuous piece of writing, in formal English. That is, the typical academic essay is not divided and subdivided by headings as is the report or paper, and it must be written in clear, academic English, with no abbreviations or slang.

Essays are never an invitation to write 'all you know' on a topic, but an invitation to explore a question, undertake targeted research and active reading, and then to structure a logical and clear response that typically answers the question one point at a time via the use of argument supported by evidence.

● **Tip:** It may be that you as tutor would like to indicate what counts as argument and evidence within your discipline at this point.

This answer has to be produced within the word limit set, for that is part of the challenge of the task, and writing too little or too much can lead to an automatic fail.

Typically essays should be well presented, looking neat and well cared for. Word-processing is a boon here in terms of offering ease of drafting and redrafting – and of presentation. With respect to layout, most lecturers want their essays 1.5 or double line spaced, with margins and written on one side of the paper only – and it is only common sense to give the lecturer what they want. You do not want an angry lecturer marking your work.

Formal convention

The academic essay also constitutes a specific academic form or genre, that is it must have a particular shape or structure. **Note:** this structure is not whimsical but is designed to facilitate effective communication – and above all your written work must communicate with a real reader.

The essay structure explained

The essay structure is comprised of introduction, body, conclusion and bibliography (see Resource 11.1), and each part has a distinct function to perform.

Introduction – plus agenda (5–7% of word limit): Tells the reader how you are going to tackle the question and in what order you have structured your essay answer. A good introduction helps the reader understand the essay and it will allow an assessor to judge whether or not the subsequent essay will answer the question set.

● **Tip:** It is difficult to write an introduction for an essay that does not exist. Write the introduction last.

The body (80% word limit): *Is* the answer and is comprised of well-structured academic paragraphs.

Typically the body is made up of rather long (can be 200–350 words long in some subjects) paragraphs. The rule of thumb is one 'big idea' or topic per paragraph. Each paragraph is structured like a mini-essay:

■ Introduction – opening sentence that introduces paragraph topic which is:

■ Defined

■ Argued

■ Supported by evidence (which is discussed) and

■ Concluded (often by relation back to the overall question).

● **Tutor tip:** Elaborate as follows – here or in a specific seminar session based around paragraph writing.

● **Student tip:** When starting to write formal academic paragraphs it can help if you use the paragraph questions (see Resource 11.1) to prompt your writing. That is, imagine you are in a dialogue with your reader. Your reader will be asking questions of your writing – you must make sure that that writing supplies the answers to the reader's questions.

Paragraph tips:

■ Write the paragraph questions on an index card and Blu-Tack the card to the top of your computer screen.

■ When writing **each** paragraph, look at the questions and attempt to answer them.

■ Do not aim for perfection first draft – always intend to draft and redraft work, refining in the redrafting stages. Aiming for perfection 'first go' leads to writing blocks.

The questions in practice

As you write answer the reader's questions:

■ **What is this paragraph about?** This invites you to introduce the subject or topic of your paragraph. In first drafts this could be as simple as: 'Now we are going to look at . . .' Hopefully you will find that you can improve paragraph introductions in subsequent drafts – this also gets easier with practice.

■ **What exactly is that?** This invites you to define or clarify what you are writing about.

■ **Tell me more . . .** This invites you to say something about your topic, in relation to the essay question that you are answering. Typically this is where you offer an argument of some sort.

■ **What is your evidence for this?** This invites you to offer relevant evidence, excavated from your research, to support your argument.

■ **What does it mean?** Here you must discuss your evidence, linking it to the argument that you are making.

■ **[Possibly also] But what about the contrasting evidence?** This invites you to acknowledge that other arguments and evidence exist.

■ **What is your final point (and how does it relate to the question)?** Here you are invited to draw the paragraph to a conclusion, perhaps by making a point that goes back to the question.

● **Tip:** Such writing is quite complex and has to be learned through practice – just as you would not expect to learn to drive a car or play the violin immediately but via ongoing and continuous practice.

The conclusion (13–15%): The conclusion is where you draw your essay together and prove that you have answered the whole question. It is the place to reiterate your main arguments and restate your main points.

● **Tips:** use the language from the question in your conclusion; this will help your reader to understand that you have answered that question. If you have strong thoughts on an essay topic, you might like to draft a **rough** conclusion first, so that you know where your essay is going. Remember to rewrite the conclusion once you have actually written the essay, for your thinking can change as you write.

Bibliography: The bibliography is where you record the sources that you have utilised in the construction of your essay, typically in alphabetical order by author surname using one of the following systems:

■ Harvard system: author (date) title, town: publisher – this is an indicative system, which means you only include in the bibliography work drawn upon in the writing;

■ British standard system – author, title, publisher, date.

■ Other – explain the system that you require of your students. Give a handout that illustrates how to cite within the body of the essay and how to construct a correct bibliography.

● **Tutor tips:** It is here that we often reiterate warnings on plagiarism that we will have first mentioned when tackling research and reading (see Chapter 8). If we feel that students are particularly unfamiliar with academic endeavour we stress that the British education system requires research – thus students are not expected to 'make it all up for themselves' (many students think that acknowledging sources is a sign of weakness!) and that it is actually good practice to reveal sources, etc. You might like to tell students how many sources you would expect to see in a typical A, B, C or D essay.

Why write essays?

There are many reasons for writing essays and, yes, they are assessment devices and your tutor will mark your essay and award you a grade that will have significance for you as a student. The problem with only focusing on the essay as assessment is that it can increase your trepidation and this can get in the way of your thinking. It also hides the fact that we 'write to learn' rather than writing what we know – writing is a **thinking** process.

Yes, essay writing produces a product that tutors can assess, but more than that, the whole planning, drafting and reviewing of your written work is a valuable learning process for you the student. Essay writing is designed to be heuristic – you are supposed to learn through all the processes involved in the generation of a written assignment.

That is, essay production encourages you to:

▪ Revisit and revise various elements of the taught programme.

▪ Extend your understanding by undertaking independent research – reading around the question.

▪ Synthesise your thinking – that is, as you read you will encounter people who argue one thing and people who argue to the contrary, and typically both will offer convincing arguments and evidence. You will be expected to form an informed opinion by judging contrary arguments and deciding which is the strongest.

▪ Struggle to write a coherent, well-structured essay that communicates clearly and effectively with an informed reader.

None of this is easy. That is why writing is a struggle – and it is in the struggle to write that learning is refined: this is very intense, active thinking and learning.

How to prepare and write an essay

When discussing 'How to write an essay', we typically cover the ten-step approach to assignment success (see the handout in Resource 11.2), discussing the points thus:

1 Preparation

We stress that typically preparation is the key to assignment success and that students have to think and read and struggle before they are in a position to answer any assignment question. Problems arise perhaps because students see a question and believe that they ought to just **know** the answer, whereas we tend to set questions that prompt students to investigate, research, think and come up with answers.

Step 1 of the ten-step programme encourages students to think – it suggests that you do not need to know answers, but it is helpful to generate questions as avenues of research. Hence we encourage starting work on an assignment early on in a programme of study. You can **tell** students the activities in which they ought to participate (see below) to successfully engage with and learn from a programme of study; it will help if you also take students through the activities in your seminar programme.

● **Tutor tip:** Get students to open an assignment research folder in the very first seminar that you have with them.

To prepare to research and learn from a whole programme it will help if students:

▪ Open a research folder.

▓ Write out the question in full (photocopy and stick on if too long to copy).

▓ Analyse the task: in terms of form and content.

▓ Check (with the tutor) the characteristics of the form that they have requested (essay, presentation, report, etc.).

▓ Investigate the question set: underline key words in the question.

● **Tips:** Make sure you understand everything it is asking. Discuss what you have underlined and why with a study partner.

▓ Make links with module aims and learning outcomes, highlighting key words in the course handbook.

▓ Make links with the syllabus: note which bits of the taught pro-gramme will relate to specific parts of the assignment question.

▓ Make links with the reading list, highlighting books that must be read to answer the question.

● **Tip:** Form reading groups.

▓ Brainstorm all the key words in the question (see box below) – typically brainstorming improves when undertaken collectively.

▓ **Seminar discussion:** *Get students into pairs to devise questions to ask of you with regard to the course, the thinking behind your course and what you intend they should gain from undertaking your course. Get them to interrogate you regarding the work that you expect them to undertake in order to meet the goals that you have in mind.*

▓ In the light of all the work undertaken above, students should devise action plans spaced over the several weeks of your programme. They should indicate across time what they will be doing to prepare for the assignment. This can involve noting relevant lectures, seminars, reading, etc that they will have to attend or the research that they will have to undertake in order to get ready for their writing.

Tutor notes: Brainstorming and question matrixing

Typically we encourage students to engage creatively with assignment topics by using the brainstorm and/or the question matrix.

The brainstorm encourages creativity by prompting uncensored thought around key words in the assignment question. If students follow up the ideas generated in a brainstorm they will often find they have an original approach to an assignment.

A question matrix can be used instead of or alongside the brainstorm. The question matrix involves turning all the key words in a question into a series of smaller questions. It is in the struggle to answer the smaller questions that students move towards answering the larger question.

A sample question matrix

A question matrix can be generated around any question in any subject. Typically it helps to use the six journalism questions – the five W's and an H or who, what, where, when, why and how – to generate matrices. For example:

Describe and discuss the characteristics of the eukaryotic cell

A quick matrix exercise might throw up the following questions:

- **Describe:** What does describe mean in this context? Can I use diagrams? How can I find this out?

- **Discuss:** What is the difference between describe and discuss? Who will know how to discuss this properly? How much should be description? How much will be discussion? Who will know?

- **Describe and discuss the characteristics:** I suppose that means saying what they are and saying what they **do**? And maybe how they are different from other forms of cells?

- **Eukaryotic cell:** What is a EU cell? What other forms of cell are there? How is the EU different from other cells? Do we have EU cells – and if so, why? Where can EU be found? What do they do? How do they do it? When were they discovered? Who by? How does knowing about EU cells help me in this course?

Discussion: Once a student has generated a matrix, perhaps like the one above, they are ready to determine just what they already know on the topic, what they will need to find out and why. Hopefully this leads the student into more focused and productive research.

2 Follow the action plan

Once students have thought about the assignment in the proactive ways described above, they should derive more benefit from the lecture and seminar programme – and they can move on to undertake targeted research and active reading (see also Chapter 8) alongside the taught programme. Typically this will involve students in adopting the QOOQRRR system:

▨ **Question:** Read with a purpose. Know why you are reading – are you a novice or an initiate? Are you searching for a general understanding or for specific arguments and evidence? How will this affect the notes that you make?

▨ **Overview:** Read with a context. Within which unit, module or programme is this reading taking place? What are the aims and outcomes? What has to be done and learned to pass the course? How will a specific reading activity enable you the student to demonstrate in the assignment that aims and outcomes have been met?

▨ **Overview:** Know what you are reading. Have you scanned the computer catalogue? Have you scanned the journals? With texts, have you scanned contents and indexes? With a chapter/journal article, have you read the introduction and conclusion?

▨ **Question:** Question once more – so why am I reading this now, and with which bit of the assignment will it help me?

▨ **Read:** Read actively and interactively, marking up as you go, noting perspective, arguments, evidence, dis/agreements with other reading, etc.

▨ **Re-read:** Re-read annotations and marginalia, construct pattern notes, consider building topic patterns – with all reading on a topic captured on distinct sheets of paper.

▨ **Review:** Review notes – think again . . .

Remind students that each bit of reading that is undertaken can lead on to yet more reading – but at some point the reading has to stop and the student will have to move on to the next step.

3 Review findings

Students will have to review their notes and make decisions about which of their notes relate to material that is relevant and will be drawn upon in their writing, and which is not.

● **Tip:** Even information that is ejected from the assignment folder might make its way into an exam preparation folder!

Students will have to decide if there are any gaps in the research – and if so, they must decide on a course of action.

● **Tips:** Index surfing books on the reading list might help to plug gaps. Similarly index surfing books from a Key Text Area or Counter Loan facility could provide a short cut to information when time is scarce.

4 Plan the outline of the essay, report, presentation ... other

Typically we recommend that at this stage students should return to the question and the key words that they have underlined. They should now plan the **body** of the essay – that is, they should think about the separate paragraphs that they would need in their essay answer. It may be possible to structure the essay in terms of what they would discuss first, second, third, etc. but equally, this structuring could come after the paragraphs have been drafted.

● **Tips:** Encourage students to write paragraphs on separate pieces of paper and to move them around physically to get a sense of the best and most logical structure for the essay. Students should not plan to write an introduction or even a conclusion at this stage unless they really need to, and if they do, they ought to learn to be happy to write incomplete ones, with ellipses and 'blah', etc. written to indicate unfinished thinking.

5 Prepare a first draft

At some point – and hopefully several weeks before an assignment deadline – students should attempt to write a rough draft of an answer.

● **Tutor tips:** Typically we recommend that students actually start writing individual paragraphs before they have finished all their reading – and this could definitely be supported in seminar work.

When writing what is an acknowledged **rough** draft, students should not be aiming for perfection – they should not yet be struggling for the right word or phrase or all the correct quotes. It helps at this stage if students utilise their plans and the paragraph questions and write with a 'flow'. Stopping for spellings, tenses, exactly the right word is fraught with problems:

▨ It embodies the notion that writing is about pouring out what you know rather than learning through writing.

▨ It encapsulates the bad practice of one-draft writing which precludes students learning through revision processes.

▨ It leads to writing blocks.

6 Leave a creative time lag

The brain likes closure; if we write with gaps – ellipses, 'blah', highlighting text in pink, etc. – we are telling our brains that work is unfinished. The brain will seek to complete unfinished work, so students should leave a time lag between the production of first drafts and the review, revise and edit process.

7 Review, revise and edit

It is in the review, revise and edit process that students – and arguably all writers – learn in their struggle with their material. There are a variety of struggles engaged with here. There is the struggle to structure work to best effect. There is the struggle to harness the best evidence to support one's arguments. There is the struggle involved in cutting out irrelevant material – especially if it cost much time to acquire. There is the struggle to actually answer the question – and to prove that to the reader. There is the struggle to harness the appropriate use of language, tone, style – and discourse or linguistic markers . . . and so forth.

At some point the writer has to judge the work that they have produced against the assessment time line and decide on an 'as good as I can get it' draft of their work. But it is not finished yet – there is still work to do.

● **Tutor tips:** When encouraging students to draft and redraft work take in an example from your own practice. For example, we might take in the seven, eight or nine drafts of an article that we have written – dropping them onto the desk one by one to illustrate the struggle involved in writing. Encourage peer review of work in process. Offer formative feedback on work in progress.

8 Proofread

All work has to be spell-checked and proofread. Here the fact that our brains like closure can work against students for often in proofreading the eye sees what should be there rather than what actually is there. (Just ask students to read their work aloud and you can see this – sometimes they read a correct version, without seeing that that is not what they have written.) To facilitate proofreading it can help to look for one problem at a time, and to distanciate or make strange the proofreading process thus it helps to:

▓ proofread from the back to the front;

▓ proofread from the bottom of the page to the top;

▓ proofread someone else's work.

9 Hand work in on or before the deadline

Remind students of just how important deadlines are in your department. Often a missed deadline leads to an automatic fail, but this will not have been true for students prior to attending university. The rigidity of the application of rules and regulations must be stressed as should the severity of the penalties imposed. Further, we always recommend that students keep copies of final drafts of work – photocopies if handwritten or submitting portfolio examples of work, or on floppy disks if word-processed. (Moreover, disks should be kept in different locations –

in case of fire!) No student should ever hand in the only copy of a piece of work – an assessment unit can always lose it. We also stress that it is worth waiting in line and getting a receipt for submitted work – this may be the only evidence that a deadline has been met. Obviously students should not lose these receipts!

10 Review

For many students the completion of an assignment absolves them of all responsibility for it – and all contact with it. We have encountered students who will not review work prior to handing it in – and who have no interest in reviewing it if it is returned to them (beyond a quick glance at the grade). Obviously we feel that much can be learned from completed work and as we indicate above, students should get into the good practice of judging the quality of their own work before they hand it in, and of 'SWOTing' it once they get it back, exploring its strengths, weaknesses, opportunities (links with exams?) and threats (fear of success as well as fear of failure?).

Concluding the lecture

If you are delivering a lecture on the what, why and how of the academic essay, do draw to a conclusion by reiterating the main points covered, stressing the information that you feel is of the most importance to your students. You might like to inform students of related seminar sessions where particular essay writing theory will be put into practice. You may like to run a quick SWOT session on the information that you have given for typically it is an idealised process that the majority of (working) students will not feel able to put 100% into practice. Encourage students to solve the problems that they themselves highlight with respect to the ten-step programme.

Practising essay preparation and writing

- Before students prepare assignments for you take them through all the assessment criteria that you will be applying and explain what they mean in real terms.

- In seminars get students to mark and grade student essays applying your assessment criteria and discuss.

- Consider giving detailed formative feedback even on summative writing, explaining how students could improve future performance in academic assignments.

- Utilise tutorial sessions to return student work and explain the grade awarded, what the student has done well, and how the work – and future work – could be further improved.

■ Encourage students to form reading groups in order to undertake research broad enough to answer one of your assignment tasks.

■ Get students to plan and prepare answers to assignment questions, and to deliver presentations on their answers – individually or in groups.

■ Photocopy useful chapters and articles and give students class time to read and make notes.

■ Allow seminar time for student reading groups to meet – perhaps allowing groups to give presentations on their reading.

■ Get students to write a well-structured paragraph in class, utilising information from the notes they have made upon the chapters and articles you have disseminated.

■ Think of particular concepts that you wish students to understand or key thinkers with whom you would like them to engage. Ask students to prepare and deliver presentations upon them.

■ With particular concepts that you wish students to understand or key thinkers with whom you would like them to engage, set different writing tasks, for example:
  – Write an article for the *Daily Mirror* newspaper upon . . .
  – Write an obituary for *The Times* on . . .
  – Write a letter to a friend in Canada explaining why Marxism (or postmodernism, etc.) is so important in this programme.

■ Disseminate a journal article from which you have removed the abstract and ask students to devise an appropriate replacement.

● **Tutor tip:** Abstract and summary writing are complex activities involving the generation of a 'right answer', therefore it is best to leave these until students are feeling confident within the academic environment. Setting 'right answer' tasks too soon discourages independent thought.

■ Run a Writing Week.

■ Run an 'overcoming writing blocks' exercise with your students (see box below).

Student activity: Overcoming writing blocks[3]

■ Writing with commentary
■ Prompted writing

Writing with commentary

Resources: Students will need pens and two sheets of paper each. They should label one sheet 'writing' and the other 'commentary'.

Activity: Tell students that they must move around the room and find a spot in which they will feel comfortable writing. If they want to lie on the floor to write, that is OK. Basically within the constraints of the room you are actually in, they must prepare themselves for writing as well as they can. Tell students that they will be expected to write for 10, 15 or 20 minutes, whichever you prefer, on any topic – perhaps something that they can see, hear or feel at the moment. Each time students stop writing, they must write their reason for stopping, no matter how trivial, on the commentary sheet.

Give students time to write. You may leave the room if you wish, read or write yourself.

After the allocated time, get students to call out their reasons for pausing and collect the points on the board – perhaps in a pattern note that links related reasons. Once all the reasons have been collected in – discuss them in as much detail as you think appropriate. We make some suggestions below.

Typical reason groups:

Thinking of words, spellings, getting it right:

- Checking a spelling
- Getting the right tense
- Thinking of the right word
- Etc.

Here students are blocking themselves by not 'going with the flow'. Remind students to write with ellipses and gaps, knowing that they will redraft later.

Searching for ideas:

- I was trying to think of a better idea
- I didn't know what to say next

Here students have started to write without a quick brainstorm/plan. Remind them that no matter what the task, a quick preliminary brainstorm/plan will give a direction to their writing.

General feelings of discomfort

- It was too hot, cold, light, dark
- The chair was uncomfortable, I was thirsty, hungry, etc.

▓ I was distracted by a noise, movement, someone leaving the room

▓ I was bored, I could not see the point of this activity

Here students have not achieved the right mental and physical conditions (see below) to promote their own study well-being.

Mental: Remind students that they will need to harness their own interest and motivation in order to succeed in anything, even a task such as this. If students are not interested in something, they should try to 'fake it to make it'.

Physical: Remind students that we all have different learning preferences and styles (see also Chapter 12 on exam success). Some people need light, some prefer shade. Some will like a quiet environment, some will prefer noise. While some students will need to sit still and think, others will require movement. There are no one perfect set of conditions for all learners – all people are different with different preferences. Students must investigate the physical conditions they will require in order to prompt their study.

Note: We have found this a very useful session not just in tackling writing per se, but also in getting students to explore particular problems they may be having with their studies. If particular issues arise it may be necessary to run a further session in order to resolve them. For example, we have found that the positive thinking lecture (Chapter 6) fits in very nicely here. We have included another writing exercise, below.

Prompted writing

Resources: Postcards, pictures and visual prompts, though the exercise may work by including some cards with key quotes upon them.

Note: The cards can be on general topics, or you could choose material relevant to your subject – pictures of key thinkers, illustrations from related textbooks, etc.

Activity: Cards are placed face down so that the contents are not seen. Students have to choose a card at random and then write for a short space of time about whatever comes into their minds upon looking at their card.

Note: This activity can be varied by having the cards face up and allowing students to select a card. This will generate a whole different set of issues with regard to what affects the assignment **choices** that students make.

Once students have written for their allocated time, hold a plenary. You may like to get students to read out what they have written and/or to discuss the issues that came up for them in this writing exercise. Get the students to suggest solutions for the problems that arose for the group.

Some issues that may arise:

'I wish I'd chosen a better card!'

'I thought that everybody else had chosen better cards.'

This is a common block for students, thinking that they could have chosen a better question – or even a different course altogether. It can relate to issues of motivation and informed choice, or it may be a personality trait. It may be necessary to unpack the implications of this for students. Should they see the careers service to check that they are on the right track, or will they need to develop a confidence in their work and ignore the doubting voice?

'I didn't know what to write.'

'I started writing one thing, then changed my mind and started writing something else . . .'

Again, issues of brainstorming and planning are evident here, but it may also be that the student does already have something to say on a topic and that a particular task (or assignment question) is not allowing them to give vent to their own ideas. Here it may be necessary for the student to write out what they need to say before they start on their assignment otherwise they will remain blocked.

How to write better reports – lecture notes

It is possible to utilise the 'what, why and how' format when tackling reports. While 'how' can be tackled drawing on the 'Ten steps to assignment success', the 'what' and 'why' might need some further elaboration. We make some suggestions below.

What is a report?

The essence of a report is that it is a document designed to deal with real issues in the real world – whether it is a laboratory experiment or the analysis of a business case study. Typically the report writer has to conduct an experiment or research a real issue, and then detail the problem, the methodology and the findings in a report that discusses the significance of those findings and that is targeted at a known reader.

● **Tutor tip:** Elaborate in as much detail as you think your students need – possibly utilising the information in Resources 11.3 to 11.6.

Why write reports?

Obviously within an academic context, the report becomes another assessment engine, one that models the academic paper and the practical writing in which students will engage once they enter their professions – from laboratory report to business case study. Thus this writing both models good academic practice and prepares students for work.

But why *this* report?

Beyond that, students will have to investigate the specific elements of any report writing activity in which they are engaged. Some questions they might ask themselves include:

- Why am I writing this report?
- What am I investigating?
- What am I trying to achieve?
- How does this report relate to the aims and outcomes of this unit?
- What do I expect to find out?
- Who will be reading my report?
- What can I expect my reader to think, believe and want before reading my report?
- What will I want them to think and do after they have read my report?
- What structure, language, tone, style, arguments and evidence would work with my real reader?
- Will I be using diagrams, tables and charts in my report? How should they be laid out and titled?

How to prepare and write reports

Take students through the ten-step process via discussion of the handout (Resource 11.2).

- **Tips:**
- Give students examples of well-written reports.
- Engage in report marking exercises.

Concluding the lecture

Obviously, if giving a what, why and how lecture on report writing, it will be helpful if you bring it to a conclusion by restating your main arguments and reiterating your main points, paying particular attention to that information you feel is of the most importance to your students at the time.

Overall conclusion

In this chapter we have explored academic writing with a particular emphasis on this as a key locus for negative debate with respect to widening participation and the 'deficit' (sic), non-traditional student. We have suggested that there are in fact social and institutional reasons that negatively affect student performance in assessment per se and academic writing in particular. These include changes in university funding involving students in paid employment alongside their studies plus the move towards modularisation, both of which reduce the amount of time that students have to engage with new material and concepts.

We suggested that one way of tackling student writing is to adopt more transparent, emancipatory pedagogical practices that reveal the forms and structures with which we want students to engage. We have also argued for an emphasis on 'writing to learn' as opposed to learning to write, suggesting that students will learn to write in academically appropriate ways through mastery of the discourse and concepts and that such mastery is promoted through active learning endeavour, including experiencing many formative writing opportunities.

We described how we tackle academic writing within learning development by means of 'what, why and how' lectures, including the ten steps to assignment success, and we suggested that student success is promoted when such approaches become embedded within subject tuition.

Resources

11.1   The structure of an academic essay
11.2   Ten steps to assignment success
11.3   The structure of a scientific report
11.4   Typical report structures
11.5   Explanation of a complex report structure
11.6   Report checklist

Notes

1   Southeast England Network and Learning Development in Higher Education Network (*http://www.jiscmail.ac.uk/lists/LDHEN.html*).
2   Sally Mitchell in the Queen Mary thinking/writing project, Writing in the Disciplines (WID), links her practice to Britton (1982) and the 'language across the curriculum' movement. With language across the curriculum it was argued that students learned to think and then write through active, language-driven engagement with material. The 1980s onwards re-emphasised curriculum

content and arguably school, further and higher education staff again privileged the transmission of content rather than the development of thinking/writing processes. See *www.thinkingwriting.qmul.ac.uk.*

3 With thanks to a Rogerian 'Counselling for Learning' programme, Tower Hamlets College, 1992, that introduced us to these activities in the first place.

Bibliography and further reading

Archer, L., Hutchings, H. and Ross, A. (2003) *Higher Education and Social Class.* London and New York: Routledge Falmer.

Bennett, R. (2002) 'Lecturers' attitudes to new teaching methods', *International Journal of Management Education*, 2 (1): 42–57.

Bourdieu, P. and Passeron, J.-C. (1979) *Reproduction in Education, Society and Culture.* London: Sage.

Britton, J. (1982) 'Writing to learn and learning to write', in Pradl, G. M. (ed.), *Prospect and Retrospect: Selected Essays of James Britton.* New Jersey: Boynton/Cook Publishers.

Bruner, J.S. (1975) *Toward a Theory of Instruction.* London: Belknap/Harvard.

Burn, E. and Finnigan, T. (2003) 'I've made it more academic by adding some snob words from the thesaurus', in Satterthwaite, J., Atkinson, E. and Gale, K. (eds), *Discourse, Power, Resistance: Challenging the Rhetoric of Contemporary Education.* Stoke-on-Trent: Trentham Books.

Burns, T. and Sinfield, S. (2003) *Essential Study Skills: The complete guide to success @ university.* London: Sage.

Cottrell, S. (2001) *Teaching Study Skills and Supporting Learning.* Basingstoke: Palgrave.

Hodge, Margaret (2003) quoted in Claire Saunders, 'Fact: term jobs damage grades', *Times Higher Education Supplement*, 7 February.

LDHEN (2003) Learning Development in Higher Education Network discussion at: *http://www.jiscmail.ac.uk/lists/LDHEN.html.*

Leathwood, C. and O'Connell, P. (2003) ' "It's a struggle": the construction of the "new student" in higher education', *Journal of Educational Policy*, 18 (6).

Lillis, T. (2001) *Student Writing, Access, Regulation, Desire.* London: Routledge.

Mitchell, S. (2003) *Developing the Potential of Student Writing for Learning in University.* Presented to Southeast England (Learning Development) Network – see *www.thinkingwriting.qmul.ac.uk.*

Rogers, C. (1994) *Freedom to Learn.* Upper Saddle River, NJ: Merrill.

Sinfield, S., Burns, T. and Holley, D. (2004) 'Outsiders looking in or insiders looking out?', in Satterthwaite, J. et al. (eds), *The Disciplining of Education: New Languages of Power and Resistance.* Stoke-on-Trent: Trentham Books.

Thompson, J. (ed.) (2000) *Stretching the Academy: The Politics and Practice of Widening Participation in Higher Education.* Leicester: NIACE.

Warren, D. (2002) 'Curriculum design in a context of widening participation in higher education', *Arts and Humanities in Higher Education*, 1 (1): 85–99.

12 How to promote effective revision and exam techniques

Introduction

In *Essential Study Skills* we call the chapter on this topic 'How to pass exams (big picture – small steps)'. This is to emphasise to students that while each course that they study will have a big picture – an overall shape, structure and design – they will typically make sense of that structure – and learn the course content – one step at a time, piece by piece. We have found that this analogy can help both staff and students make sense of the examination process; it also benefits students if they harness information on memory and learning styles in order to promote their success in examinations. In this chapter we will explore some issues with respect to examinations, including some student fears with respect to the examination process. We shall give some tips on memory and learning style that we pass on to students and finally we will explore SQP4, our whole-course approach to passing exams.

Exams – the feared event

Many students fear examinations with responses ranging from the mildly terrified to the pathological, and for many the whole examination process is wrought with fear: they have never performed well in exams and they see no way of being able to turn this around. In fact student perceptions of exams may be one of the drivers towards the use of alternative modes of assessment, including an emphasis on coursework which we cover in Chapter 3 on how to assess. However, examinations themselves are not necessarily the problem. The best written, discursive exam allows students to demonstrate a combination of surface and deep learning. That is, students are invited to use the information that they have learned over a programme of study, including such surface details as the key names, dates and events, to answer new questions which require them to select and shape material in appropriate and deep ways.

Arguably the problem therefore is not in the examination per se, but in the way that students have or have not been taught to study and learn, how they have or have not been taught to use and harness their memories, and how they have or have not been taught to prepare for examinations.

Some student fears with respect to exams

▓ **I'm dyslexic and I write really slowly:** Whether or not a student is dyslexic, if they feel that they write too slowly to demonstrate their learning to good effect in an exam situation, they will fear that exam. One thing that we recommend here is that students investigate just how much they can write in the different times that they will be allocated in their different exams. Once they have an idea of their individual word limits, they must practise planning and writing information-packed exam answers within their particular word and time constraints.

● **Tips:** Set word-constrained rather than time-constrained examinations. Caveat – as students will be unfamiliar with these they will need careful explanation. Encourage potentially dyslexic students to go for testing. Often the dyslexic student will be allocated extra time in an exam – and may possibly be allowed computer assistance. This latter has really made a difference to students we have known enabling them to move from a 100% failure rate in exams, to achieving 2:1 grades and above.

■ **How can I learn all that material in a couple of weeks?** Typically students work through any course that they are on – modular or whole-year – without thinking about the exams until a couple of weeks before they arrive. This is not effective practice. The best way to learn material is through active ongoing learning and revision practices and where the student is immersed in their studies (see also the ongoing revision cycle, p. 160). Unfortunately even where students are aware of these positive learning conditions, the need for paid employment works against them.

● **Tips:** Promote active learning by formative exercises, including the preparation of revision notes. In revision sessions encourage students to generate potential exam questions, and then to plan and prepare perfect answers in groups or individually.

■ **I'll never pass an exam, I have a really bad memory:** We have found that the majority of our students believe that they have bad memories. We feel that this is a result of not consciously learning how to learn, and of not understanding how the memory works.

● **Tips:** Give students information on short- and long-term memory and the revision cycle. Give information on learning styles.

How we do it

We have a series of activities that we put into practice with students when preparing them for exams. While we tend to run one long session on 'Memory, learning style and revision and exam success' it is possible to spread the activities over several sessions and it is for you to decide which of the following to cover with your students, and when. Note, when we do cover this material we emphasise to students how they have encountered the information before – the revision cycle when looking at note-making and learning styles when considering how to study. In this way we attempt to reinforce notions of good practice and of the transferability of study and learning skills.

Session structure:

■ Lecture/discussion around memory and learning style plus tips and tricks

■ Lecture/discussion on SQP4 plus examination day tips and tricks

Memory and learning style plus tips and tricks – lecture/discussion notes

When running a session on memory and learning style we tend to set the scene by drawing on the board the diagram shown in Figure 12.1.

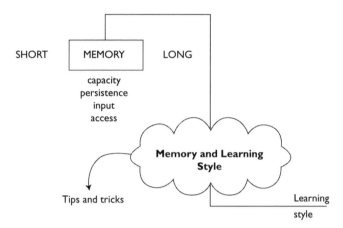

Figure 12.1 Board diagram for lecture/discussion on memory and learning style.

Typically we introduce the session by asking students whether or not they have good memories, we take responses and then feed in a lecture/discussion that first looks at short- and long-term memory, that explores how we remembered when at primary school or kindergarten, and then revisits the revision cycle (mentioned in Chapter 9 on note-making). We move on to discuss learning styles and how to utilise them in study practice and we conclude the lecture with some tips and tricks for success. We have included the information that we cover here. It is possible to lecture straight from the following, or use it to seed your own work with students on these topics.

The main attributes of short- and long-term memory

When people feel they have a bad memory it is often because they do not understand the difference between the short- and the long-term memory – nor do they understand just how active they have to be in their own learning. Note: The table shown in Figure 12.2 lists the main characteristics of short- and long-term memory.

● **Tip:** Build the table on the board, discussing the items as you go.

Short-term memory	Attribute	Long-term memory
Relatively small – holds 5–9 pieces of information	Capacity – size	Infinite – can build an infinite number of memories in the brain
Brief – piece of information number 8 comes along – and a piece of information falls out	Persistence – how long information stays	Infinite – with reactivation and barring brain trauma information can stay there forever
Is immediate – either it goes in or it does not	Input – how to get information in	Relatively slow – see revision cycle. It takes time and effort to build memories
Is immediate – if it is there you can access it	Access – how to get information out	Depends on input. How you put it in is how you get it out

Figure 12.2 Board diagram for lecture/discussion on memory and learning style.
Taken from Tom Burns and Sandra Sinfield (2003) *Essential Study Skills: The complete guide to success @ university.*
London: Sage.

Additional discussion: What this tells us is that most people rely too heavily on their short-term memory – hence they are always forgetting information. In order to learn you need to:

▓ choose what you want to remember;

▓ decide how you are going to remember it;

▓ take steps to remember – perhaps using the revision cycle.

If appropriate, say: 'we have already covered the revision cycle – have any of you started to use this system?' Typically no one will be using revision cycles! Remind students that the information that you give will only work if students put it into practice. If necessary, remind students of the revision cycle – and the fact that unless we revise material that we encounter we forget 98% of it after just three weeks (Buzan, 1989).

The revision cycle:

▓ When encountering new information that you want to remember spend some time revising that information immediately. Typically, some time the same day spend ten minutes producing short, effective and memorable notes.

▓ A day later spend two minutes recalling the key data – utilise your memory triggers and fill any blanks or gaps.

■ Do this again a week and a month later.

■ Reactivate the memory every six months.

How we learn

Student activity: Think back to how you learned things in primary school or kindergarten. Quickly jot down how you learned things in your earliest days at school – you might like to think of how you learned the alphabet or spellings, for example.

Take the student responses and discuss them with reference to examples of your own or with regard to examples from other students selected from the list below:

■ A, B, D, E, F, G (♫ ♪) – I learned the alphabet song by singing along to a little jingle.

■ Being an older student, I learned the colours of the rainbow by the mnemonic: Richard of York gave battle in vain – take the first letter and this gives the rainbow: **r**ed, **o**range, **y**ellow, **g**reen, **b**lue, **i**ndigo, **v**iolet. It is easier to remember the sentence than the colours in a list.

■ I learned spellings that way – 'because' came from '**b**ig **e**lephants **c**an **a**lways **u**nderstand **s**mall **e**lephants'.

Ask students: How do these compare with your strategies? Can you see anything in all the strategies covered – those here and your own – that could help you now?

Discussion: Typically learning is promoted by the use of rhythm and rhyme, by repetition and by mnemonic (memory) strategies. Something else that helps is the use of the bizarre to aid recall – the Von Rostorff effect (in Palmer and Pope, 1984). All these are really useful to you as a student now!

● **Tip:** Choose what you need to remember, devise a jingle or other mnemonic strategy – first-letter sentences, for example – and then use repetition, a revision cycle, to learn.

Use your learning style

When learning in primary school we tend to use 'see, hear, say and do' learning strategies or learning styles. Typically we all have a primary learning style or pathway – we are visual, auditory or kinaesthetic. That is, we might learn first by seeing, hearing/saying or doing/feeling, although we learn best when we do all of these.

Query: What do you think is your primary learning style. How do you think this will help you?

One way to check your primary learning pathway is to examine the language that you use in your everyday life. For example, do you normally say: 'I see what you mean' *or* 'I hear what you're saying' *or* 'It feels good to me'?

■ 'I see what you mean' could indicate that you are a visual learner and that you might favour a visual learning style.

■ 'I hear what you're saying' indicates that you are an auditory (hear/say) learner.

■ 'It feels good to me' could indicate a preference for kinaesthetic learning. Here you might need to be emotionally involved with the subjects you study or you might need to use physical activity in your learning.

Still confused about your style? Well, how do you remember a spelling? Would you:

■ write out the word and see if it looks right (visual)?

■ spell out the word and check that it sounds right (auditory)?

■ look at or say the spelling and check if it feels right (kinaesthetic)?

Now ask students to think what strategies to employy to harness see, hear, say and do strategies in their learning.

● **Learning style tips**

● **Visual:** If you are a visual person you may enjoy reading, watching film, TV and video. You will profit from using pattern note-making systems supplemented by the use of colour, space, highlighting and cartoons or other visual images.

● **Auditory:** If you remember sounds best you will benefit from discussion or explaining things to other people. You may need to speak aloud when you are learning something, and you can supplement this by making key word tapes of topics that you need to remember, possibly using jingles, tunes and funny voices to stimulate your memory.

● **Kinaesthetic:** If you remember kinaesthetically you will need to love your subject, and possibly to build movement into your learning strategies. You will not learn by sitting in one place hour after hour. Make charts and patterns of the key topics that you need to remember or act out or role-play in some way.

● **Super tip:** See, hear, say and do to really learn – whatever your primary pathway.

Key points

When inputting information on memory and learning style we also stress to students the importance of **key word** revision strategies (see also Chapter 9 on note-making). That is, we do not encourage the passive rote-learning of already pre-digested material – lecture notes or essay texts for example. For students to be effective in their learning they need to develop their abilities to strip back what they need to learn to the bare essentials, the key words or phrases that stand for the essential data. Students then learn by **using** information for themselves in discussion, in their writing and in other academic endeavour, including preparing for exams.

When preparing for exams it is especially important for students to reduce information to bare essentials, and then to practise using that information in a variety of contexts, including using it under the specific exam conditions for which they are preparing.

● **Tips:** Encourage students to inject some fun into their learning – to have sport with ideas: . . .
● Get students to devise revision materials for a programme of study utilising see, hear, say and do data.
● Get students to design some form of revision game for your course or module, also using learning styles information.

When we have set such activities with students they have prepared complex information packs that would adequately resource future teaching of a programme! Further, students have designed quizzes and even detailed board games that have excavated a course for key information and that require knowledge of that information in order to play the game.

Tips and tricks

Typically we will conclude our session on memory and learning style with a brief summary of the data covered under the heading 'tips and tricks'. We emphasise that for students to study and learn effectively they must:

■ want to do well;

■ be interested in the programme that they are following;

■ understand key data and how the whole programme has been put together – they must have an overview or the global picture (aims, outcomes, syllabus);

■ check the specific exam format for which they are preparing;

- prepare key word revision notes;
- learn key data using see, hear, say and do strategies;
- practise using information under a variety of conditions, including exam conditions.

This leads logically into the next session – or part session – on the whole-course approach to passing exams, below.

SQP4 plus examination day tips and tricks – lecture/discussion notes

We might preface a session on SQP4 thus: 'We are now going to look at a whole-course approach to active learning and exam success. We will conclude this session with some advice on how to survive your examination day. As you make notes, please think how knowing this information will help you in the particular exams for which you are preparing.'

Optional preliminary activity

Utilising individual effort or a pyramid discussion,[1] give students five minutes to jot down how they would prepare for a driving test. Discuss student responses as follows:

When preparing for tests that students themselves choose to undertake they typically do know and practice good strategy. That is, they will:

- find out exactly what will be required of them in the test – written and practical;
- learn the things that they need to learn;
- practise using the information – testing themselves on their knowledge of the written test contents and practising their driving;
- practise under exam conditions – and until they feel ready for the test;
- if they fail, they will reflect on where they went wrong and practise those items further.

If they could only apply such strategies to their studies students would be much more successful.

The SQP4 system

The SQP4 system is a way of applying such strategies to academic contexts (notes below). SQP4 stands for survey, question, predict, plan, prepare and practise.

S = Survey

At some time during a course or programme of study (preferably at the beginning) students should work to gain an overview of the whole course and should use this to make sense of their learning and to plan their exam strategies. To gain their overview students should survey:

▨ module or course outlines and handbooks;

▨ course aims and learning outcomes which detail exactly what the student has to do and learn to pass a course;

▨ syllabus;

▨ assessment criteria;

▨ past exam papers – such that they understand the exact format of each exam for which they are preparing – different formats will require different practice.

● **Tutor tip:** Tell students where the past papers for your subject are kept – online, with the departmental secretary, in the library, etc.

Q = Question

Students need to ask themselves: 'What do I need to do and learn to pass this course?' That is, after a detailed review of all the available information, students should determine exactly what they would need to do in order to succeed on each course that they are studying.

● **Tips:** Students should:
● draw up a list for each course of everything that must be undertaken and everything that must be learned in order to succeed;
● draw up such lists with a study partner;
● for each exam, make a list of the topics that will come up;
● link exam topics to course aims and outcomes;
● link exam topics to on-course assignments;
● pin lists in personal study space;
● put lists in topic folders.

P = Predict

In class, get students to predict the topics that will come up on your exam paper – perhaps get everyone to write out what they think will be a potential question. Give feed back in general terms on how accurate they have been. If desired, unpack the thinking that has gone into their questions and your exam strategies. Get students to say what their next step should be – this leads us in to P for plan.

P = Plan

Once students have predicted potential exam topics they must devise effective learning and revision strategies for each exam they will undertake. Typically they should plan on undertaking the following:

▨ Open a revision folder for each exam topic that they will prepare for each exam.

▨ Note on the folder key aims and outcomes that answering a question on such a topic would allow them to address.

▨ Note which items from the reading list should be read to answer questions on such a topic.

▨ Place relevant lecture, seminar and research notes in the folder.

▨ Put relevant press cuttings and journal articles in the folder.

▨ Review each folder once a month and reduce key information to key words on a revision crib sheet.

▨ Build a revision pattern for each topic (see also Chapter 9 on note-making and Chapter 8 on research and reading) utilising key words, names and dates, and memory triggers.

● **Tip:** Undertake some of these strategies in a seminar session.

P = Prepare

Of course it is not enough for students to have great plans – they must actually **do** the things that they have planned to do. They must prepare themselves for exams over time. Typically this involves the following:

▨ Maintain a revision cycle for each exam topic, in each subject.

▨ Keep revision folders up to date – pruning and revising regularly.

▨ Keep revision pattern notes up to date.

▨ Reduce key points onto index cards and carry the cards, revising from them in bus queues, in lifts, when travelling, etc.

▨ Illustrate notes with memorable cartoons.

▨ Make key word tapes and sing along to them.

▨ Design quizzes and board games, and play revision games with study partners.

P = Practise

Typically coursework requires completely different strategies to examinations. Whereas in coursework we might have 1,500–5,000 words to answer a question, in an exam we might have an hour or less per question or we might be set a word limit. Hence students have to familiarise themselves with completely different writing strategies in order to prepare for exams. Typically students should practise for exams in the following ways:

- Practise brainstorming and planning answers to questions – develop the ten minute brainstorm/plan strategy.

- Brainstorm every question in a course handbook for ten minutes.

- Find past exam papers and brainstorm every exam question for ten minutes.

- Divide exam time into reading time, planning time, writing time and reviewing time. Once students know how much time they will have per question per exam, they can practise timed writing.

- Practise brainstorming, planning, drafting and reviewing under the conditions that will operate in each different exam.

- Practise timed writing with notes.

- Practise timed writing without notes.

- Check timed writing with study partner, course tutor, learning development.

Conclusion: examination tips

It is possible to conclude the SQP4 lecture here, reiterating the key points. The tutor can then conclude the session by feeding in the following examination tips.

Exam time tips

- Always read the paper carefully.

- Always plan before you write.

- Always start answers.

- Don't worry about finishing answers. (The law of diminishing returns means that more marks are picked up at the start of an answer than at the conclusion.)

- Only write the number of answers requested – no more or less.

- Always read through what you have written.

> ■ What will work for you:
>   – Brainstorm and plan every answer before starting to write anything?
>   – Brainstorm and write your favourite answer, then brainstorm all the rest and answer least favourite last?
>   – Brainstorm and write the answer for one question at a time?

And finally – examination day!

There are several things that students can do on and around examination day in order to promote their success. You could advise the following:

■ **Positive thinking** (see also Chapter 6)**:** Students need to want to do well in a particular exam – if they are not motivated to succeed, then they will not. While fear is normal, students can be reminded to enjoy their fear – it means that they are still facing new challenges, and that adrenalin can be harnessed to help them 'think on their feet'. Students should practise positive thinking such as: 'I am looking forward to this exam. I am enjoying this opportunity to show what I know' rather than: 'I'm no good at exams! I'm going to have a horrible time.'

■ **Relaxation:** In Chapter 7 – especially when we looked at how to study – we mentioned that it is useful for students to build stress-busting/relaxation techniques into their everyday lives as students so that when exam time comes around they can just use more of them. Furthermore, if students think that they will encounter sleep problems during exam time, it will be useful to practise using sleep-inducing tapes before exam time so that they will work when needed.

■ **The night before:** If students have put SQP4 techniques into practice they should not be cramming in new data the night before an exam, neither should they be trying to learn essays by rote. They might like to recall the topics that they have predicted will appear on the exam and practise recalling the key points that they will utilise in answering possible questions. Students can get their supplies ready for the next day – pens, calculators, case study books, glucose tablets, watch/clock – but mainly students should relax and get an early night before the exam.

■ **Examination day:** On exam days students should plan to get up early, eat a light meal and get to the right room at the right time – and obviously on the right day! (We have heard of students five minutes before a start time wandering around a confusing building saying 'where is room XXX again?') The meal is necessary because thought uses up a lot of energy but a heavy meal will drain all the blood to the stomach – not a good thing!

■ **What examiners like to see:** The correct number of questions answered. Correct use of key data, including concepts used appropriately and with understanding. Formulated answers – not all you know on the topic. The correct format – essays, reports, short answers as requested. A focus on the question set drawing on course material appropriately and analytically. Well-structured answers. Good use of time. Neat presentation.

■ **After the exam:** Avoid post-mortem sessions – these tend to intimidate. Withdraw and prepare for the next exam.

We have included two resources to use with your students – the three-minute test (Resource 12.1) and the exam preparation checklist (Resource 12.2). The former reveals to students whether or not they can follow instructions; the latter might fit into a seminar handbook so that you can prompt your students to adopt an SQP4 strategy if you wish.

Alternative conclusion

If concluding the lecture on SQP4 here, please reiterate main points as you see fit.

SWOT it

The SQP4 strategy, while practical and successful, can seem like a very labour-intensive strategy – especially to the student who already dislikes examinations or who is working more than 20 hours per week on top of their study timetable. It might benefit your students if you run a quick SWOT session on the strategy: what do they think are its strengths, weaknesses, opportunities and threats? Pay particular attention to the threats that they suggest, and perhaps ask the students to suggest solutions to the weaknesses/threats that they have indicated.

Extension activities

■ As part of a portfolio of assessment tasks, set students the task of either devising revision materials or a revision game. Evaluate the materials in class with specific reference to their potential efficacy. To inject some fun, where students have devised games, play them.

■ In a revision session get students to predict possible exam questions. Tease out the reasoning behind their predictions. Explain the rationale behind your exam strategy.

■ Have students brainstorm all the predicted questions or all the questions on an old exam paper.

■ Get students to plan and prepare perfect answers to possible exam questions – individually or in groups.

■ Get students to complete an 'exam-preparation checklist' nearer to exam deadlines. Require students to complete detailed revision timetables.

■ To enable students to appreciate the role of personal motivation with regard to exam success, require students to complete a learning contract (see p. 40) for your examination.

Overall conclusion

In this chapter we have revealed some apprehensions that our students tend to express with respect to examinations per se and we have outlined how we tackle revision and exam preparation with our students, paying particular attention to how we cover memory and learning style and the SQP4 whole-course preparation strategy.

Resources

12.1   The three-minute test
12.2   Get ready for exams checklist

Note

1 The pyramid discussion system involves students working first individually, then in pairs and fours, and then holding a plenary session.

Bibliography and further reading

Buzan, B. and Buzan, T. (1999) *The Mind Map Book*. London: BBC Publications.
Buzan, T. (1989) *Use Your Head*. London: BBC Publications.
Gibbs, G. and Habeshaw, T. (1992) *53 Interesting Things to Do in Your Lectures*. Bristol: Arrowsmith.
Palmer, R. & Pope, C. (1984) *Brain Train: Studying for Success*. London: Spon.
Rogers, C. (1992) *Freedom to Learn*. Upper Saddle River, NJ: Merrill.
Rose, C. and Goll, L. (1992) *Accelerate Your Learning*. Aylesbury: Accelerated Learning Systems.
Sutherland, P., Badger, R. and White, G. (2002) 'How new students take notes in lectures', *Journal of further and higher education*, 26 (4): 377–88.

13 How to promote effective group work

Introduction

In HE, whether it takes the form of tutor- or student-led interactions, we have a tradition of using group work to support learning. Tutor-led group work can take the form of one-to-one engagements between tutors and students, tutorials with one tutor and three to five students or seminars where a tutor may lead a session including 15–20 students or more. For student-led group work we might encourage students to work together either in relatively informal discussions or more formally to lead academic seminars. We might set group activities wherein we ask students to work together to produce a presentation, report or some other product, from a group video to a dramatic performance. Some 40% of HE work is said to fall into one or more of these categories (Bennett et al., 2002).

There are many roots to our valuing of the group interaction as a positive learning process. These might stem from a belief in Socratic dialogue as a route to the acquisition of knowledge to a drawing on education theories based on interactionist, cognitive or social theories of learning. There are economic factors to the utilisation of group work, from the decreasing unit of resource available to HE (Leathwood and O'Connell, 2003), which leads inexorably to more reliance on student/ student as apposed to staff/student interactions, to the notion of education as a factor in the generation of social prosperity – thus students need group work experience to prepare them for their collaborative roles in the arenas of work in which they will have to engage. Further we may have ideological reasons for group work based on the belief that rather than being independent, we are interdependent beings and as such group work fosters a value of collaborative effort (Leathwood, 2001). Here we might also believe that group work can facilitate the development of interpersonal skills such as assertiveness, compromise and tolerance.

Whatever our pedagogical reasons for using group work in our own practice we can have many specific goals for particular group activities. Perhaps you require that students discuss new ideas and information as a route to understanding and as a precursor to written assignments. Perhaps you are setting tasks to develop specific study or academic skills like the others contained in this handbook – organisation and time management, effective research and reading strategies, the production of presentations, seminars or written assignments, or to help students revise and prepare for exams. In these instances you might be content with the collaborative generation of an end product. Increasingly, however, we have found that tutors are also requiring that students produce some sort of written reflection on the group work process per se as a part of the assessment. In either event we have found that students benefit from both theoretical and practical guidance to help develop their group work skills and their thoughtful reflections upon their group experiences. Typically, as with other areas covered in this text, we find that students benefit from a consideration of the what, why and how of group work – plus clear assessment criteria with respect to the group activity and the reflection exercise that is set.

Tutor activity

Take a few moments to think about your own experiences of using group activities with your students.

1 In what forms of group activities do you expect your students to engage?

2 Which of these do students seem to prefer? Which do they appear to dislike?

3 What are your reasons for setting group activities? Do you communicate these to your students?

4 What do you think are the strengths, weaknesses, opportunities and threats of group work?

Here are some responses from other tutors:

In what forms of group activities do you expect your students to engage?

▨ I ask students to discuss topics in class to develop their understanding and aid their learning. I do also set group tasks, but at the moment I do not grade these.

▨ I set a group presentation but give individual marks. I know of other tutors who only award group marks.

Which of these do students seem to prefer? Which do they appear to dislike?

▨ I find that students resent getting a group mark when they do not feel everybody has pulled their weight.

▨ I used to find that students would not engage in large group discussions – it would always be the same people talking. Eventually I realised that they were just too scared to speak. I now use buzz groups as a way of loosening people up and I find that the majority of my students do enjoy group discussion now. Similarly my students appear to enjoy other group tasks now – but I do know that many tutors say that students really resent group work.

What are your reasons for setting group activities? Do you communicate these to your students?

▨ I believe that we learn by active engagement with material, so I don't think students can learn unless they discuss new ideas with other people. I also firmly believe that group discussion promotes active learning. Hence group work increases understanding, facilitates learning and even deepens learning. And, yes, I do tell my students that. I think that if they know why I am doing something 'to' them, then they will accept it.

▨ I teach in the Business Department, I set group work to prepare students for work. I would have thought that was obvious!

What do you think are the strengths, weaknesses, opportunities and threats of group work?

▨ **Strengths:** Active and interactive learning. When it works well can it can create a positive and happy learning environment and a rich and enjoyable experience.

▨ **Weaknesses:** Some students just do not want to engage in group activities, and there is a range of reasons for this – frustration with the lack of motivation or engagement in others or an overall lack of awareness of what it takes to do good group work. They might hold back in discussions, contribute little to group projects, etc. Another weakness tends to be the reflection on the group activity. Typically these never seem to go deeper than 'we had some problems but we overcame them'. There is very little thought as to the purpose of group work – or the purpose of the reflection itself.

- **Opportunities:** Supportive, collaborative learning. Group work shares out the workload and increases understanding. It offers social support rather than academic isolation, which is always good, but especially helpful for students with low self-esteem – it gives them someone to talk to before they quit.

- **Threats:** Students who do not know how to engage in group work or students with low motivation can hold back the success of an otherwise good group. Also, students who dominate, especially if they do not know what's going on. Where grades are being awarded, this can increase stress on already typically over-stressed students.

Query: Were any of these responses like your own? Where any different? Have they made you rethink group work slightly?

Discussion: There are many reasons for setting group activities and there are many advantages to group work, but there are some problems attached. Hopefully we can help students to deal with some of their own issues with respect to group work and we can work to mitigate the negative impact of the non-motivated student in the group activities that we set.

How we do it

Typically, we tackle group work under the banner of 'integrated skills'[1] when invited by subject tutors to help a class prepare for a specific group activity – a presentation or seminar, say. We also offer specific sessions on group work in our own study and academic skills programme in learning development. In both instances we will briefly detail information on the what, why and how of group work, followed by suggestions for a teambuilding activity. We do find that students resist sessions on group work – we are told that this is because they now resent assessed group activities. However, we do find that students who undertake a session on group work with us do go on to do better in their group activities and often write useful and considered reflections on their group activities, reflections that also receive good grades.

Tutor tips: Group work made simple

When initiating a group discussion or project first get the students into buzz groups or utilise the pyramid discussion format.

- **Buzz groups:** Divide the class, lecture or seminar group into sub-groups of three to five people. Give each group a topic to discuss – either all the same topic or a different one per group. Allow a few minutes for discussion then hold a plenary session.

- **Pyramid discussion:** Move students into group work from individual thought to plenary session. Start by allowing two minutes for individual thought, then gather into pairs (10 minutes), then fours (10–20 minutes) – finally hold a plenary.

- **Plenary sessions:** Can be really informal – call for one point per group and go round the room until all the information is collected on the board – to the quite formal where each mini-group presents their findings to the larger group.

In this section of the guide we shall detail the information that we give students on the 'what, why and how' of group work. We will make suggestions as to how to improve student performance in group work and also on how to improve the reflections that they write upon their group work experiences. We move on to offer suggestions for building and extending group work skills in your students. You can use the information as a lecture yourself or utilise the resources so that students can develop their skills themselves.

Tutor tip: SWOT student groups

- Before starting a group activity, get your students to SWOT their own approaches to group work: What are their group work strengths? What are their weaknesses? What are the opportunities and threats of group work?

- Collect points from the group and discuss ways of building on the strengths and opportunities and resolving the weaknesses and threats.

- Mention that this could be a starting point for their subsequent reflection on their experience of group work.

Group work: what, why and how – lecture notes

Introduction

As a preamble to any lecture on the what, why and how of group work it is useful if you explain the purpose of group work in your unit, module or programme. Inform students as to what you will be looking for in their group processes and, if appropriate, explain how you will be assessing their written reflections.

What is group work?

A group is defined as having a membership of two or more people with a shared sense of identity – a sense of being in a group with shared goals. Group members should experience a sense of interdependence as they interact and collaborate to achieve common goals. Perhaps this is where the problems stem with academic groups. Arguably very few student groups (or groups of academics for that matter) could be said to interact and relate in this way. (*One issue for us as tutors is definitely to work to build that positive, interactive and collaborative feeling around the group activities that we set.*)

In school, college and university there are many forms of group work in which students have to participate. Group activities range from the relatively informal classroom discussion, through the tutor-led tutorial and seminar, to the student-led seminar and culminating in the group project. In the latter, the product of the group enterprise – and perhaps a reflection upon that exercise and experience – will be formally assessed and thus will contribute to a student's final grade. Beyond the tutor-led or the tutor-initiated group activity, it is also advisable for students to engage in their own positive group activities – finding a study partner or building a study group – in order to share out the workload and improve learning through discussion and other interactions.

Why groups?

Whether lecturers introduce group activities from psychological, sociological or economic perspectives (*explain more if desirable – as above*), there are many benefits to group work for the student. A good group promotes active and interactive learning – which promotes understanding and a shift from surface to deep learning. Further, a good group helps to share out the workload, thus decreasing the pressure on the individual while increasing the benefits of the work undertaken. A positive group also breaks down the isolation of academic study. Further, if students participate positively in group interactions they can refine their interpersonal skills as they learn to discuss ideas and negotiate problem-solving strategies with diplomacy and tact – with assertiveness rather than aggression.

Of course there can be negatives attached to group work. Increasingly students are becoming grade conscious, and many thus resent the imposition of group work whereby their grade will in part be determined by the efforts and abilities – or lack of them – of others. Typically students become resentful of students who do not pull their weight, who do not stay on track, who fail to meet their obligations. Similarly people will resent those who bully, dominate or, conversely, fail to speak or contribute in any way.

Now some tutors note these problems but argue that, as this is a preparation for work, then students just have to resolve these issues for themselves. However, we can put a more positive 'spin' on this if we remind students that whether or not they are able to resolve group problems and conflicts, if they note what problems they had – and suggest possible strategies for resolution – they will be gathering useful data for their reflection exercise (and for future curriculum vitae).

Typically we stress to students that every disadvantage can be turned into an advantage if students work to resolve the problems that they encounter. Typically students should note the different sorts of behaviours that are exhibited in their own groups and the ways that negative behaviours were turned around.

● **Student tip:** Put such notes in a curriculum vitae file. Hence when going for that job interview they can give real examples to back up the 'I can work as part of a team' bit of their application form.

How to succeed in group work

▨ Choosing groups

▨ A business-like approach

▨ Ten steps to assignment success

A very simple and basic tip for students preparing to engage in group work is to approach the task positively, determined to get the most from it. Feelings of resentment will not facilitate success in any activity – and group work is no different. We also cover choosing groups business approaches to group work and ten steps to assignment success.

Choosing groups

● **Tutor tips:** Allow students to choose their own groups. If you want to direct the group forming process try the Celtic method: get the youngest member of the class to the front. Inform them as to how many groups you want formed. This person then picks out group members one by one till everybody is in a relatively randomly formed group.

If allowing students to form their own groups, advise them to choose wisely. There is no necessary value in just teaming up with the people who happen to be sitting next to them in class – or, worse, in working with those great people they were clubbing with till three in the morning. Typically, it is useful if students pair up with others having the same degree of commitment and motivation that they themselves have. In some ways, while it may be frustrating for the tutor, it is better to have several really committed groups and a couple of really appalling ones than to impose a mix of committed and non-committed students in the groups that you form from the class as a whole. Such imposition does not really motivate the unmotivated – but it can really depress the once-motivated.

Of course the modular system that operates in many universities these days can work against such student choice. Many students will not pass through a degree programme with a consistent cohort. Hence they will not be able to pick out fellow travellers with necessary accuracy. Even so, here students might be allowed to form their groups around specific topics – hence they will be drawn together by shared interest, if not necessarily from a shared degree of motivation and commitment.

A business-like approach

When preparing students for success in group work we were very influenced by expertise from the world of business. Hence we focus on Belbin's roles and Adair's processes (see Resources 13.1 and 13.2 for student handouts) as ways of getting students to consider how they might understand and enjoy group work – and improve their own reflections upon their group experiences.

> ● **Tutor tip:** Either deliver a brief lecture on Belbin and Adair from the handouts, or give the students the handouts and inform them that you expect them to reflect on the handout information thus:
> ● How will knowing this help me in this group task?
> ● How will it help me write a better reflection?

We would also remind students of (or take them through for the first time) the 'Ten steps for group assignment success' (set out in the box below and adapted from Resource 11.2). As a group activity is no different from any other it will still help students to follow the ten-step plan.

Ten steps for group assignment success

1 Open a research folder on the group task. Students should write out the assignment in full and then analyse the task, making links with the module aims and learning outcomes. To inject a little creativity, first individually and then as a group, they should brainstorm the task and then draw up an action plan stating who, will do what and when. (See also Chapter 10 on presentations and seminars and/or Chapter 11 on assignment writing.)

2 Follow the action plan – undertake targeted research and active reading (see Chapter 8 on research and reading) making key word patterns or Cornell notes (see Chapter 9 on note-making).

3 Review findings as a group. What has been discovered? What does it mean? What gaps are there in the research? Who will plug the gaps?

4 Plan the outline of the essay, report, presentation . . . other.

5 Prepare a first draft.

6 Leave a creative time lag.

7 Review, revise and edit – agree on a final draft.

8 Proofread – and rehearse if an oral event.

9 Hand work in on or before the deadline – or perform the oral activity with confidence and to time.

10 Review
 – Review the product of the group experience and acknowledge its strengths and weaknesses.
 – Move on to review the group experience, especially if required to produce a formal reflection upon it. Here it helps to pay attention to the initial SWOT and the steps taken to build on strengths and overcome weaknesses. There should be a focus on the what, why and how of group work, and some reference made to Belbin's roles, Adair's processes and the quality of the final product.

Conclusion

Conclude the group work lecture/discussion session, reiterating key arguments that you have made and restating the points upon which you want students to focus.

● **Tutor tips:**
● When addressing step 10 of the ten-step programme above, give sufficient information to assist students in their preparation of thoughtful and useful reflections upon their group work experience.

● Explain your own assessment criteria in detail.
● Show students a model of a reflection on a group activity that you have felt to be useful.
● Distribute samples of good and bad reflections without revealing which is which and ask students to mark and grade them, individually or in groups. Get students to justify their grades, then reveal the grades actually awarded, compare with student grades and discuss the differences.
● Include the student grading and discussion of peer work as part of the assessment process – either formatively as a stage in the preparation of their own work or summatively as part of their overall assessment for the unit, module or programme.

Practising group work

If you have the time, there are several ways of practising group work:

■ Use the paper tower exercise. This can be a light-hearted way of enabling students to appreciate their own traits with respect to group work.

■ Ask students to prepare formative group presentations or seminars on a summative assignment topic – graded or un-graded.

There are many management team building games that you might like to experiment with to develop your group work skills – and for the fun of it. We have included one below; you can search out others if you wish.

The paper tower

In this activity you will need to gather together some students who want to develop their group work skills and some simple resources.

The goal will be for groups to construct a paper tower with a given supply of resources. Variations on this include: designing, producing and testing a non-breakable egg container or balancing a spoon on a paper tower. The egg container is the more dramatic!

Aim

To develop group work skills through practical activity, observation and feedback.

Learning outcomes

By the end of this activity participants will have developed:

■ a sense of the social support offered by group work

■ an idea of their own approach to group work

- a sense of the fun of group work

- an idea of the positive benefits of undertaking tasks in a team rather than alone

- some strategies for successful group participation.

Resources

Large quantities of newspaper, cellotape, paper clips and rubber bands – sufficient for all participants.

The paper tower exercise

1 Divide participants into groups of 5–6 people. Each group has to choose an observer who will not participate but who will note how the other people do so. The participants have to build a tower with the resources to hand. Each group will 'present' their tower to the other groups. Each observer will feed back how his or her group performed. (Allow 20–30 minutes tower building time.)

2 While the students build their towers the observer makes notes as to the roles adopted by individual members or the processes engaged in by the group. The observer notes how people engage in the group task.

3 Groups report back on the criteria they had chosen for their tower, the tower itself and how they felt the group performed. The observer feeds back (in constructive terms) on the roles and/or processes of the group.

4 Plenary: hold a plenary to discuss what the participants have learned from the activity – and how they will draw on this in the future.

Review points

When reviewing this activity participants might note that they:

- enjoyed it – it was fun

- benefited from being part of a team

- have some idea of how they performed in a group activity

- have learned something useful about group work that they will build on in the future.

Taken from Tom Burns and Sandra Sinfield (2003) *Essential Study Skills: The complete guide to success @ university*. London: Sage.

Overall conclusion – mourning the group

In this chapter we have looked at the role of group work as part of teaching and learning – and also with respect to the part that it can play in the assessment process. We explored the 'what, why and how' of group work paying particular attention to how we would cover the material with students. We have tried to stress the positive effects of group work while at the same time acknowledging some of the problems that occur around group work at the moment, not least in that many students are ill-prepared for group work or resent having to work with other students who are ill-prepared or unmotivated. We have made links between this section of the guide and others, especially useful if the group activity is to be formally assessed. For further help with regard to preparing students to write written reflections upon their group work, see Chapter 14 on reflective practice.

Resources

13.1   A business-like approach to group work: Belbin's group roles
13.2   A business-like approach to group work: Adair's processes

Note

1 Integrated skills is a term used to describe the delivery of study or academic skills tuition within subject delivery; integrated skills are often seen as a way of facilitating the development of subject-specific rather than generic study and academic skills.

Bibliography and further reading

Adair, J. (1987) *Effective Team Building: How to Make a Winning Team*. London: Pan. (Students are recommended to carry out an author search around the name J. Adair to find further useful texts by this author.)

Belbin, R. M. (1981) *Managing Teams: Why They Succeed or Fail*. London: Heinemann.

Bennett, C., Howe, C. and Truswell, E. (2002) *Small Group Teaching and Learning in Psychology*, LTSN Psychology Report and Evaluation series, No. 1. Available at: *www.psychology.ltsn.ac.uk*.

Leathwood, C. (2001) 'The road to independence? Policy, pedagogy and the "independent learner" in higher education', in West, L., Miller, N., O'Reilly,

D. and Allen, R. (eds), *Travellers' Tales: From Adult Education to Lifelong Learning and Beyond*. Proceedings of the 31st Annual SCRUTEA Conference, Pilgrim College, University of Nottingham.

Leathwood, C. and O'Connell, P. (2003) ' "It's a struggle": the construction of the "new student" in higher education', *Journal of Educational Policy*, 18 (6).

14 How to promote reflective practice

Introduction

Becoming a reflexive student is akin to becoming a reflective practitioner in any field, and one model that we use to promote reflective practice in our students in learning development is arguably akin to Kolb's 'active learning model' (Kolb, 1984), which is used in many professional development programmes. The model as applied to our practice could be described thus:

- Concepts are offered (here learning/study theory).

- Concepts are tested in new situations (here, putting theory into practice as a student).

- Observations are made and reflected upon (prompted by discussion, note-making and learning log entries (below)).

- Concepts and generalisations are evolved and adapted and are again –

- Tested in new situations, etc.

That is, students are offered concepts and models of good practice with respect to study and academic skills. The students are then given a space in which to rehearse the models of good practice; this rehearsal is followed by structured reflection where students are encouraged to consider their experiences so that they can further understand, adapt and use effective study and academic skills, techniques and practices – self-consciously and appropriately. While sometimes accused of being mechanistic (Holmes, 2001, 2002), in practice this is not only a thoughtful, mature and respectful way of introducing students to the good practice that will facilitate their success as students, it is also a model of behaviour and reflection that will facilitate the development of the emergent graduate persona within other disciplines and subject areas. (See Chapter 15 on how to promote overall success for models of how this translates into teaching and learning practice.)

This reflective practice can be linked to reflective learning practices that we have also covered elsewhere in this text, where active learning is promoted through the use of considered organisation and time management strategies, creative note-making techniques, targeted research and active reading practice, study partners and groups, discussion and rehearsal, formative exercises, including formative writing opportunities, and the use of the revision cycle[1] in active learning. That is, we argue that students need to engage in ongoing (revision) activities in order to promote understanding, to make learning conscious, to move from surface to deep learning and to transfer information from the short- to the long-term memory and into practice. The implicit argument here is that without reflection there is no learning. In learning development, while we encourage such good practice throughout all our work with students, we also focus on the learning diary or log – also known as the professional development journal – as a means of overtly developing the student as a reflective, reflexive practitioner. We shall detail our practice with respect to the learning log below, moving on to briefly discuss recent developments with respect to the Personal Development Portfolio (PDP) which is gradually being introduced into many universities as the official vehicle for these sorts of processes.

Learning development and the learning log

As learning development practitioners we build student learning diaries or learning logs into our own module: 'An introduction to academic studies' (which we cover in more detail in Chapter 15 on how to promote overall success), but the learning log can be introduced as a reflective learning tool in any programme of study. Put simply the learning log is where the students engage in focused, concise and analytical reviews of their own practices, processes and learning – for a specific learning or study activity and/or across a whole programme of study.

Tutor activity: Thinking about logs

1 Have you utilised learning logs or similar in your practice already?

2 What do you like about learning logs?

3 What do you dislike about logs?

4 How did you introduce the logs to your students?

5 What do you want from this section of this book?

Here are some responses from other tutors:

Have you utilised learning logs or similar in your practice already?

■ Yes – we introduced them last year. It was my first experience of this device.

What do you like about learning logs?

■ I like the fact that they are designed to encourage self-conscious learning.

What do you dislike about logs?

■ I hate it where the student writes pages and pages of description but seems to have no idea of what the log itself is for – or what specific formative activities were for.

How did you introduce the logs to your students?

■ I suppose that I did not introduce the topic very well. I think I was caught between two poles – not wanting to stifle a creative and interesting response to the task but, at the same time, not wanting students to be descriptive, definitely wanting concise and analytical journals.

What do you want from this section of this book?

■ I would like some tips as to how to help my students write better logs. I want them to understand the purpose of the log itself, and I want them to demonstrate real understanding as to the form, content and purpose of the course as a whole.

■ I want to help students write reflective journals alongside their group work activities.

> **Query:** Were any of these responses like your own? Do you now have goals for this section of the book?
>
> ● **Tip:** We have found that being told exactly what you would like in a learning log or journal does not in fact limit students. Typically the less inducted student is empowered to give you what you want more swiftly while the stronger student is prompted to exceed your expectations.

Model it first

If thinking about using learning logs with your students it is useful if you think first of what you want the log to achieve for the student, and then of how you will be assessing that these learning goals have been met. Draw up a model log for yourself first, and then gently lead students towards making the sorts of entries that you feel would benefit them as active learners of your subject. (For a model log entry please see Resource 14.1.)

● **Tip:** You can photocopy this resource as a model for your students if you feel that it embodies the qualities that you wish to encourage in them. Typically we find that models are under-used in academic endeavour – perhaps for the reasons mentioned by the tutor in the 'box': not wanting to stifle creativity. Perhaps we fear that students will only copy the content of what we offer rather than drawing inspiration from the form. Whatever the reasons, we find that students are desperate for models while tutors tend to be loathe to offer them. However, because the learning log is often as original a format for the tutor as it is for the student, we do find that we have leverage – if the tutor would benefit from a model of a good log surely the student could benefit also?

A model of good behaviour

In our programme, we expect students to write a learning log after every taught session, and we introduce this in the very first session that we have with our students. We might relate the activity to the Personal Development Portfolio or similar if appropriate. While learning logs will be assessed in our programme, we emphasise that they are designed to encourage active learning – to move students from surface to deep learning. Basically we emphasise that the idea of the log is to help students become more successful students in the first instance (and thus to assist with the evolution and development of a successful graduate identity (Holmes, 2002)) and that the practice, if continued, will enable students to become ever more thoughtful, reflexive practitioners.

How we do it

The learning log or diary is an essential part of our own study and academic skills programme. It is something that we introduce in the very first session of such a programme and that we insist that students maintain session by session. We collect and mark – not grade – logs each session, so that students receive feedback on their log generation and we also receive feedback on how well the programme is progressing.

Rather than having a formal 'what, why and how' lecture or discussion around the learning log (as we have provided in other sections of this text for other academic forms), students learn to write logs by doing them and by constantly receiving formative feedback upon them (a possible model for other writing?). In this way we feel that we do not problematise an academic form that has not yet acquired the negative accretions associated with the essay, exam or presentation. However, the more such logs are introduced as vehicles of assessment without adequate explanation and formative feedback, the more this will become another such mysterious and problematic academic form or practice.

Typically we stress that the role of the log is to rehearse students in good active learning practice. That is, students will be taken through a series of reflections designed to make their learning conscious in analytical ways and this will improve both the quantity and the quality of their learning. At the same time, for us, learning logs become an excellent tool for our own course monitoring, telling us where topics have been covered adequately or inadequately, where material has been fully understood and where it will need further elaboration.

We have a particular structure that we recommend that students use when starting their learning logs (see Resource 14.2), with students compiling entries under the headings:

- What
- Why
- Reaction
- Learned
- Issues
- Goals.

And we lead students through the completion of their first log in class, perhaps handing out the sample log (see Resource 14.1), to prompt the production of the sort of entries that we want to see. We stress that we want concise and targeted reflections rather than descriptive accounts of their activities.

Assessing logs

In our own study and academic skills module, student logs are a part of the formal assessment and students have to submit a completed log for each session of the programme (whether or not they attended that session). In other modules, tutors might request a specific number of logs – the best six, say. In still other modules a whole workbook might be provided for students in which reflections (such as learning logs) and other activities have to be recorded. The whole workbook will be submitted at the end of the programme and will be awarded a certain proportion of the overall marks for the module.

● **Tip:** If using this latter device do make clear to students just where marks are awarded across the workbook as a whole.

Even where each log completed has to be submitted for evaluation in a final assessment portfolio, we allow students to revise their logs following formative feedback from the tutor. In this way we feel that we can emphasise the developmental rather than the assessment function of the log. If you have a group of a sufficiently small size, logs can be collected in frequently, even every week. Where we are able to do this, we mark but do not grade these formative logs – still reminding the students that the logs as a whole will receive a grade in the final portfolio. Formative marking is designed to prompt the production of concise but effective logs so that students are encouraged to produce very brief *descriptions* but more thoughtful analysis of the content and purpose of those learning or study events.

Thus students are encouraged to put down concise yet detailed write-ups of the learning that took place, with analysis prompted in the 'why' section of the log. In the 'why' section of the review, the student should be encouraged to demonstrate understanding not only of the content per se, but of how it relates to the course structure, the underlying principles and connections. For example, you might want the student to understand why there was a lecture on the eukaryotic cell or postmodernism in your programme. Here you might like them to be able to relate a specific lecture or seminar topic to your course aims and outcomes, for example, and how it relates to the assignment set. (See also the Cornell note-making system discussed on p. 103.)

When seeking 'reactions' from our students, we stress that they should be as honest as possible when noting their personal reaction or response to an activity. There is no necessarily right or wrong 'reaction' to a learning event, only the one that the real student has encountered. Obviously this requires that the student not be penalised for 'inappropriate' reactions – or for encountering problems rather than just sailing untroubled through a course.

● **Tutor tip:** You have to be honest with yourself here and if you feel you will tend to judge more harshly the student who is bored or who could not find the key text area first go, it might be necessary to omit this part of the learning log.[2]

Note: Some students will instantly enjoy the learning log. Others may really resent this practice – especially if they feel that you are peering inside their minds in ways that get them to reveal their innermost fears and failings. We have heard students say that they feel 'betrayed' by the log or that they resent and distrust this revelatory process. Hence this is an area requiring real sensitivity and empathy from the tutor.

Introducing the learning log

In the session where you are going to introduce the learning log you might like to flag this up in the session agenda that you write on the board. Tell students that you are going to take them through their first learning log at the end of the session and that it will be based upon the activities engaged with in that session.

When it comes to taking students through that first log, we suggest that you write the categories that you would like students to include in their logs on the board. We recommend what, why, reaction, issues, learned, goal setting – but do choose your own. For example, some tutors would include a 'starting point' section where students can note their understanding of a particular topic prior to engaging with the lecture or seminar; similarly a section requiring a brainstorm could open every log. Whatever categories you decide to utilise we recommend that you briefly explain the purpose of each of category – possibly as we have in the student handout in Resource 14.2.

● **Tips:**
● Complete the first learning log by getting class members to call out responses to the various headings.
● Get students to complete the first log in pairs.
● Collect the first logs the very next time you see the students. Mark and return as soon as possible.
● Hand out the model log after you have collected in the students' first log and before you get them to complete a second log.

Personal development portfolios

PDPs are being encouraged in universities by the Southern England Education Consortium as a way of developing employability skills in students. As such they may be related to Key Skills if a university has opted to make explicit Key Skill development at Level 4. Similarly they may be linked to study and academic skill development or they may be located within that aspect of the curriculum that explicitly focuses on employability, graduate attributes or personal professional development. As a developing activity it can be seen that this is an area that is still ripe for further definition and exploration.

Critics of such developments argue that again this is a negative response to mass higher education (see also the discussion of widening participation and the skills debate in Chapter 1 and a related discussion in Chapter 6 on how to promote self-confidence) and actually confirms the negative impressions of widening participation students. That is, while some students acquire degrees that do lead to employment, other, typically non-traditional, students have to demonstrate value addition, that is skills development beyond that bestowed by the acquisition of the university degree. Moreover, it has been argued that if employability skills are to be truly relevant they could only be measured by employment outcomes. Thus it is not enough to focus on developing these skills or attributes in students, there is a need to demonstrate that such developments, **in your institution**, do lead to your students acquiring jobs, albeit that students from a particular institution would not get a job if in competition with students from a higher status institution, no matter what additional skills portfolio they had compiled.

What now?

Whatever the political ramifications of this debate, if your institution is currently moving towards PDPs, then you would be advised to investigate the system that is being introduced at your university and which departments or units will have some or overall responsibility for this enterprise. Further, you might like to investigate how you and your particular courses or modules are supposed to articulate with the central thrust of the PDP project. For example, in our institution there is to be a three-pronged development of employability and related skills. In the first year there will be a focus on HE orientation ensuring that students do become inducted into academic practices per se and in the specific practices of their subject (or subjects if on joint degrees). In the second year there will be a focus on employability with the encouragement of work placement or work-related modules and in the third year the emphasis will be on the development of dissertation or project skills. The PDP process will be expected to articulate with all these developments.

The PDP enterprise will be clearer for students if:

- University promotional material refers explicitly to PDP;
- The rationale for PDP is made explicit – at every stage of a degree programme;

■ PDP opportunities within courses are made explicit.

Who is responsible?

Alongside the three-tiered shape to our institution's Undergraduate Modular Scheme and its articulation with PDP opportunities, the careers service has a particular expertise with respect to PDP in terms of supporting students with their career prospects. Initially subject staff are being invited to develop PDP initiatives within their modules – and they can coordinate with the careers service if they so wish. The positives of such an approach allow for the initiatives to move forward via staff that are enthusiastic and motivated towards the project. It also allows for a variety of approaches to evolve which can subsequently be evaluated to generate models of good practice. Critics might dispute this perhaps by arguing that when everyone is responsible for something, then no one really takes responsibility and energy is dissipated and opportunities are lost.

How we do it

Learning development and careers personnel discuss HE orientation development and PDP initiatives. Particular schemes are identified as loci for proactive engagement. Initiatives are set in motion and good practice will be identified by end-of-course feedback from students and staff.

Where HE orientation opportunities are set up, students can be introduced to the way that these will articulate with PDP development. Within the context of reflexive, reflective practice, students can be alerted as to how the learning log relates to the PDP and both can be linked to the curriculum vitae – that aspect of the PDP which is typically developed in either second- or third-year professional development modules.

Overall conclusion

In this chapter we have considered how we in learning development facilitate the evolution of the student as a reflective, reflexive practitioner. We have focused particularly on our use of the learning log or diary, sometimes termed a professional development journal. We stress that at this time the log per se is not experienced as a problematic agent of assessment, thus it is perhaps uniquely poised to be introduced in positive ways and developed through scaffolded and sensitive formative experiences: that students learn to write logs by doing rather than failing them. We detailed how we in learning development introduce, use and scaffold the learning logs that we utilise, even though they are also vehicles of assessment. We moved on to briefly consider the Personal Development Portfolio as the process that will probably become the one that most universities adopt with regard to developing students as effective practitioners. We hope that you have found this section of the book useful – not only in terms of the learning log in itself, but in that it also offers a model of how we could introduce students to other academic assessment vehicles, for students can learn how to write essays and how to deliver presentations in just such scaffolded and formative ways.

Resources

14.1   Example of a student learning log (on a research and reading session)
14.2   The reflective learning log – or professional development journal

Notes

1 The revision cycle: revise learning after ten minutes, a day, a week, a month and six months.
2 Certain programmes – as with education and QTS or with social work – require the production of reflective journals of some form that will be subject to legal as well as evaluative scrutiny. Ethically here tutors should warn students with regard to making statements that would be in contravention to government laws or institutional codes of practice: complete honesty may not be at all appropriate.

Bibliography and further reading

Cottrell, S. (2001) *Teaching Study Skills and Supporting Learning*. Basingstoke: Palgrave.
Holmes, L. (2001) 'Reconsidering graduate employability: the "graduate identity" approach', *Quality in Higher Education*, 7 (2): 111–19.
Holmes, L. (2002) Available at: *www.re-skill.org.uk/thesis/*, accessed February 2002. (See also: *www.re-skill.org.uk*; *www.graduate-employability.org.uk*; *www.odysseygroup.org.uk*.)
Kolb, D. (1984) *Experiential Learning*. Englewood Cliffs, NJ: Prentice Hall.

15 How to promote overall success

Introduction

In this chapter we explore several strategies for adopting an embedded approach to teaching, learning and study skills across the whole university. While universities will and do have distinct (or combined) units for teaching, learning and professional development, these units are only effective when they work closely with professional staff on the theory and practice of teaching and learning – and on the real business of promoting the academic achievement of all the university's students. For if 'employability' initiatives for students must be defined by employment outcomes (Chapter 14), then teaching, learning and study skills development must also have measurable outcomes in terms of student success. In this chapter we detail ways of approaching teaching, learning and study skills across university departments and within specific HE orientation initiatives. We are using the expression 'HE orientation' to describe both those practices designed to make transparent the forms and processes of academic discourse and those that introduce students to and rehearse them in the constituent study and academic skills and practices that will enable them to succeed within higher education.

An embedded approach

Student success is not just the responsibility of teaching and learning development units or departments within universities. It is not just that widening participation is changing the make-up of the university student body – there is an ethical case to be made for the university to problematise its own rather than its students' discourse (Lillis, 2001) and that when this happens the success of all students is promoted (Warren, 2002). Within our university it is believed that, at its best, learning development is facilitated by all professional staff and is expressed:

▦ Through creative and academically rigorous programmes.

▦ Through modules embodying key curriculum themes – including HE orientation courses or parts of courses at preliminary level (see Appendix A for HE orientation websites). Employability and project orientation occur at intermediate and honours levels.

▦ Through integrated skills development within modules.

These three aspects are 'owned' by departments, module convenors and teaching staff – but may be supported by the Centre for Academic and Professional Development and Learning Development.

▦ Through teaching and learning expertise, supported by staff induction and resources and by professional development programmes, including staff workshops and the MA in Teaching and Learning in Higher Education.

These are run by our Centre for Academic and Professional Development (CAPD) and can include liaison with Learning Development.

▦ Through additional study and academic skills programmes, pre-sessional and sessional, accredited and unaccredited.

▦ Through drop-in workshops where students can receive one-to-one support with study issues.

▦ Through teaching and learning resources, including a study skills collection maintained by the library and paper and online resources collected and/or produced by Learning Development.

These three are led by Learning Development.

There is no one model of how this variety of approaches to learning development translates into actual practice, but at the time of writing three general models of HE orientation either exist or are in development across our institution which we shall explore as case study exemplars:

▦ the bolt-on course – the Learning Development Module EA199;

- the universal module in one key location – the business skills module;

- the universal programme disseminated across the whole year – the humanities programme.

Generic accredited learning development module

Learning Development itself operates an accredited 'module in a week' (see Appendix B) which is offered to students pre-sessionally in auditor or creditor modes and elements of which also constitute our voluntary, unaccredited study and academic skills programme. Developed under the aegis of access, retention and progression, this is an intensive module that covers the key academic skills involved in successful learning, studying and communicating that are detailed in this text (see Appendix B for module handbook). The student body attending the module is mixed and composed of:

- prospective students – foundation, under- and postgraduate level who typically choose to attend the course to prepare for study;

- students already on-course – who typically choose to attend to acquire a missing first-year module or to improve their study performance.

The advantages of offering an accredited generic module in this way are that it grants choice to the student; attending students tend to be highly motivated, interested and 'ready' for the course and typically acquire much benefit from it. Further, a programme like this allows students to make positive contacts with learning development staff and resources so that they can utilise them again if the need arises. Potential negatives are that this is seen as a bolt-on, quick-fix solution to the 'problem' of the non-traditional student, and also that the study, learning and communicating techniques are delivered distinct from a meaningful subject context and hence epistemological aspects may not be adequately explored. However, the programme is designed to mesh with other HE orientation initiatives that students will encounter on-course; furthermore, the tutors also emphasise that the acquisition of a graduate persona (Holmes, 2001, 2002) that confidently and appropriately uses constituent academic skills and practices will require rehearsal of and reflection upon the same in a variety of contexts and at all university levels.

Business skills module

The Business Department currently offers one compulsory first-year module to all its incoming students. A committed team of business staff with an interest in the psychology of learning have first ownership of the programme which has been designed with contributions from learning development, especially in the form of teaching and learning resources and materials. The programme runs with a lecture programme delivered by the core team and that covers key aspects of university study – from the financing of the university system to coverage of learning styles and problem-solving. Seminars are supported by a detailed student handbook that has information and activities to do associated with topics that are covered in this text, for example organisation and time management, note-making, how to prepare and deliver a presentation and how to prepare and write an essay. Relevant subject specialists lead the seminars, thus leisure and tourism staff support leisure and tourism students and so forth. In this way generic advice can be shaped and tailored to specific epistemological practice. The advantage of such a scheme is that subject staff take ownership of the programme while at the same time maintaining and developing relationships with learning development – which benefits both staff and students. Possible disadvantages are that as a compulsory programme it is delivered to the students when the university is ready rather than when the students are ready to learn (Rogers, 1994); furthermore, it could be thought that HE orientation is covered in just one first-year module and by just one staff team, rather than it being understood that constituent academic skills and practices are developed and refined over time in a variety of contexts and with the guidance of all professional staff.

Humanities programme

Currently one humanities programme is proposing to undertake HE orientation across the whole first year, with key academic skills and practices being introduced and rehearsed across the first semester and further refined in the second. The proposal is that while one module is nominated in the capacity of HE orientation, all four first-semester – and some second-semester – modules will play some nominated and overt part in developing the following:

- processing given information – appropriate note-making in lectures, enabling active, critical and relevant note-making

- evaluating materials (texts, etc.) – enabling the evaluation and excavation of texts for informed use

- academic discussion – enabling academic discussion and interaction

- presentation skills – enabling the preparation and delivery of presentations and seminars

- assembling arguments – involving the preparation and refinement of written pieces and enabling written argument and the logical use of argument and evidence.

These various practices are reinforced by a student buddy system plus staged and coherent assignments thus:

Module 1

(a) Ten bullet point summary of lecture (task 1)

(b) Class discussion (task 3)

(c) Presentation (task 4)

(d) Assembling argument for assessment (task 5)

Module 2

(a) Second library introduction (task 6)

(b) Research project (task 7)

Module 3

(a) Summary of textual fragments (task 2)

(b) Back-up of class discussion (task 3)

(c) Back-up of presentation (task 4)

Module 4

(a) Reflective practice (task 8)

(b) Peer observation (buddy system)

(c) Presentation, observation and feedback skills

(d) Observation skills: self-observation, peer observation, object/subject-specific observation skills

The advantages of such a system is its universality, its dissemination over time and space and the ownership of the staff team; furthermore, no one module has to assume responsibility for assessing all the constituent study and academic skills. A possible disadvantage is that the initiative becomes so self-contained that it does not articulate sufficiently with other support networks and resources within the university, which could disadvantage students if additional study or other problems arise.

Conclusion

Throughout this text we have argued that teaching, learning and study skills are in fact the responsibility of all professional staff in a university. We have returned to that proposition here, arguing again that learning development at its best necessitates an embedded approach, that is that student success is promoted within subject tuition supported by articulation with teaching, learning and professional development units and by an emancipatory pedagogy that draws upon creative and various teaching and learning development initiatives including:

- generation of teaching and learning resources;

- staff development;

- study and academic skills programmes and workshops for (staff and) students.

In this chapter we have detailed some of the ways in which this operates at our university, and we have briefly described just three modes in which this might translate into practice with respect to HE orientation initiatives, with 'HE orientation' encompassing those practices that make transparent the forms and processes of academic discourse and those that facilitate student adoption and adaptation of constituent study and academic skills and practices.

While the 'study skills' debate is a hot one (see Chapter 1) we have attempted to stimulate debate with respect to teaching, learning and study skills for our readers rather than to offer a prescriptive, formulaic approach to this topic. If you are involved in learning development and wish to continue this debate, you are welcome to join the Learning Development in Higher Education Network and to engage with other practitioners: *http://www.jiscmail.ac.uk/lists/LDHEN.html*.

Bibliography and further reading

Anie, A. (2001) *Widening Participation – Graduate Employability Project*. University of North London (now London Metropolitan University).

Archer, L. (2002) 'Access elite', *Times Higher Education Supplement*, 18 January.

Archer, L., Hutchings, H. and Ross, A. (2003) *Higher Education and Social Class*. London and New York: Routledge Falmer.

Bennett, R. (2002) 'Lecturers' attitudes to new teaching methods', *International Journal of Management Education*, 2 (1): 42–57.

Blalock, A. (1999) 'Evaluation research and the performance management movement: from estrangement to useful integration?', *Evaluation*, 5 (2): 117–49.

Bourdieu, P. and Passeron, J.-C. (1979) *Reproduction in Education, Society and Culture*. London: Sage.

Burn, E. and Finnigan, T. (2003) 'I've made it more academic by adding some snob words from the thesaurus', in Satterthwaite J., Atkinson, E. and Gale, K.

(eds), *Discourse, Power, Resistance: Challenging the Rhetoric of Contemporary Education*. Stoke-on-Trent: Trentham Books.

Burns, T. and Sinfield, S. (2003) *Essential Study Skills: The complete guide to success @ university*. London: Sage.

Clarke, K., Secretary of State for Education (1991) *Hansard*, 20 May.

Cottrell, S. (2001) *Teaching Study Skills and Supporting Learning*. Basingstoke: Palgrave.

Giddens, A. (1996) *Consequences of Modernity*. Cambridge: Polity Press.

Hodge, Margaret, Secretary of State for Education (2002) *What Is College and University Education for?* Keynote speech, Church House, Westminster, Education Conference, 24 January.

Hodge, Margaret (2003), quoted in Claire Saunders, 'Fact: term jobs damage grades', *Times Higher Education Supplement*, 7 February.

Holmes, L. (2001) 'Reconsidering graduate employability: the "graduate identity" approach', *Quality in Higher Education*, 7 (2): 111–19.

Holmes, L. (2002) Available from *www.re-skill.org.uk/thesis/*, accessed February 2002. (See also: *www.re-skill.org.uk*; *www.graduate-employability.org.uk*; *www.odysseygroup.org.uk*.)

hooks, b. (1994) *Teaching to Transgress*. London: Routledge.

LDHEN (2003) Learning Development in Higher Education Network discussion at *http://www.jiscmail.ac.uk/lists/LDHEN.html*.

Leathwood, C. and O'Connell, P. (2003) ' "It's a struggle": the construction of the "new student" in higher education', *Journal of Educational Policy*, 18 (6).

Lillis, T. (2001) *Student Writing, Access, Regulation, Desire*. London: Routledge.

Luttrell, W. (1997) *Schoolsmart and Motherwise*. London: Routledge.

Medhurst, A. (2000) 'If anywhere: class identifications and cultural studies academics', in Munt, S. (ed.), *Cultural Studies and the Working Class*. London: Cassell.

Munt, S. (ed.) (2000) *Cultural Studies and the Working Class*. London: Cassell.

Noble, D. (2002) *Digital Diploma Mills: The Automation of Higher Education*. New York: Education Monthly Review Press.

Reay, D. (1998) *Class Work*. London: UCL Press.

Rogers, C. (1994) *Freedom to Learn*. Upper Saddle River, NJ: Merrill.

Sinfield, S., Burns, T. and Holley, D. (2004) 'Outsiders looking in or insiders looking out?', in Satterthwaite, J. et al. (eds), *The Disciplining of Education: New Languages of Power and Resistance*. Stoke-on-Trent. Trentham Books.

Tett, L. (2000) 'I'm working class and proud of it – gendered experiences of non-traditional participants in higher education', *Gender and Education*, 1 (2): 183–94.

Thompson, J. (ed.) (2000) *Stretching the Academy: The Politics and Practice of Widening Participation in Higher Education*. Leicester: NIACE.

Warren, D. (2002) 'Curriculum design in a context of widening participation in higher education', *Arts and Humanities in Higher Education*, 1 (1): 85–99.

White Paper (2003) *The future of higher education*. Available at *http://www.dfes.gov.uk/hestudents/hestrategy/exec.shtml* (accessed 25 November 2003).

Appendix A: Bibliographic and online resources for 'HE orientation'

Bibliographic websites

http://www.bbk.ac.uk/lib/study.html
http://www.ncl.ac.uk/library/training/study/stan.html
http://www.uwe.ac.uk/library/resources/general/info_study_skills/books/

UK skills websites

The following are UK-based websites that contain online or downloadable guidelines or tips on specific types of academic/study skills (such as how to write essays). The Wolverhampton site also has something on punctuation and the Bradford page contains tips and rules about spelling.

http://www.wlv.ac.uk/lib/systems/tipsweb.htm#essay
http://www.studyskills.soton.ac.uk/
http://www.leeds.ac.uk/ics/study.htm
http://www.mantex.co.uk/ (free downloads)
http://www.bradford.ac.uk/acad/civeng/skills/spelling.htm
http://www.lgu.ac.uk/ldu/ldu/courses/essayandreportwriting.htm

US skills websites

The following are US websites dealing with study and academic skills (time management, essay writing, etc.), but the approaches obviously reflect the American context (e.g. the advice that an essay introduction should include a 'thesis statement').

http://www.ucc.vt.edu/stdysk/stdyhlp.html
http://www.jcu.edu.au/studying/services/studyskills/online.html
http://www.und.edu/dept/ULC/handout.htm

Compiled by Digby Warren (CAPD), London Metropolitan University, November 2003

Appendix B: EA199: An introduction to academic studies: reflecting, learning and communicating

Preliminary level

15 credit points at CATS level 1

Prerequisites

Students should normally have a commitment to personal development including academic study.

Insert graduate attributes

Think critically and produce solutions: The student is able to make links between learning, study and communications theory and their own practice as students.

Communicate effectively in context: The student is able to present material clearly in oral and written media, showing an elementary understanding of the discourse of presentation and the target audience.

Module aims

To enable students to:

- make connections between experiential knowledge, including work-based and academic knowledge;

- relate their own learning, study and work experience to the professional context of their subject pathway;

- recognise the value of both individual and collaborative learning;

- have an appreciation of all aspects of academic discourse, written and oral;

- develop confidence within the academic environment.

Syllabus

The module will be run as a series of practical workshops where students will be given the opportunity to note, practise and reflect on their own strategies for learning and study. Emphasis will be placed on personal responsibility and on collaborative work. Aspects of academic discourse will be focused on and their role in subject studies explored. The module will include an introduction to the library with an emphasis on the use of electronic information systems and the Internet.

Note: The module can run as normal or be offered as an intensive one-week programme.

Learning outcomes

By the end of the module students should be able to:

1 Think critically about significant issues relating to their own learning and identify strategies to develop and strengthen their approach to study.

2 Demonstrate an ability to keep to deadlines for independent and collaborative work and to work in cooperation with others.

3 Present material in appropriate academic forms, with a clear sense of audience.

4 Make use of a range of sources of information, showing awareness of the need for academic reference.

Teaching and learning methods

Lectures, discussion, group work, practical activities and group and individual presentations.

Lectures, workshops and seminars (including online)   30 hours
Assessment related independent study (including tutorials)   100 hours
Seminar preparation (including tutorials)   20 hours
Total   **150 hours**

Assessment instruments

Portfolio containing:

Assessment A: Coursework, including learning contract, reflective learning logs, notes (from spoken source and from written source), presentation plan, essay plan and learning self-assessment.

Assessment B: Reflective essay or report utilising appropriate formal convention and identifying the learning achieved from the module.

Assessment item	Assessment instrument	Words	Weighting	Learning outcomes	Graduate attributes
A	Course work	N/A	50%	1	
B	Essay or report	1,500–2,000 words	50%	2, 3, (4)	

Indicative bibliography

Indicative bibliographies will be reviewed annually to ensure that up-to-date references are included in course programmes.

Essential reading

Burns, T. and Sinfield, S. (2003) *Essential Study Skills: The complete guide to success @ university*. Sage: London.

Buzan, B. and Buzan, T. (1995) *The Mind Map Book*. London: BBC Publications.

Jeffers, S. (1987) *Feel the Fear and Do It Anyway*. Century.

Recommended reading

Buzan, T. (1989) *Use Your Head*. London: BBC Publications.

Cottrell, S. (2003) *The Study Skills Handbook*. Basingstoke: Palgrave Macmillan.

Northedge, A. (1993) *The Good Study Guide*. Milton Keynes: Open University Press.

Rogers, C. (1996) *Freedom to Learn*. Upper Saddle River, NJ: Merrill.

Sinfield, S. (1999) *The Work Smart Series*. London: Learning Curve Productions (Learning Resource Collection, London Metropolitan University).

Preliminary level module

15 credit points at CATS level 1

> The module will be run as a series of practical workshops where students will be given the opportunity to note, practise and reflect on their own strategies for learning and study.
>
> Emphasis will be placed on personal responsibility and on collaborative work. Aspects of academic discourse will be focused on and their role in the student's subject pathway explored. The module will include an introduction to the library with an emphasis on the use of electronic information systems and the Internet.

General information about the module

Prerequisites: Students should have a commitment to personal development including academic study.

This is a preliminary level module. Preliminary level modules provide a foundation of knowledge and understanding from which you will be able to build, developing links with your practical experience.

Module aims

This module aims to help you to:

■ make connections between experiential knowledge, including work-based and academic knowledge;

■ relate your own learning and work experience to the professional context of your subject pathway;

■ recognise the value of both individual and collaborative learning;

■ develop an appreciation of all aspects of academic discourse, written and oral;

■ become more confident within the academic environment.

Graduate attributes

Insert graduate attributes

Learning outcomes

By the end of the module you should be able to:

- think critically about your own learning and be able to identify strategies to develop and strengthen your approach to study;

- demonstrate a growing knowledge of significant issues relating to your own learning and how they relate to the context of your subject pathway;

- demonstrate an ability to keep to deadlines for independent and collaborative work and to work in cooperation with others;

- present material in both written and oral forms, with a clear sense of audience;

- make use of a range of sources of information, showing awareness of the need for academic reference.

The module programme
Session I

Introduction to module. Introductions exercise. Good and bad learning exercise. Learning Contract. Reflective Learning Log.

Learning outcomes

This session gives a practical demonstration of the importance of the 'overview' to give a 'meaningful context' to student learning. In the course of this session students are encouraged to:

- develop oral communication skills by speaking to others in the group and speaking to the group;

- begin collaborative learning via an exploration of their previous good and bad learning experiences;

- draw on their knowledge of the unit structure and previous learning experiences to devise a personal learning contract;

- begin to develop reflective learning strategies (the reflective learning log).

Suggested reading

Burns, T. and Sinfield, S. (2003) *Essential Study Skills: The complete guide to success @ university*. Sage: London. **Note:** This text will support the whole module.

Students are encouraged to engage regularly with the 'quality' press, e.g. the *Guardian* and *The Times*, and to begin to build up press cuttings and assignment files.

Intersessional task

Complete individual learning contract and personal reflective learning log.

Session 2

Note-making; brainstorm; linear versus non-linear and perfect notes; note-making practice; 'note-making from lectures'; revision of notes; comparison of notes.

Organisation and time management issues will be raised focusing on when, where and how to study.

Learning outcomes

By the end of this session students:

▪ will have engaged in further collaborative learning via class brainstorm on lecture topic and discussion of note-making practice;

▪ considered the active nature of learning, especially with respect to preparation for learning and with note-making and revision strategies;

▪ will have been introduced to organisation and time management concerns.

Suggested reading

Burns, T. and Sinfield, S. (2003) *Essential Study Skills: The complete guide to success @ university*. London: Sage.
Buzan, B. and Buzan, T. (1995) *The Mind Map Book*. London: BBC Publishing.

Intersessional task

Complete detailed reflective learning log for session, preferably utilising smart note strategies.

Session 3

Targeted research and active reading strategies (QOOQRRR) – theory and practice.

Learning outcomes

▪ By the end of this session students will have been introduced to research and reading strategies, theory and practice.

▓ Transferable learning is encouraged as students make links between smart note practice in lectures (Session 2) and in reading.

Suggested reading

Burns, T. and Sinfield, S. (2003) *Essential Study Skills: The complete guide to success @ university*. London: Sage.

Northedge, A. (1993) *The Good Study Guide*. Milton Keynes: Open University Press.

Periodicals (journals) in the Learning Centre that would facilitate subject study.

Intersessional task

Complete detailed reflective learning log on the session identifying aspects of research and reading that will require further attention and strategies to improve research and reading skills.

Session 4

Library visit and induction. Students to make smart notes of the session.

Learning outcomes

By the end of this session students will:

▓ have been introduced to the Learning Centre;

▓ be expected to identify the potential of the Learning Centre to support their studies – this will include noticing the Writing and Communication Workshop facilities and relevant text areas including the Key Text Area and the Study Skills Collection.

Suggested reading

Burns, T. and Sinfield, S. (2003) *Essential Study Skills: The complete guide to success @ university*. London: Sage.

Intersessional task

Complete detailed smart notes and reflective learning log on the session.

Session 5

Presentations: what, why, how. Positive thinking in the academic environment.

Learning outcomes

By the end of this session students will have been introduced to:

■ what: the various features of the academic presentation including the formal convention and aspects of interactive communication including notions of audience;

■ why: the heuristic qualities of the presentation, including the potential of the presentation to bring about active learning in the presenter;

■ how: successful planning, preparation, practice and presentation techniques;

■ the notion that a lack of self-confidence and self-esteem can have a negative effect on the student;

■ successful positive thinking strategies designed to directly address and tackle the fear associated with formal academic study.

Suggested reading

Burns, T. and Sinfield, S. (2003) *Essential Study Skills: The complete guide to success @ university*. London: Sage.

Jeffers, S. (1987) *Feel the Fear and Do It Anyway*. London: Century.

Sinfield, S. (1997) *Smart Presentations* and *Smart Thinking*. London: Learning Curve Productions (Learning Resource Collection – London Metropolitan University Learning Centre).

Intersessional task

Complete detailed reflective learning log on the session. Prepare three-minute presentation on a topic of student's own choice – with AVA.

Session 6

Student presentations with self-evaluation and tutor feedback. Group work discussion.

Learning outcomes

By the end of this session students will have:

■ delivered a personal presentation;

■ viewed and evaluated the presentations of their peers;

■ engaged in self-evaluation with respect to their own presentations;

- considered the benefits of all the above activities;

- engaged with a consideration of the what, why and how of group work.

Suggested reading

Burns, T. and Sinfield, S. (2003) *Essential Study Skills: The complete guide to success @ university*. London: Sage.

Sinfield, S. (1997) *Smart Groups*. London: Learning Curve Productions (Learning Resource Collection – London Metropolitan University Learning Centre).

Intersessional task

Complete a detailed reflective learning log of the session. Update assignment 'envelope' ready for following session on academic writing.

Session 7

Academic writing: why, what (essay and report), how. Essay presentation groups.

Learning outcomes

By the end of this session students will have considered:

- what: aspects of academic writing including the formal conventions of the essay, the report and the paragraph;

- why: the reasons behind the setting of academic writing tasks with a special emphasis on the heuristic (active learning) function of writing;

- how: successful preparation, planning and drafting techniques with a special focus on brainstorming and question matrixing, cross-referenced with the sessions on targeted research, active reading and smart note-making.

Students will also have been organised into study groups and will have:

- engaged in further collaborative learning;

- begun preparation for a group presentation;

- begun preparation for their first written assignment.

Suggested reading

Burns, T. and Sinfield, S. (2003) *Essential Study Skills: The complete guide to success @ university*. London: Sage.

Cottrell, S. (1999) *The Study Skills Handbook*. Basingstoke: Palgrave.

Northedge, A. (1993) *The Good Study Guide*. Milton Keynes: Open University Press.

Intersessional task

Complete a detailed reflective learning log of the session. Engage in tasks pertinent to preparing the group presentation.

Session 8

Memory, learning style, revision and exam techniques. Collaborative work on group presentations.

Learning outcomes

By the end of this session students will have further engaged in collaborative learning and will also have considered:

- differences between short- and long-term memories;

- the active nature of learning;

- the active nature of selecting and remembering relevant information;

- notions of visual, auditory and haptic learning styles.

Suggested reading

Burns, T. and Sinfield, S. (2003) *Essential Study Skills: The complete guide to success @ university*. London: Sage.
Jeffers, S. (1987) *Feel the Fear and Do It Anyway*. London: Century.
Sinfield, S. (1997) *Smart Exams*. London: Learning Curve Productions (Learning Resource Collection – London Metropolitan University Learning Centre).

Intersessional task

Complete detailed reflective learning log of the session. Engage in tasks pertinent to preparing the group presentation.

Session 9

Group presentations and discussion. Writing exercise (time permitting).

Learning outcomes

By the end of this session students will have delivered group presentations and will have acted as critical audience to the presentations of others. This will have developed:

- individual presentation skills;

- group presentation skills;

- an awareness of the value of collaborative learning.

Suggested reading

Burns, T. and Sinfield, S. (2003) *Essential Study Skills: The complete guide to success @ university.* London: Sage.
Buzan, B. and Buzan, T. (1995) *The Mind Map Book.* London: BBC Publications.
Cottrell, S. (1999) *The Study Skills Handbook.* Basingstoke: Palgrave.
Jeffers, S. (1987) *Feel the Fear and Do It Anyway.* London: Century.
Northedge, A. (1993) *The Good Study Guide.* Milton Keynes: Open University Press.
Sinfield, S. (1997) *The Work Smart Series.* London: Learning Curve Productions (Learning Resource Collection – London Metropolitan University Learning Centre).

Intersessional task

Complete detailed reflective learning log of the session. Engage in tasks pertinent to preparing individual assignment – with a special emphasis on having an essay plan and a sample paragraph prepared for an individual tutorial.

Session 10

'Bringing it all together' – lecture on the 'six steps to success' that revisits the whole programme from another perspective. Guidance on self-evaluation for assessment portfolio. Course evaluation. Individual tutorials.

Learning outcomes

By the end of this session students will have:

- engaged in an academic exercise that revisits the course content from an alternative perspective (this is an important learning exercise for it is a form of revision. It is also an important study skills exercise for it also demonstrates how material delivered or encountered in one way, can be creatively re-presented);

- prepared for their assessment activities in terms of engaging with notes towards self-assessment and an individual tutorial;

- engaged in course evaluation, contributing to ongoing course development.

Suggested reading

Burns, T. and Sinfield, S. (2003) *Essential Study Skills: The complete guide to success @ university*. London: Sage.

Sinfield, S. (1997) *Six Smart Steps to Success*. London: Learning Curve Productions (Learning Resource Collection – London Metropolitan University Learning Centre).

End of module assessment

You will be asked to put together a **portfolio** containing **two assessment tasks**.

The first will be **coursework**, including learning contract, reflective learning logs, notes (at least one set of notes from a written source and one set of notes from a spoken source), presentation plan, essay plan and self-assessment of learning.

The second will be a **reflective essay** or **report** identifying the learning achieved from this module (see **EA199 Writing tasks** below).

You must pass each task in order to pass the module. The coursework and writing task (essay or report) will each carry 50% of your final grade.

In addition to the guidance given in the student handbook about the way in which assignments are marked, the criteria detailed below will be applied to your work.

Assessment criteria

The **coursework** will be marked on the extent to which it:

- shows that you are thinking critically about your own learning and are able to identify strategies to develop and strengthen your approach;

- demonstrates your growing knowledge of significant issues relating to your own learning and study skills, techniques and strategies;

- draws on practical experience and the reflective process you have been applying to your own learning.

The **essay or report** should have between 1,500 and 2,000 words and will be marked on the extent to which it:

- demonstrates your growing knowledge of significant issues relating to your own learning and study skills, techniques and strategies;

- shows that you are developing a sense of academic discourse in your writing, with a sense of audience;

■ makes use of information from a variety of sources, showing awareness of the need for academic reference;

■ demonstrates that you are developing a capacity to study independently.

EA199 Writing tasks

The object of any assessment assignment is to get the student thinking about and using that which they have learned over their course of study. This assessment is no different. There are two assignment options detailed below, an essay and a report; you only have to do **one**.

Essay option

Utilising the essay convention answer **one** of the following:

1 Describe and discuss one or more of your learning experiences on the Study Skills module that you think will be of value to you as a student of _____

2 'In the end all learning is active learning.' Discuss with particular reference to the Study Skills module.

3 'Being a successful student depends as much on dealing with our feelings as on developing good study techniques.' Discuss.

4 How has the Study Skills module prepared you for 'lifelong learning' (Dearing Report, 1997)?

OR

Report option

Utilising the report convention devise a formal report on one element of your own learning/studying/communicating practice. Analyse your proficiency and make recommendations as to your continued development (for example a formal report evaluating your academic writing strategies or your memory techniques).

Indicative bibliography

Indicative bibliographies will be reviewed annually to ensure that up-to-date references are included in course programmes.

Essential reading

Burns, T. and Sinfield, S. (2003) *Essential Study Skills: The complete guide to success @ university*. London: Sage.
Buzan, B. and Buzan, T. (1995) *The Mind Map Book*. London: BBC Publications.
Jeffers, S. (1987) *Feel the Fear and Do It Anyway*. London: Century.

Recommended reading

Buzan, T. (1989) *Use Your Head*. London: BBC Publications.

Cottrell, S. (1999) *The Study Skills Handbook*. Basingstoke: Palgrave.

Northedge, A. (1993) *The Good Study Guide*. Milton Keynes: Open University Press.

Rogers, C. (1996) *Freedom to Learn*. Upper Saddle River, NJ: Merrill.

Sinfield, S. (1997) *The Work Smart Series*. London: Learning Curve Productions (Learning Resource Collection – London Metropolitan University Learning Centre).

Resources

Resource 5.1   OK, I've been accepted – what do I do now?

Summer reading

You have just finished your A levels, you feel that you have worked really hard and you deserve a break! OK – but you have a long summer vacation with plenty of time to undertake some reading before you actually start at university. If you do actively prepare for university it will help you feel in control and you can hit the ground running when you start. Things to read include:

Study skills books

Burns, T. and Sinfield, S. (2003) *Essential Study Skills: The complete guide to success @ university.* London: Sage.
Cottrell, S. (1999) *The Study Skills Handbook.* Basingstoke: Palgrave.
Northedge, A. (1991) *The Good Study Guide.* Milton Keynes: Open University Press.

Other books

Sometimes universities send out pre-course **reading lists**. It can be useful to dip into these – especially if you already feel competent and able to read at the level required. However, if you are feeling a little bit swamped it may be useful to dip into simpler pre-degree texts just to get a flavour of what you will be doing later on.

● **Tips: For many subjects the 'Beginners Guide . . .' series by Writers and Readers Press are great. Have a look at:**

DNA for beginners
Freud for beginners
Philosophy for beginners

Find the Beginners Guide that will help you with your university subject.

Summer programmes

Many universities offer summer programmes in topics like study and academic skills, maths and information technology. It is a good idea to undertake some of these courses – not only to help you really understand what studying at university will entail, but – and perhaps even more importantly – they will get you through the door – you can meet other students, visit the library, find out where learning development support/study skills help are situated. All this means that when you arrive to enrol at your university the place will hold no – or very little – fear for you.

▶

Resource 5.1   OK, I've been accepted – what do I do now? *(continued)*

Induction and enrolment

Most universities offer some form of induction programme alongside their enrolment procedures.

● **Tip:** Enrolment and induction, while necessary and useful, are also usually extremely time consuming – and will include much potentially frustrating time spent in queues. Take a good book with you and keep smiling!

Enrolment is where you actually register to become a student. Typically you will receive a Joining Pack containing information on what to prepare, what to bring (photographs, etc.), where to go and when.

● **Tip:** Read this carefully – follow instructions!

Induction may happen alongside enrolment or at another time. Induction usually involves a series of activities designed to introduce you to the workings of your particular institution, sometimes with a departmental party included in the package. Induction activities might include introductory sessions with **librarians, IT staff, learning development and student support services**. While these sessions may not always appear the most exciting or stimulating, they do allow you to see the real people you will have to deal with throughout your time at a university.

● **Tip:** Go, be positive, and note the names of the staff who appear friendly and approachable – you may need these people later!

Resource 5.2   Places to go, people to meet and things to do at university

Your first weeks at university may be busy, challenging and even frightening. Here is some advice on places and people that could become very important parts of your time as a student and who could play key roles in your success. Read through this list and note the important information – then act upon it!

■ **Subject librarians:** Subject librarians are not just there to point you at the right book – though they do this as well. These are people who are subject experts in their own right. They can point you towards the books, the journals and the online resources – including websites and online journals – that can help you study.

● **Tip: When asking for help be polite, know what you want, listen.**

■ **IT staff:** Many universities have a range of IT support systems for their students. These may vary from quite basic support in terms of computer access that allows you to word process your assignments to a website presence for each module that you undertake. You will need to know how to set up your IT access and accounts.

● **Tip: When meeting IT support staff have a list of questions that you need answered – How do I get my account? What journal accounts will I need? Can I access resources from home? Make notes of the answers.**

■ **Learning Development and Support** (also known as Study Skills, Study and Academic Support, etc)**:** Typically universities have some sort of service these days that is dedicated to helping students achieve to their potential. There may be courses or units on note-making, essay writing, preparing presentations and passing exams – all these can be very helpful indeed. Further, there may be drop-in workshop support wherein you can get help with individual assignments.

● **Tip: Unhappy with that D, C or B grade? Go to Learning Development – find out what it would take to get the grade that you want!**

■ **Student Support Services (SSS):** This can often break down into a range of smaller units:
　– **Accommodation:** Most universities have accommodation offices that you would approach if you wished to find a place in student accommodation or in local 'digs'.
　– **Careers:** You might think that the careers service is something that you might search out two weeks before you leave the university to get that glorious well-paid job! Not so. The best way to get the most from the careers service is to go and have a look at what it offers in your first few

Resource 5.2   Places to go, people to meet and things to do at university (*continued*)

weeks at university. Often there will be information available on different career opportunities, including jobs that you have never heard or thought of. Once you know what is available you can ask for advice as to what modules, options or whole courses and work placement or voluntary work will help you achieve your goals.

● **Tip:** Leaving this visit until your third or fourth year is a wasted opportunity.

– **Work placement:** As with careers, the work placement (WP) service offers an opportunity to increase your employment prospects while still a student. Typically, WP staff will find you a work opportunity in an area related to that in which you will eventually work. Sometimes your university will offer you the chance of getting module accreditation for this work placement – that is, it will actually count as part of your degree.

● **Tip:** WP allows you to see if you really do want to work in a specific field – but more than that, many students find that they can make a good impression on their placement such that they have a job waiting for them when they finish their degrees.

– **Student development or voluntary work:** Many universities offer alternatives to WP in the form of voluntary work. This can take many forms from peer mentoring (assisting students with their work) or mentoring of school children to much more. Again, these are good opportunities to try out career choices in advance – and to make a good impression on prospective employers.

● **Tip:** All forms of placement – voluntary or paid – offer excellent curriculum vitae (CV) building opportunities. Your CV is your statement of education and employment experience that you may send to prospective employers in order to apply for posts. The better your CV, the more likely you are to get a job interview.

– **Programme planning:** While not typically a part of SSS, programme planners are there to help students in a semester-based university choose the modules that they will take as they work through their degree programmes.

● **Tip:** Once you have visited careers, you might like to go to programme planning to see how to tailor your degree to your future career.

▶

Resource 5.2 Places to go, people to meet and things to do at university *(continued)*

- – **Counselling:** Life – and student life especially – can at times be very stressful. Most universities offer confidential counselling services to students to help them with particular problems when they arise. Find out what is on offer at your university – even if you never intend to use it.

● **Tip:** Feeling homesick? Don't just sit there, speak to someone – and counselling might be a good place to start.

■ **Dyslexia and disability:** Some students arrive at university already knowing that they are dyslexic (dyslexia is a term that covers several forms of problems with words) or with a diagnosed disability and thus they just need to connect with the **dyslexia and disability service** to see what specific help is available to them in their institution.

● **Tip:** If you think you are dyslexic, or if you become disabled while at university, you will need to go to the dyslexia and disability service to find out what steps you will need to take to get support.

■ **Chaplaincy:** Many universities offer spiritual support either in terms of generic chaplaincy support that is open to people of all faiths or in faith-specific modes. If religious support is important to you, make sure that you discover what is on offer at your university.

■ **Student union:** Your student union is there to offer a range of activities and services to students. Not only will they be able to advise you if you are having problems with the university, they will run clubs and societies for your benefit.

● **Tip:** You may feel that you have too many commitments and no time for any form of social life – but clubs and societies are great way to meet other students – and enjoy yourself more as a student. Also, more worldly-wise students tend to join the society that is most closely linked with a future career choice: the television society if they intended to go into the media, the union newspaper if thinking about journalism and so forth. Do this, too!

● **Big tip:** Do something with this information! It is not enough for you as a student to just go and look at these places or people. **Think:** how will knowing this help me as a student? What should I do next? When will I do it? And then **act**!

Resource 5.3   For study success think SOCCER

Learning how to study and learn effectively can make all the difference to your time as a student. Here are some quick tips on study success. Read them and think – How will knowing this help me as a student? What will I have to do about the things that are suggested here? When will I do these things?

▪ **S** = **Study techniques.** You are not born knowing how to study and learn, but you can develop these abilities.

● **Tips:** Find information on note-making, research and reading, revision and exam techniques and organisation and time management. Practice what you learn – make a commitment to get better at these study and academic skills and practices.

▪ **O** = **Overview.** Studying can be like a big jigsaw puzzle – and like a jigsaw it is easier to put the puzzle together if you have the 'big picture' on the box to guide you. Find out how your university works – from the organisation of its support systems to how your particular degree programme is put together. Find out how your degree prepares you for work, and discover what other things you can do at university to make that job opportunity happen for you. **Also** – degrees are made up of particular units, modules or courses, so get the overview of each particular unit, module or course that you take.

Typically course tutors put together some form of course booklet that will help you here. Things to read and understand are the **aims** and **learning outcomes** of the programme. The **aims** tell you what the course is intending to do or offer – it is a snapshot of the course as a whole. The **learning outcomes** spell out exactly what the student has to do and learn to pass the course. This is important information that will help your understanding of the course and help shape your choices of what to read and why. Finally, this information will really help you to understand the sorts of things that you should be addressing in any assignment that you undertake for the course.

▪ **C** = **Creativity.** While you may have chosen to study something from a pure love of the subject or from a really practical intention of getting a good job, it is never enough just to plod through the course as the tutor lays it out for you. Just parroting back to the tutor what the tutor has handed out will only ever get students an average grade. If you want more than that for yourself as a student you will need to think 'outside the box', you will need to inject some creativity into your study techniques and approaches – and into your reading.

● **Tips:** Find out about pattern note-making or mind mapping and find out about brainstorming – these will inject a little creativity into your learning and studying and will help you perform better – and enjoy yourself more.

▶

Resource 5.3 For study success think SOCCER *(continued)*

■ **C = Communicate effectively and in the correct form or convention.** University lecturers often have very specific things in mind when they ask for an essay, report or academic paper, similarly when they ask you to give a presentation or a seminar. Take the time to find out exactly what they are talking about and what the final product should look like.

● **Tip:** Go and see the learning development/study skills people at your university. Find out what is meant by essay, report, paper, presentation and seminar.

■ **E = Emotions matter too.** All students will be affected by their emotions – positive or negative. It is really useful to acknowledge this as early as possible and take steps to do something about how you feel about yourself as a student – and about your studies. Typically you will like some subjects better than others, you will like some tutors more, some less – you will also find that certain study techniques or assessment procedures come easier to you than others. Moreover, many students find themselves fearful at university – frightened of making mistakes, of 'being found out' as not being good enough, of looking, sounding or feeling foolish. While all these things are perfectly natural emotions they can sometimes hinder your performance as a student. It does not help if you are frightened all the time – and you can't learn if you daren't make a mistake.

● **Tips:** Find a positive thinking book – like Susan Jeffers' *Feel the Fear and Do It Anyway* – and practice positive thinking. Make some positive friends. Get an optimistic and enthusiastic study partner . . . all these things will make a difference.

■ **R = Review, review, review.** Without review there is no learning. Sometimes we enter university knowing very little about how our memories work or how to actually learn all the material that we will have to. Perhaps we just hope that the things that we will need to learn will just seep or percolate into our brains. However, studying – and especially learning – is much more active than that. Typically you will need to make conscious decisions about what to learn and how to learn it, and you will have to build active revision systems into your study and learning programmes if you want to succeed.

● **Tips:** Make sure you have that overview (aims and learning outcomes) and find out about revision and exam techniques now, not just before your exams!

For detailed information on these topics you could look at Burns, T. and Sinfield, S. (2003) *Essential Study Skills: The complete guide to success @ university.* London: Sage.

Resource 5.4 Teaching and learning in university demystified

University can be very different from sixth form or FE college: suddenly you are expected to participate in lectures, seminars and tutorials, you may be given an academic or a personal tutor, you will be expected to undertake independent research and to 'read around the subject' – all these things may be new to you or at least different from what you have been used to. Here is a quick guide to studying at university.

The university as a whole: Developed from the Platonic notion of the Academy, universities are designed to foster logical thought in a reasoned environment. The capacity for rational and reasonable thought is developed via the process of student research (study) under tutor supervision. The teaching/learning process at university is designed to be a dialectical engagement between tutor and student that involves talking, listening and thinking.

Subjects/disciplines: Plato's pupil Aristotle was the first to divide knowledge into specific forms that, he argued, had distinct characteristics. Aristotle's forms ranged from logic to poetics, but at that time history did not count as a serious subject, just as some people argue over the value of leisure and tourism now. Perhaps the thing to realise here is that what counts as knowledge – and the way that we know – is not natural or inevitable but created, decided upon. What counts as knowledge or knowing in a particular subject is called its **epistemology**. It is important for you as a student to get to grips with the epistemology of your subject: with history, say, as a subject you would need to understand the nature of thought and enquiry as it relates to history and that this might involve different forms of argument and evidence to biology or physics.

HE orientation: Many universities now have HE Orientation programmes, courses or modules that are designed to introduce students to the forms, practices and processes of the institution as a whole and to the specific practices of particular subjects. It is here that students could be introduced to the teaching and learning practices of HE – and also perhaps to the thinkers and writers not only of their subject but in their society as a whole. The trick for students is to make the most of these programmes – this is the time to find out the what, why and how of your subject, and what it means to be a student of that subject.

The lecture: Many university programmes still contain quite a high proportion of lectures. A lecture is where there is one lecturer speaking to a large group of students – 150 or even more. Sometimes there will be more people in your

Resource 5.4   Teaching and learning in university demystified
(continued)

lecture than there were in your whole school or year. The lecturer is the subject expert, often a researcher in that area, and gives the student a shortcut to a large amount of information; if you are sensible you will make notes of that useful information during the lecture. However, no one lecture – or book or journal article – is designed to give you 'all you need to know' on the subject. Lectures are designed to introduce you to key ideas and people, and you are supposed to note what these are to seed your own research.

● **Tips: Note names mentioned by the lecturer – look these people up in the library after the lecture. Notice how the lecturer uses the language of your subject – use this as a model for your own use of that language. Always prepare before a lecture – and reflect on a lecture afterwards.**

The seminar: The tutor-led seminar usually consists of one tutor plus 10 to 30 students. The name comes from semen or seed and, as with the lecture, the idea is that the seminar seeds student thinking and research. Typically the seminar is where you can discuss key themes from the lecture programme, for if you can discuss what you are learning it becomes easier to write about it. Sometimes you will be expected to prepare for seminars in certain ways – undertake a piece of reading or prepare a small piece of writing – or you will be expected to research a topic and lead a seminar yourself.

● **Tip: Be active: prepare what you have to prepare, engage in the discussion and try to get the most from your seminars.**

The tutorial: The tutorial typically consists of one tutor plus two to five students. It offers the opportunity for quite intense interactions between staff and students (the Platonic model), and while it is becoming less common now it is being revived in an HE orientation role – that is, it can be a small intense space that offers the student the opportunity to get to grips with the content of their subject – and the study and academic skills necessary for engaging with that subject. If this is the case, it is often called an **academic tutorial**.

● **Tip: With so few students in a tutorial there is no hiding place! Prepare for tutorials and always participate in them.**

The academic tutor: This will be a tutor who is expected to get to know you – and your strengths and weaknesses – as a student. This person may be with you throughout your time at university, being the one who writes you a job reference, perhaps, or the one to intercede for you if you are having academic problems.

▶

Resource 5.4   Teaching and learning in university demystified
(continued)

Personal tutor: The personal tutor system runs in some universities instead of the academic tutorial system. Here the personal tutor also has the task of keeping an eye on you as a student, and may still be someone to intercede on your behalf or write references for you, but typically the personal tutor is seen as having a pastoral rather than an academic engagement with you. That is, they are supposed to be more directly concerned with your personal, human needs as opposed to your academic ones.

● **Tips:** Whether you have a personal tutor or an academic tutor, get to know that person. Introduce yourself before you have any problems – and if you do then have a problem it will be that much easier to see them again. If you cannot get on with your tutor, find out how to change tutors without upsetting anyone!

Independent study: Independent study incorporates your research and the way that you organise and manage your way through the planning and preparation of your assignments – independent study **is** being a university student. This can be very different from sixth form or FE college where your tutors tend to guide you through your programmes of study, telling you what to read and what to write – and when. In HE this becomes your responsibility and you have to decide how much effort you will put into being a student.

To aid independent study:

■ **Know your library:** Find out where your books and journals are – dip into them every week.

● **Tip:** Pick out the key words from an assignment question. Do a 'key word' search in the electronic catalogue in your library. See which books are flagged up as useful – scan them and see how they will help you answer your assignment question.

■ **Key text area or counter loans:** Crucial texts for every subject may be kept in a special area of the library (key text area) or be available over the counter (counter loans). Find out what system operates at your university, then make a habit of seeing what texts are there and use them.

■ **The books:** Yes, there are too many books to read! But you must start to dip into the key texts in your subject. Armed with the key words from an assignment question, select from the reading list and look up your key words in the index of several different books. Get used to seeing what different writers have to say on the same subject.

Resource 5.4   Teaching and learning in university demystified
(continued)

■ **Journals/periodicals:** While books are a vital part of your studies, in order to keep your work up to date you will also have to read up on your topics in the research journals or periodicals for your subject.

● **Tips:** Ask your subject librarian where your journals are, see if they are available online, see if you can access them from home.

■ **Quality press:** Many subjects that we study – education, the media, business, technology – are also written up regularly in the quality press – *The Times*, *Independent* and *Guardian*. Make a habit of reading the quality press every week.

● **Tip:** Keep a press cuttings file – put sourced cuttings (with date and newspaper title) in your file. Dip into your file when you are putting assignments together.

■ **Electronic information systems:** Not only can you access journals and the quality press on-line, you will be able to access many useful websites to support your research. Ask your subject librarian which are the useful sites for your subject.

Resource 7.1 Blank 24/7 timetable

Time	MONDAY	TUESDAY	WEDNESDAY	THURSDAY	FRIDAY	SATURDAY	SUNDAY
1.00							
2.00							
3.00							
4.00							
5.00							
6.00							
7.00							
8.00							
9.00							
10.00							
11.00							
12.00							
13.00							
14.00							
15.00							
16.00							
17.00							
18.00							
19.00							
20.00							
21.00							
22.00							
23.00							
24.00							

Taken from Tom Burns and Sandra Sinfield (2003) *Essential Study Skills: The complete guide to success @ university*. London: Sage.

Resource 7.2   Events and deadlines timetable

EVENTS AND DEADLINES				
Write down the dates of the following events each term:				
	Course 1	Course 2	Course 3	Course 4
Course title:				
Exam(s)				
Essay deadline(s)				
Laboratory report deadline(s)				
Seminar presentations				
Field trips/visits				
Project report or exhibition deadlines				
Bank holidays or other 'days off'				
Other events (specify)				

Taken from Tom Burns and Sandra Sinfield (2003) *Essential Study Skills: The complete guide to success @ university.* London: Sage.

Resource 7.3   Term/semester plan

Term Plan – what is happening over your term/semester?							
	Mon	Tue	Wed	Thurs	Fri	Sat	Sun
Week 1							
Week 2							
Week 3							
Week 4							
Week 5							
Week 6							
Week 7							
Week 8							
Week 9							
Week 10							
Week 11							
Week 12							
Longer term deadlines:							

Taken from Tom Burns and Sandra Sinfield (2003) *Essential Study Skills: The complete guide to success @ university.* London: Sage.

Resource 7.4   **Weekly timetable**

Keep a WEEKLY PLAN – key events and activities each week							
Week Number:	Mon	Tue	Wed	Thurs	Fri	Sat	Sun
8am							
9am							
10am							
11am							
12noon							
1pm							
2pm							
3pm							
4pm							
5pm							
6pm							
7pm							
8pm							
9pm							
10pm							
11pm							
12midnight							
1am							

Taken from Tom Burns and Sandra Sinfield (2003) *Essential Study Skills: The complete guide to success @ university*. London: Sage.

Resource 8.1 Library worksheet

Introduction to the library
Find your college library. If you find it an intimidating place hopefully this worksheet will take you through the library in a useful way so that you start using as much of the library as possible, as soon as possible – and it will not be intimidating any more.

For each activity, tick the box when you have completed it, and write in details where indicated.

Books Find the part of the library that houses the books for your subject.

▨ My books are _____

▨ Write in the Dewey decimal number (the numbers on the spine of the book) for your subject _____

Journals

▨ When studying it is important to read the relevant journals for your subject. Where are your journals kept? _____

▨ Write in the title of two journals that you could be reading:
Journal one _____
Journal two _____

Newspapers

▨ With most subjects it is also important to read the 'quality' press. Where are the newspapers kept? _____

Key text area (counter loans)

▨ The key text area holds the most important texts for each subject – find it. My key text area is _____

Study areas What facilities are there for independent study in your library?

▨ My library offers quiet study areas? _____

▨ My library offers group study areas? _____

Workshops Some libraries contain student help workshops – does yours?

▨ My library does/does not have workshops.

▨ They are located _____

▨ Opening times are _____

Resource 8.1   Library worksheet *(continued)*

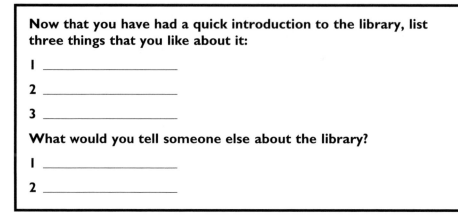

Now that you have had a quick introduction to the library, list three things that you like about it:

1 _____

2 _____

3 _____

What would you tell someone else about the library?

1 _____

2 _____

Taken from Tom Burns and Sandra Sinfield (2003) *Essential Study Skills: The complete guide to success @ university.* London: Sage.

Resource 8.2   Overview: choose what to read – know what you are reading

---

Sources of information

Before you read you need to choose what to read very carefully. Overviewing the following sources of information will help you get to the information that you want – quickly.

- **Books:** Find some of the books on the reading list and have a look at them – do they seem easy or difficult to read? How do you know? Will you read on your own or with a study partner? When will you do this reading?

- **Contents pages:** Look for a word from the assignment question in the Contents pages – have a look at those bits of the book. Choose small sections of the book to read. Decide when you will do the reading.

- **Indexes:** Look for the word in the index at the back of the book. If it is mentioned, note the page numbers that are given. Go to these pages first. Once you have read these pages, decide whether or not you will read any more of that book.

- **Wider searches:** Go to the electronic catalogue in your library, use the key word, author or subject search facilities and see what books come up. Find some of them and then repeat the Contents/Index strategy with them.

- **Using people:** Ask your tutor, other students or the subject librarian for assistance. Any of these might be able to narrow your search for you.

- **The Internet:** As well as helping with the key word searches, your subject librarian can help you find the most useful Internet sites for your subject. The Internet is vast and not all of the search engines are useful to you. The trick is to find the search engines that take you to useful sites. Your librarian will know this.

- **Use the journals:** Ask your subject librarian to point you towards the most useful journals on your subject. Books are good, but, typically, once you progress from gaining a basic understanding of a subject to extending your knowledge of that subject, journals come into their own. Journals publish the most recent research; thus they will keep your research fresh and interesting. Typically universities will have actual journals and access to journals online. Find out – have a look – always use journals as a starting point for research.

Resource 8.2   Overview: choose what to read – know what you are reading *(continued)*

Knowing what you are reading – chapters and paragraphs

All the above overview activities lead you **to** information. Once you have chosen something that you are going to read, you must know what it is about before you start to read it, and you must decide how much of it you are actually going to read.

So, once you have a chapter of a book or a journal article in your hand, get the overview of that as well:

■ Read the **introduction** (first paragraph) and **conclusion** (last paragraph): these tell you what the piece is about.

■ Once you know that, you can decide whether or not you really do want to read it – and you can more clearly define why you are reading the bits that you will read.

■ Read the first sentence of every **paragraph**. First sentences tell you what the paragraph is about.

■ See which paragraphs are on your topic. Decide which ones you will read in depth.

■ **Now** you should have a skeleton understanding of the whole chapter/article and you have started to plot your course through the article/chapter. You are being an active learner.

Taken from Tom Burns and Sandra Sinfield (2003) *Essential Study Skills: The complete guide to success @ university.* London: Sage.

Resource 8.3   How to move to pattern notes from your reading

When making notes from reading consider taking notes in stages:
1. Underline key words in text
2. Summarise key points in sentences (first column)
3. Reduce sentences to key words (second column)
4. Construct pattern notes with the key words

Reduce to key words →

Use the words to construct a pattern →

SUMMARY	KEY WORD
Older people are an increasing proportion of our population, yet their presence is not equally reflected in adult education programmes. Participating in learning opportunities offers many benefits to older people. However, they often feel excluded because of their age and life circumstances.	Older people ← Educational opportunities →
Islington Age Concern set up the Older Learners' Project to address these issues. Over the last year the group has been meeting weekly to look at the learning needs and ambitions of people over 55 years of age. It particularly wants to involve people who were not able to take up the learning they wanted when they were younger, or who feel they have not been able to make much use of their knowledge and skills.	55 knowledge and personal skills
On the day, there were information stands providing up-to-date information on learning opportunities locally and nationally, which gave people the opportunity to speak to specialists, find out about training and, most importantly, develop confidence in trying new things. The event also included a number of workshops on study skills, creative writing, access to funding and older people as tutors.	Opportunities New things Confidence

Sum up in sentences or phrases

Taken from Tom Burns and Sandra Sinfield (2003) *Essential Study Skills: The complete guide to success @ university.* London: Sage.

Resource 8.4 Student notes on QOOQRRR: targeted research and active reading

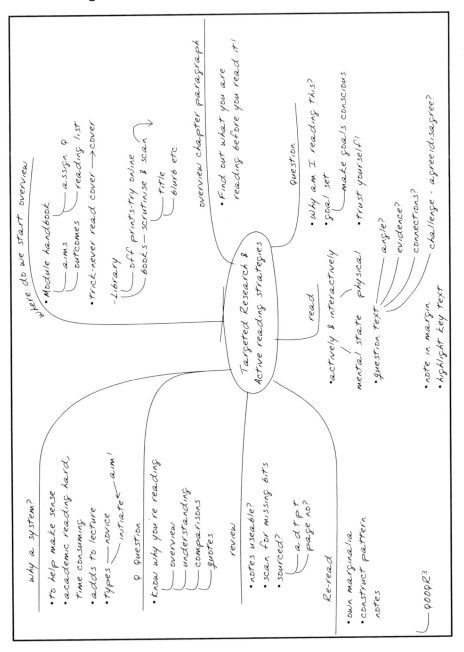

Taken from Tom Burns and Sandra Sinfield (2003) *Essential Study Skills: The complete guide to success @ university*. London: Sage.

Resource 8.5 Student notes on Tony Buzan: QOOQRRR theory into practice

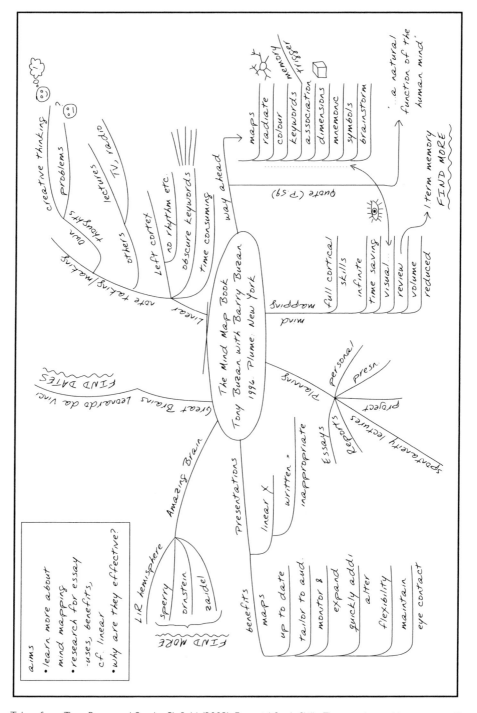

Taken from Tom Burns and Sandra Sinfield (2003) *Essential Study Skills: The complete guide to success @ university*. London: Sage.

Resource 9.1 Beginner's guide to pattern notes

You can make key word notes from lectures and from your reading. There are several stages that you can go through – the trick is to remember that you can draft and re-draft notes. You do not need to get them right first go!

1 Get an overview of the lecture or chapter before you start. With books, you know to read the beginning and end of chapters. With lectures, you should get the sense of what the lecture is to be about from your syllabus or scheme of work.

2 Once you know what the lecture or text is about, brainstorm – identify what you know on the topic and what you need to find out.

3 Then goal set – that is, work out the sort of information that you want to take away (an overview, key points, key names and dates, key quotes . . .). Remember to look at your assignment question to help you here.

4 With your goals in mind, engage with the lecture or the text in an active way – searching for and identifying key words, points, etc.

5 Put the key points down in a 'rough' way first. With a book, we have suggested that you make notes on the text itself. With the lecture, you might put the title in the centre of a piece of paper and draw points away from the title. If things connect directly to the central topic, branch them off. If they connect with each other, draw them off from the sub-branches.

6 Review your rough notes – make up your mind just what you need to keep and what you do not need. Think about how to connect ideas with each other.

7 Construct your own key word pattern – adding colour, pictures and diagrams to illustrate points and to act as memory triggers.

● **Tips: The Von Rostorff effect – our minds are playful by nature and the triggers that work best with our minds are funny, dramatic, obscene or colourful (in Palmer and Pope, 1984).**

Resource 9.1   Beginner's guide to pattern notes (continued)

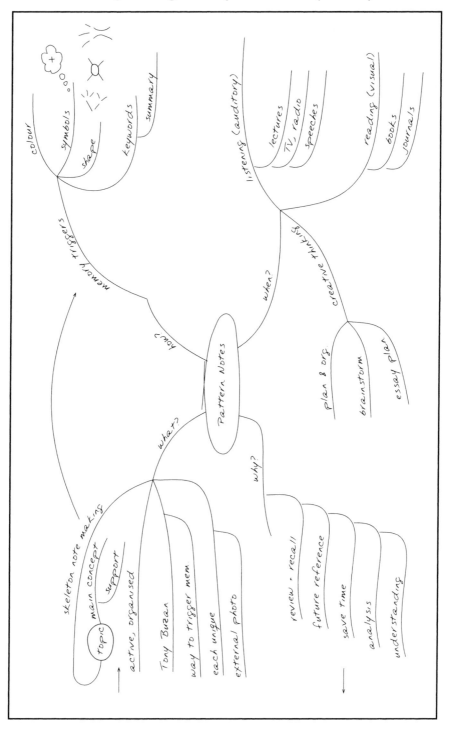

Taken from Tom Burns and Sandra Sinfield (2003) *Essential Study Skills: The complete guide to success @ university.* London: Sage.

Resource 9.2 Student notes on the lecture 'Note-making from lectures'

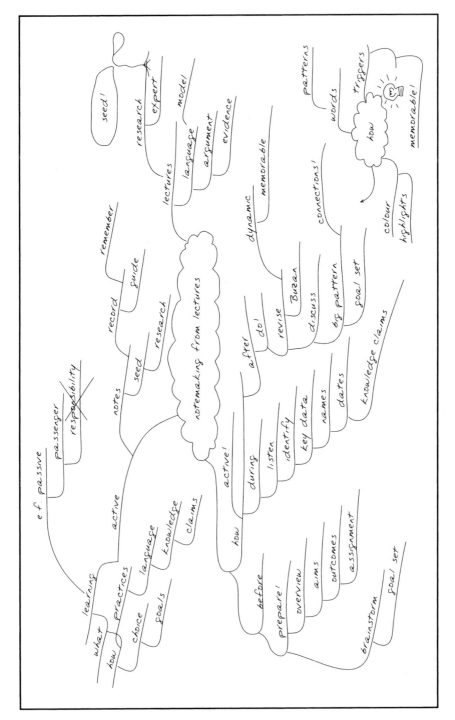

Taken from Tom Burns and Sandra Sinfield (2003) *Essential Study Skills: The complete guide to success @ university.* London: Sage.

Resource 10.1 The structure of an academic presentation

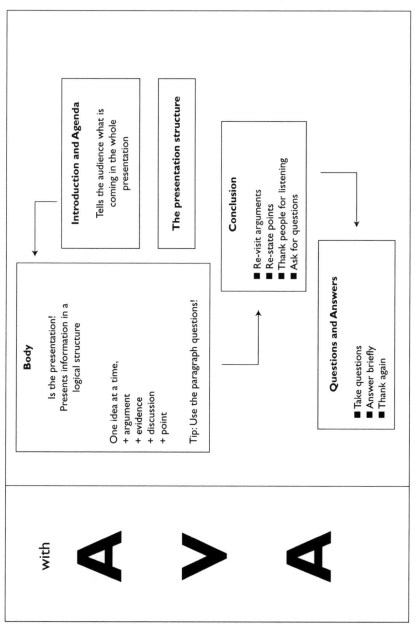

Adapted from Tom Burns and Sandra Sinfield (2003) *Essential Study Skills: The complete guide to success @ university.* London: Sage.

Resource 10.2   Using the paragraph questions for presentations

When giving a presentation we are addressing an audience of real people. As you prepare your presentation, imagine your audience asking you questions – your presentation should answer such questions.

Think about the following questions for **each separate section** of your presentation body.

What is this section about?

■ This prompts you to **introduce** a separate point/section of the presentation.

What exactly is that?

■ This invites you to define, explain or clarify a point in the way that would be useful to your audience.

Tell me more.

■ This invites you to say something interesting about the topic (in relation to the question set). Typically it is where you offer an argument of some kind.

What is your evidence?

■ This invites you to offer supporting evidence for the argument you have made. This can be in the form of referring to or quoting from relevant experts; it can mean giving a practical example from life or a case study that you have covered.

What does your evidence mean?

■ This invites you to explain or discuss your evidence in some way. Remember, it is not enough just to cite evidence – you need to use it.

How does this all relate to your topic?

■ This invites you to explain the significance of the point you have raised, the argument you have made and the evidence you have discussed in relation to the overall question you are answering.

Resource 10.3 Assessment pro forma: the presentation

Tutor:

Student:

Title:

Date:

Tick as appropriate:

- ☐   Student introduced self and topic
- ☐   Presentation had a clear and relevant introduction – with a 'hook'
- ☐   Presentation had a useful agenda
- ☐   Presentation had a clear structure
- ☐   Arguments were offered logically
- ☐   Each argument was supported by relevant evidence
- ☐   Evidence was sourced
- ☐   Evidence was discussed
- ☐   Appropriate AVA were used – sensitively
- ☐   A conclusion was offered
- ☐   Main arguments and points were restated
- ☐   The whole topic was covered/question answered

Other:

- ☐   The student built a rapport with the audience
- ☐   Eye contact was developed and maintained
- ☐   Positive body language was utilised
- ☐   The student used prompts and did not speak from a script

Overall comments:

Grade:

Resource 11.1   The structure of an academic essay

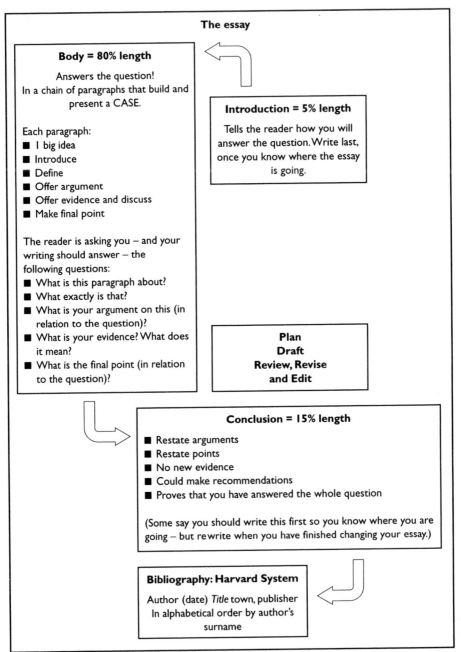

The essay

Body = 80% length

Answers the question!
In a chain of paragraphs that build and present a CASE.

Each paragraph:
■ 1 big idea
■ Introduce
■ Define
■ Offer argument
■ Offer evidence and discuss
■ Make final point

The reader is asking you – and your writing should answer – the following questions:
■ What is this paragraph about?
■ What exactly is that?
■ What is your argument on this (in relation to the question)?
■ What is your evidence? What does it mean?
■ What is the final point (in relation to the question)?

Introduction = 5% length

Tells the reader how you will answer the question. Write last, once you know where the essay is going.

Plan
Draft
Review, Revise
and Edit

Conclusion = 15% length

■ Restate arguments
■ Restate points
■ No new evidence
■ Could make recommendations
■ Proves that you have answered the whole question

(Some say you should write this first so you know where you are going – but rewrite when you have finished changing your essay.)

Bibliography: Harvard System

Author (date) *Title* town, publisher
In alphabetical order by author's surname

Taken from Tom Burns and Sandra Sinfield (2003) *Essential Study Skills: The complete guide to success @ university*. London: Sage.

Resource 11.2   Ten steps to assignment success

1 Preparation: open a research folder on the assignment.
   - Write out the question in full (photocopy and stick on if too long to copy).
   - Analyse the task in terms of form and content. Use the correct form (essay, presentation, report, etc.) and analyse the specific question. Underline key words in the question – think about all of them.
   - Make links with module aims and learning outcomes.
   - Make links with the syllabus.
   - Make links with the reading list.
   - Brainstorm all the key words in the question: let uncensored thoughts come to you to inject creativity in your work.
   - Action plan – think: 'What will I do, and when, in order to get an answer together?'

2 Follow the action plan – attend relevant lectures and seminars in a positive frame of mind; undertake targeted research and active reading; make key word pattern notes.

3 Review findings. What has been discovered? What does it mean? What gaps are there in the research? How and when will you plug the gaps?

4 Plan the outline of the essay, report, presentation . . . other.

5 Prepare a first draft.

6 Leave a creative time lag.

7 Review, revise and edit – this is the struggle to write, and it happens over time. Eventually settle on a final draft.

8 Proofread (rehearse if an oral event).

9 Hand work in on or before the deadline.

10 Review:
   - Before handing in work, judge it – what grade will it get and why?
   - When you get work back, compare your estimate with the actual grade. Are there discrepancies? What could that mean? What will you do next?
   - Review the returned essay and acknowledge its strengths and weaknesses.
   - Resolve to build on your strengths and work on your weaknesses.

Resource 11.3   The structure of a scientific report

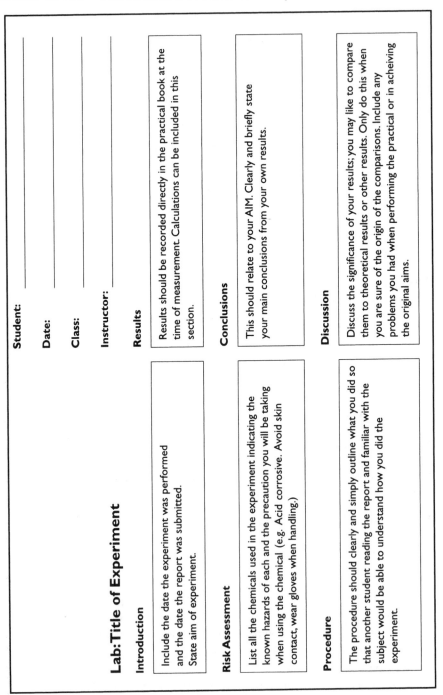

Student: _____

Date: _____

Class: _____

Instructor: _____

Lab: Title of Experiment

Introduction

Include the date the experiment was performed and the date the report was submitted. State aim of experiment.

Risk Assessment

List all the chemicals used in the experiment indicating the known hazards of each and the precaution you will be taking when using the chemical (e.g. Acid corrosive. Avoid skin contact, wear gloves when handling.)

Procedure

The procedure should clearly and simply outline what you did so that another student reading the report and familiar with the subject would be able to understand how you did the experiment.

Results

Results should be recorded directly in the practical book at the time of measurement. Calculations can be included in this section.

Conclusions

This should relate to your AIM. Clearly and briefly state your main conclusions from your own results.

Discussion

Discuss the significance of your results; you may like to compare them to theoretical results or other results. Only do this when you are sure of the origin of the comparisons. Include any problems you had when performing the practical or in acheiving the original aims.

Taken from Tom Burns and Sandra Sinfield (2003) *Essential Study Skills: The complete guide to success @ university.* London: Sage.

Resource 11.4 Typical report structures

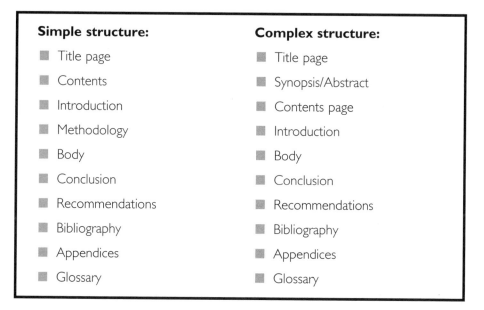

Simple structure:

- Title page
- Contents
- Introduction
- Methodology
- Body
- Conclusion
- Recommendations
- Bibliography
- Appendices
- Glossary

Complex structure:

- Title page
- Synopsis/Abstract
- Contents page
- Introduction
- Body
- Conclusion
- Recommendations
- Bibliography
- Appendices
- Glossary

Taken from Tom Burns and Sandra Sinfield (2003) *Essential Study Skills: The complete guide to success @ university.* London: Sage.

Resource 11.5   Explanation of a complex report structure

Title page
This is the front sheet of the report. This should include: title, sub-title; date; authors name and position; distribution list (reader(s)' name(s)); reference number/course details/statements of confidentiality:

■ **Title and sub-title:** Usually divided by a colon. The title gives the big picture of the report – the sub-title narrows this down. Thus the sub-title gives an indication of the scope of the report – the **'terms of reference'** of the report.

■ **Date:** Places the report in real time.

■ **Author's name and position:** When you write a college report you are often told to assume a position – public relations expert, tax consultant . . . You have to write the report as though you were that person. Revealing who you 'are' tells the reader where the report is 'coming from' – and thus it reveals what angle you might be expected to adopt on the topic.

■ **Distribution list:** As your position as writer might be revealing with respect to the report, so might the list of readers. You would write a different report for the bank manager than for the trade union rep.

Abstract
The abstract – synopsis or summary – is the essence or gist of your report. The abstract might include:

■ overall aims

■ specific objectives

■ problem or task

■ methodology or procedures

■ key findings

■ main conclusions

■ key recommendations.

● **Tips:**
● Journal articles typically begin with an abstract – read the journals and see how they do it.
● Check with your tutors to see what they expect.
● As the abstract refers to the whole report – write it last!

Resource 11.5   Explanation of a complex report structure *(continued)*

Contents page
The contents clearly list **all** the major sections of the report, including subsections and appendices – with page numbers.

The contents page allows the reader to navigate your report. Thus use detailed, clear headings in the report – and put them all in the contents.

 ● **Tip:** Check out the contents pages of books. Do they help you as a reader? How? Make yours just as useful.

Introduction
The introduction should help the reader understand the what, why and how of your report. It needs:

 ▪ **Background** to the report: either why you were interested in the topic or why the report was necessary

 ▪ **Terms of reference:** the aims or scope of the investigation – its purpose or goal, any specific limitations

 ▪ **The methodology:** the research methods you used to put the report together – literature review or something more practical: interviews, questionnaires . . .

The body
This small word refers to the major part of your report. You do not call this section the **body**, but clearly label the different sections of the report, perhaps thus: **Findings** and **Discussion**. Each section gets its own large number, and each sub-section gets its decimal point.

Note: When writing reports, as with essays, we have to use clear but formal English – there is no room for abbreviations or slang.

The conclusion
Each part of the body should have a conclusion. Conclusions point out the **implications** of your findings, that is you tell your reader what they mean – tactfully.

Recommendations
Each conclusion should lead to a recommendation. While the conclusions tell us what the findings mean, the recommendations tell the reader what to **do** about them (or more tactfully, suggest a range of things that might be possible).

▶

Resource 11.5 Explanation of a complex report structure *(continued)*

Appendices
An appendix is something added on or attached to something. 'Appendices' is the plural of this. In this section you can show your reader some of the things that you have used to compile your report. For example, if you used interviews, you would place the interview questions there. If you circulated a questionnaire, you would place a sample questionnaire there.

Appendices do not count in the word limit for your report – but this does not mean that you can just put everything in there. Only put useful things there – and only things that you direct the reader to.

Bibliography
As with the essay:

Harvard System: Author (date) Title, town of publication and publisher
British Standard System: Author, Title, publisher, date

Glossary
A list of unusual words. Especially useful in a report that has more than one reader: for example, a technical report that will also have to be read by a layperson (member of the public).

Presentation and style
■ Neat and easy to read

■ Word processed

■ Consistent style: simple basic layout used consistently throughout your whole report.

● **Tip: Decide where you will number, underline, embolden, italicise; save a template (pattern) and use it every time you start work; check for a department style – use that!**

Taken from Tom Burns and Sandra Sinfield (2003) *Essential Study Skills: The complete guide to success @ university.* London: Sage.

Resource 11.6 Report checklist

☐ What was my aim in writing this report? Have I achieved my goals?

☐ Is the title page adequate: title and sub-title; author and position; reader and position? Date?

☐ Is the title/sub-title appropriate?

☐ Was an abstract necessary? Is there one? Is it clear?

☐ Is there a contents page? Is it clear?

☐ Is there an introduction? Does it reveal: background? Terms of reference? Methodology?

☐ Are the sections and subsections of the body clearly labelled?

☐ Does the reader get sufficient information to make the decisions I desire?

☐ Is all the information necessary or have I written too much?

☐ Can the reader follow the development of my ideas? Are they laid out logically?

☐ Is the layout simple and consistent?

☐ Are the language and tone suitable for the actual reader?

☐ Is the style appropriate to the subject and reader?

☐ Do I offer sufficient evidence to 'prove' my points? Do I discuss my evidence?

☐ Does my conclusion follow logically from my arguments Is there a 'conclusion' for every section of the body?

☐ Have I really laid the groundwork for my recommendations? Is there a recommendation for each conclusion?

☐ Should there be a glossary? Is it comprehensive?

☐ Are the appendices clearly labelled? Is the reader directed to each appendix in the body of the report?

☐ Is the bibliography adequate? Is it laid out in the correct way? (Remember, alphabetical order by author's surname.)

Obviously if the answer to any of these questions is No then you must make the necessary changes!

Taken from Tom Burns and Sandra Sinfield (2003) *Essential Study Skills: The complete guide to success @ university*. London: Sage.

Resource 12.1   The three-minute test

Settle down and give yourself just three minutes to work through this short test.

Three-minute test

Instructor: Name:

Class:

Time:

Date:

Read the paper carefully before answering any questions. This is a timed test – you have three minutes to complete the paper.

1 Before answering any questions, read through the whole paper.

2 Print your name, class, time and date in the appropriate sections of this paper.

3 Draw five small squares in the bottom right-hand corner of this sheet.

4 Circle the word 'name' in question 2.

5 Put an 'x' in each of the five squares.

6 Sign your name at the top of this paper.

7 In front of your name write 'YES, YES, YES'.

8 **Loudly**, so that everyone can hear you, call out your name.

9 Put a circle around question number 3.

10 Put an 'x' in the lower left-hand corner of this paper.

11 Draw a triangle around the 'x' that you have just put down.

12 In your normal speaking voice count down from ten to one.

13 **Loudly** call out, 'I am nearly finished, I have followed directions!'

14 Now that you have finished reading everything, do only questions one and two.

End of exam

Taken from Tom Burns and Sandra Sinfield (2003) *Essential Study Skills: The complete guide to success @ university*. London: Sage.

Resource 12.2   Get ready for exams checklist

This is a checklist that you could follow for each course that you do that has exams. Why not photocopy this checklist – then fill it in for each examination that you have to sit?

Subject _____

Survey: I have:

☐   received course outline

☐   read the course aims and learning outcomes

☐   read through outline and thought about the course structure and design

☐   found and analysed past exam papers
      paper is _____ hours
      I have to answer _____ questions

☐   I know the typical language used

☐   I know the topics that come up every year

Question: I have thought about this programme.
      I need to know _____
      I need to learn _____

Predict: I have:

☐   Predicted the likely questions for this subject

☐   Chosen _____ topics to revise in depth

Plan: I have:
   Opened a revision folder on:
      Topic 1: _____
      Topic 2: _____
      Topic 3: _____
      Topic 4: _____
      Topic 5: _____
      Topic 6: _____

☐   made links between learning outcomes, course work, assignments and my revision topic

☐   placed coursework notes, press cuttings, assignment notes and assignments into the topic folders; on a big pattern on the wall; and on my index cards

▶

Resource 12.2   Get ready for exams checklist *(continued)*

Discovered that I prefer learning:
- ☐ by sight
- ☐ by sound
- ☐ by feel/movement

thus my preferred revision system will utilise mainly:
- ☐ pattern notes of the key points
- ☐ tapes of me reciting the key points
- ☐ making condensed charts of the key points

I will **see it, hear it, say it, do it**

Prepare: I have:
- ☐ gone through my exam folders and have prepared condensed notes of everything that I need to remember for the exam for:

Topic 1: _____

Topic 2: _____

Topic 3: _____

Topic 4: _____

Topic 5: _____

Topic 6: _____

I am learning this by
- ☐ memorising my key point patterns/charts
- ☐ reciting my key points along with my tape
- ☐ testing myself and friends
- ☐ carrying index cards with the key points on them

I have drawn up a revision timetable for this exam subject. It includes:

Practising
- ☐ positive thinking
- ☐ brainstorming and planning answers
- ☐ planning and writing 'perfect' answers with friends
- ☐ writing with notes
- ☐ writing without notes
- ☐ timed writing without notes

I am ready and confident

Taken from Tom Burns and Sandra Sinfield (2003) *Essential Study Skills: The complete guide to success @ university.* London: Sage.

Resource 13.1 A business-like approach to group work: Belbin's group roles

There are eight key roles that management experts like Belbin (1981) have identified in group activities. We have listed these below indicating the possible strengths and weaknesses involved:

■ *Company worker* – a dutiful, organised person, who may tend to inflexibility

■ *Chair* – a calm, open minded person, who may not shine creatively

■ *Shaper* – a dynamic person who may be impatient

■ *Creative thinker* – one who may come up with brilliant ideas, though these may be unrealistic

■ *Resource investigator* – an extrovert character who may respond well to the challenge but who may lose interest

■ *Monitor* – a sober, hard-headed individual who keeps everything on track but who may lack inspiration

■ *Team worker* – a mild social person with plenty of team spirit – may be indecisive

■ *Completer/Finisher* – conscientious, a perfectionist, maybe a worrier.

Let's pause here to go over the list.

■ Which description most fits you?

■ Are you happy with this?

■ What are you going to do about it?

● **Tips:**

● Experiment with group work. Adopt different roles in different academic groups. Each time you vary your role in a group you will develop different aspects of your personality; this is a good thing.

● Decide to use your group work experiences to develop your CV – and get you that job. So as you move through team worker, leader, information gatherer, creative thinker, completer, etc. make notes on your experiences for your CV folder.

● While eight roles are indicated here, research indicates that academic groups work best if they only contain four or five people – any more and you start to get passengers.

● In a small group, allocate roles wisely, but make sure that you have a chairperson and that everyone does know what the task is, what they are doing – and when it all has to be completed.

Resource 13.2   A business-like approach to group work: Adair's processes

As there is theory as to the **roles** adopted in group situations, so there are arguments as to the **processes** that groups go through. Adair argues that groups have distinct forms, or pass through distinct transformations, as they encounter the task, settle down to it and finally pull it off. These are known as forming, storming, norming and performing – some people also speak of a fifth stage, mourning.

Forming is where the group comes together and takes shape. This forming period is a time of high anxiety as people work out:

■ who is in the group – and what they are like

■ what the assignment is – what it involves

■ what the 'rules' are – about behaviour, about the task, about assessment

■ what they will have to do to get the job done – and who will be doing 'all the work'.

Storming is where conflict arises as people sort out all the confusions highlighted above. This is where people seek to assert their authorities – and get challenged. Typically this is a 'black and white' phase – everything seems all good or all bad: compromise is not seen. At this stage people are reacting emotionally **against** everything as they challenge:

■ each other

■ the value of the task

■ the feasibility of the task (you cannot be serious!).

● **Tip: If you do not like group work, ask yourself, is it because you do not like conflict? Perhaps you just find this phase uncomfortable? If this is so, remind yourself that this phase passes.**

Norming, as the name suggests, is where the group begins to settle down. Here that sense of interdependence develops as:

■ plans are made

■ standards are laid down

■ cooperation begins

■ people are able to communicate their feelings more positively.

▶

Resource 13.2   A business-like approach to group work: Adair's processes (continued)

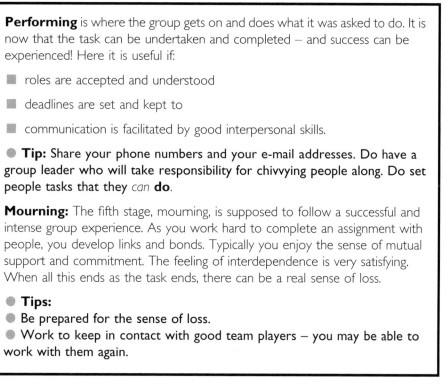

Performing is where the group gets on and does what it was asked to do. It is now that the task can be undertaken and completed – and success can be experienced! Here it is useful if:

■ roles are accepted and understood

■ deadlines are set and kept to

■ communication is facilitated by good interpersonal skills.

● **Tip:** Share your phone numbers and your e-mail addresses. Do have a group leader who will take responsibility for chivvying people along. Do set people tasks that they *can* **do**.

Mourning: The fifth stage, mourning, is supposed to follow a successful and intense group experience. As you work hard to complete an assignment with people, you develop links and bonds. Typically you enjoy the sense of mutual support and commitment. The feeling of interdependence is very satisfying. When all this ends as the task ends, there can be a real sense of loss.

● **Tips:**
● Be prepared for the sense of loss.
● Work to keep in contact with good team players – you may be able to work with them again.

Taken from Tom Burns and Sandra Sinfield (2003) *Essential Study Skills: The complete guide to success @ university.* London: Sage.

Resource 14.1   Example of a student learning log (on a research and reading session)

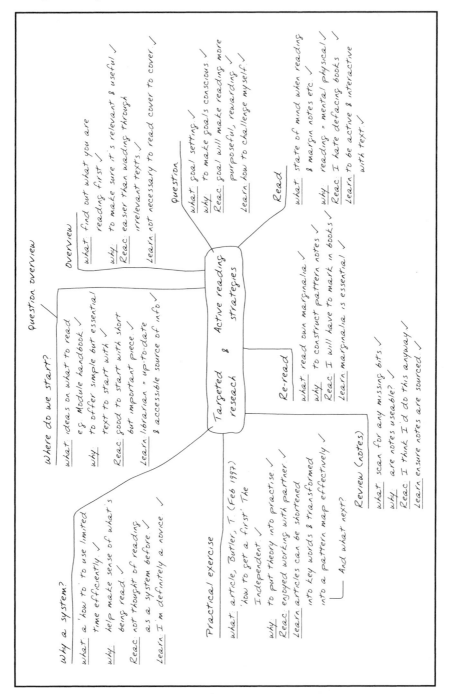

Taken from Tom Burns and Sandra Sinfield (2003) *Essential Study Skills: The complete guide to success @ university*. London: Sage.

Resource 14.2   The reflective learning log – or professional development journal

The reflective learning log is designed to structure an intense and active review of a learning activity or session. For your first few logs we recommend that you write your diary entry in response to the headings that we give below. After a while you can decide which particular headings you would like to continue to use in your own logs in order to ensure that they are useful to you and that they meet any assessment criteria that your tutor has indicated.

The structure that we recommend that you use first has six parts: what, why, reaction, learned, issues, goal setting. Each of these topics prompts you to useful thought, as described below:

- **What:** It is useful to briefly describe the activity in which you have engaged for it is very easy to forget once a session is over.

- **Why:** Make brief analytical notes explaining the purpose of the activity (your own purpose if an independent activity, or the tutor's purpose if a tutor-led activity). For example, if you have read Tony Buzan after a lecture on note-making, you might write: 'To follow up ideas on mindmapping seeded in lecture – so that I can improve my own practice.'

- **Reaction:** Make brief notes of your emotional response to the activity in which you engaged or the information that you received. **Note:** This is where you notice the *affective* (emotional) dimension of your learning. It allows you to build a picture of yourself as a learner and as a student. An entry, after a session on group work, could be like this: 'I did not think that I would like group work, but actually the people in my group were really interested in the topic and I really enjoyed the discussion.'

- **Issues:** Make brief notes on any problems that you encountered – and any solutions that you discovered – in the session itself or in the follow-up activity related to the session. For example, if asked to use at least two journal references in an assignment you might have an entry like this: 'Could not find any journals in the library. Went to a subject librarian session and discovered the paper journals – and the journals online. Brilliant!'

Resource 14.2   The reflective learning log – or professional development journal *(continued)*

■ **Learned:** Make brief notes on all that you think you learned from the lecture, class or your reading. This is where you make your learning conscious, which improves both the quantity and quality of that learning. It is a quick revision of a learning activity. An entry on note-making could be something like this: 'Learned the what, why and how of note-making after a structured brainstorm and lecture. Realised that the brainstorm did help me get more from the lecture – will use again. Also learned the Cornell and the pattern systems of note-making. I think that they are both useful. Will have to devise a system for myself where I use patterns – and where I indicate how a particular lecture relates to course aims, outcomes and the assignment.'

■ **Goal setting:** Make brief notes on possible follow-up activities in which to engage after a study session. Typically note **when** you will do the follow-up activities or they tend not to get done. Follow-up activities can include engaging in further research or in writing a section of an assignment. For example: 'Wednesday at 2.00 will look for two articles on pattern notes online. Will write a draft paragraph on pattern notes for my Business Skills essay.'

● **Tips:** Keep description to a minimum, be concise, focus on the analysis – this increases your understanding of what is happening in a course and why. When completing the 'reaction' section, be honest. You will not get a helpful picture of yourself as a student if you just say that you enjoyed everything.

Index